England's military heartland

Manchester University Press

England's military heartland

Preparing for war on Salisbury Plain

Vron Ware, Antonia Lucia Dawes, Mitra Pariyar
and Alice Cree

MANCHESTER UNIVERSITY PRESS

Published by Manchester University Press
Oxford Road, Manchester, M13 9PL
www.manchesteruniversitypress.co.uk

British Library Cataloguing-in-Publication Data
A catalogue record for this book is available from the British Library

ISBN 978 1 5261 7483 3 hardback
ISBN 978 1 5261 7484 0 paperback

First published 2025

EU authorised representative for GPSR:
Easy Access System Europe – Mustamäe tee 50, 10621 Tallinn, Estonia
gpsr.requests@easproject.com

Typeset
by Cheshire Typesetting Ltd, Cheshire

Say, rulers of the nations, from the sword
Can ought but murder, pain, and tears proceed?
Oh! what can war but endless war still breed?
William Wordsworth, *Salisbury Plain* (1793–94)

For David Gee
Philosopher, poet, gardener, activist, friend

Contents

Introduction: Hidden in plain sight

The A303 is one of England's most important trunk roads connecting London to the south-west. Sliding off the M3 motorway at Basingstoke, this 'highway to the sun' is a road of 'magical properties' and has been deemed worthy of a book in its own right.[1] Before crossing the county border between Hampshire and Wiltshire, the dual carriageway passes an incongruous phenomenon known as Solstice Park, a startling but soulless outcrop of warehouses the size of aircraft hangars and generic fast-food outlets with gigantic logos. Drivers who are weary of sluggish or standstill traffic are offered the chance to fill up on fuel, eat without getting out of their cars, shop, and even spend the night in the Holiday Inn.

After the next roundabout the carriageway narrows to a single lane as it enters the area of expansive downland that characterises Salisbury Plain. The road carries on down a curving incline, and then, suddenly, the unmistakable profile of Stonehenge can be seen on the brow of the hill. The A303 passes just 165 metres from the stone circle, allowing motorists to marvel at its compact shape regardless of the state of the traffic.

The closeness of Stonehenge to the busy road has presented a notorious headache for local residents, motorists, transport planners and governments. Proposals to widen the A303 have been rejected many times, largely because this is a UNESCO World Heritage site containing rich archaeological material dating back six thousand years. While numerous long barrows and other Neolithic earthworks have been listed, scientists believe there are further remains

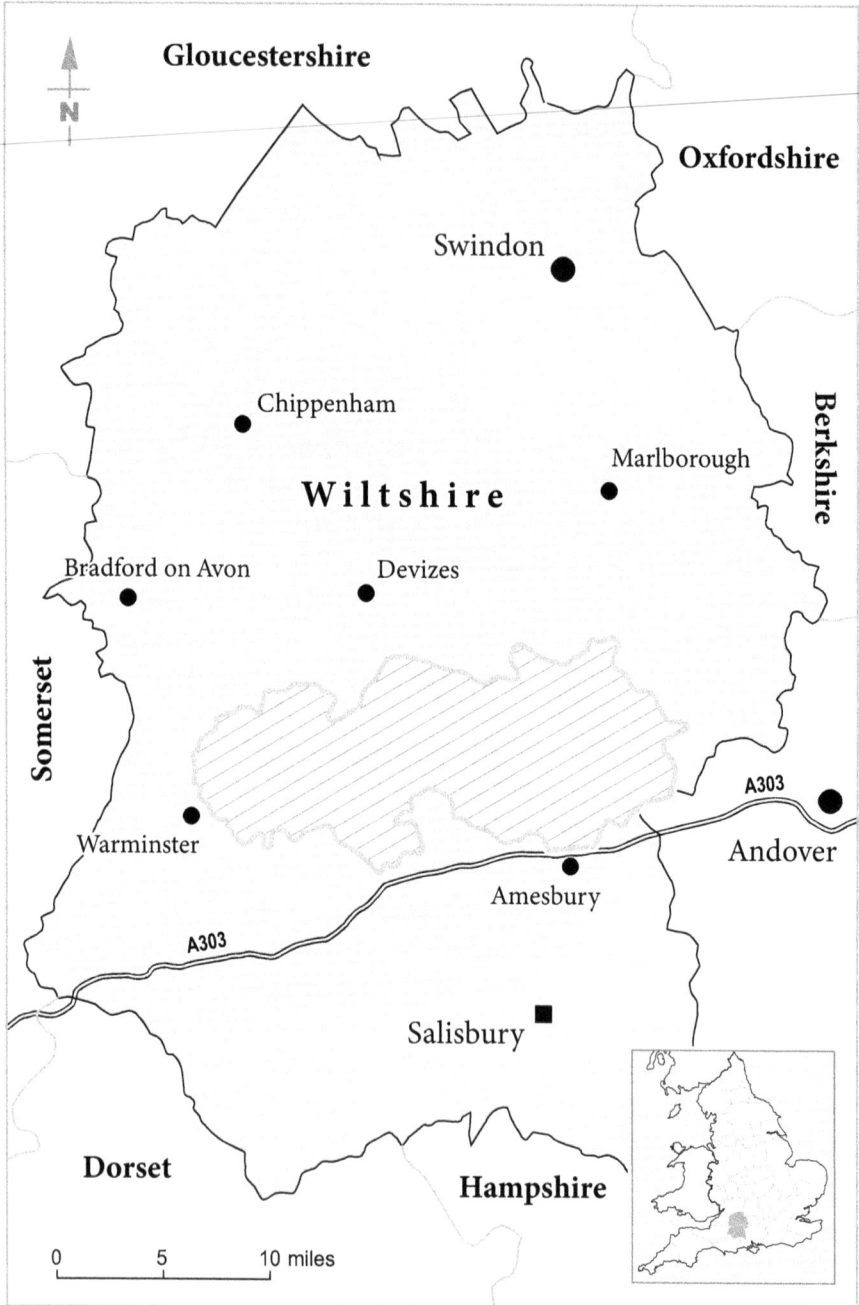

Gloucestershire

N

Oxfordshire

Swindon ●

Chippenham ●

Marlborough ●

Wiltshire

Berkshire

Bradford on Avon ●

Devizes ●

Somerset

A303 ●

Warminster ●

Andover

A303

Amesbury ●

Salisbury ■

Dorset

Hampshire

0   5   10 miles

0.1 Map showing the Salisbury Plain Training Area (cross-hatched) in relation
to Wiltshire and surrounding counties. Inset shows location of Wiltshire in UK.

of ceremonial and domestic structures to be found in the area, many of them even predating Stonehenge. In the 1990s a tunnel was put forward as a solution. regardless of the threat to the human heritage underfoot – or the cost. After three decades of controversy and numerous legal challenges, the project, by then estimated to cost £2 billion, was scrapped by the incoming Labour government in 2024.

In addition to the prehistoric obstacles and the sheer expense, there are also environmental barriers to road-widening schemes. There are no fewer than three designated Areas of Outstanding National Beauty nearby, and Salisbury Plain itself is a Special Area of Conservation and therefore a protected habitat for rare birds, insects and plants. But a more intransigent problem, seldom mentioned, is that the World Heritage site is bordered on one side by the largest military training area in the UK.[2]

While the mystery of Stonehenge casts us back to the complex social and cultural lives of our ancestors, it also acts as a decoy, diverting attention from more immediate ways of comprehending the history of the Plain. For well over a century the Ministry of Defence – formerly known as the War Office – has had possession of an area measuring 25 by 10 miles, roughly the same size as the Isle of Wight.

The army's long occupation has seen this strange landscape transformed into one of the country's most important arenas for preparing soldiers for lethal combat, a space that bears the scars of generations of ingenious death-dealing weaponry.[3] Less spectacular but no less significant, the bleak edifice of institutional life that props up the modern military workforce lies over the horizon, rarely subjected to public scrutiny.

The military in our midst

The Salisbury Plain Training Area may be tucked away in a relatively secluded part of the country, but it is also one of the country's most prized military assets. The Ministry of Defence owns 240,000 hectares of land throughout the UK, making it the second biggest landowner in the UK, after the Forestry Commission.[4] In 2008,

3

faced with the global financial crisis as well as the mounting cost of deploying troops in Afghanistan as well as Iraq, the government was forced to 'optimise' the way it managed its entire estate. Officials at the Ministry of Defence came up with the idea of creating four 'super garrisons' as a way of maintaining fewer, larger sites within the UK.

This solution would combine the armed forces' training needs with the expanded and improved infrastructure that was urgently needed to support military communities. Given the size of the area and the poor condition of existing accommodation, Salisbury Plain was a perfect candidate.

Three years later, the coalition government announced that UK residential bases in Germany would be closed and that the affected regiments were to be relocated in the UK, mainly in the camps and garrisons of Salisbury Plain. The Army Basing Programme, as it was called, was formally launched in 2014, coinciding with the withdrawal of the NATO-led International Security Assistance Force from Afghanistan.

The Salisbury Plain Masterplan, published the same year, revealed that 4,300 more army personnel and their families were to move to the area. Initial proposals included new accommodation for single soldiers, more than a thousand new service family homes and the construction, conversion or refurbishment of nearly 250 buildings such as offices, garages, workshops and mess facilities. The cost for the government was estimated at £1.4 billion.

This book is the culmination of more than ten years' observation of the social, cultural, political, ecological and economic dimensions of life on and near this 'super garrison'. Thanks to funding from the Leverhulme Trust, we carried out ethnographic research from September 2018 until the start of the global pandemic in March 2020. Originally entitled 'The military in our midst', this project enabled us to conduct both a study of a particular place and an evaluation of what it might mean to live alongside (and in an area dominated by) a secretive, inward-facing organisation devoted to training people for organised violence.

That initial title was supposed to reflect the way that the institution is able to hide in plain sight, whether camouflaged on home ground in rural England or disguised in civilian dress in public. The phrase 'in our midst' was deliberately ambiguous, referring both to the interrelationship between military and non-military communities on and around a particular base, and to the pervasive but less obvious influence of the military in other areas of national life and culture.

But while it made a picture, this working title did not begin to tell the story that emerged as we continued with the research. By foregrounding the word 'military', the phrase suggested that this might be a study of the British Army, which was certainly not our intention. It was partly the proximity of the Salisbury Plain Training Area to the UNESCO World Heritage site of Stonehenge that prompted us to look more closely at the land itself. Our aim was to emphasise the incongruity between the remote grasslands of rural Wiltshire and the way the Plain has been transformed and exploited in the course of war preparation.

In addition to the politics of environmental stewardship, which also encompassed rich archaeological resources, we wanted to emphasise the fact that the 'super garrison' was home to complex communities of dependent families whose social and cultural needs made particular demands on already stretched local services. In 2006 Wiltshire Council had entered into the Military Civilian Integration Partnership, a unique arrangement with the Ministry of Defence in an attempt to remedy years of disconnect between local and national government.

One of the early benefits of this pact was the publication of research that for the first time established the impact of the 'military footprint' in Wiltshire and the whole South West, addressing decades of inattention and neglect. Although not replicated elsewhere, the Military Civilian Integration Partnership pre-empted a more overtly political intervention, the Armed Forces Covenant, launched by David Cameron's coalition government in 2011. Devised at a time when public unease about the war in Afghanistan was at its peak, the Covenant signalled a decision to shift some of the burden of maintaining a large military workforce on to local government, industry and the third sector. By examining some of the repercussions of the

Covenant on a local scale, we hope that this raises awareness of comparable developments across the UK.

As we found ourselves moving between the different scales of local, regional, national and global, we were indebted to Rachel Woodward's pioneering body of work, especially her writings on the impact of military activity in rural areas of the UK. Even in unremarkable places, she insists, 'military geographies are everywhere. But often you have to know where to look.'[5] This provocation seemed especially relevant in the context of Tidworth garrison's main street, where soldiers, their families and local residents mingle in the most mundane settings.

But her analysis pointed to more than social interactions in shared spaces, and she was not just referring to the UK armed forces. 'Every corner of every place in every land in every part of this world of ours is touched, shaped, viewed and represented in some way by military forces and activities,' she wrote in the introduction to her 2004 book.

> Military geographies are made by a bewildering range of actions – a soldier's footprint, a landowner's custody, an invader's force, an occupier's presence. The manufacture of weapons, the destruction caused by armed conflict, the construction of military facilities, and the pollution of conventional and nuclear weapons all mark the earth. Military activities, an endless cycle of preparation for waging war, and war itself, define countless lives.[6]

Less obvious perhaps are the numerous technological innovations that map, analyse and surveil the entire planet, enabling the domain of war to be extended into outer space. As a joint report by the UK-based Drone Wars and Campaign for Nuclear Disarmament warned in 2022, 'space-based operations affect many aspects of modern life and commerce ... [but] space is also, unfortunately, a key domain for military operations'.[7]

Woodward's reference to the 'endless cycle' of war preparation draws attention to the fact that military geographies are temporal as well as spatial. The existence of historic garrisons and other military places has been largely excluded from recent assessment of colonial heritage in England. The first encampments, including the main garrison of Tidworth, were founded during the South African War, also known as the Boer War (1899–1902). The history of that war and other episodes of martial violence and rapacious expansion carried out in the name of empire is cemented into the built environment from its foundations to street level.

Nor is it just the older buildings that bear the imprint of this past: the naming of new estates continues the tradition of recalling battles, generals and other emblems of war heroism. Yet unlike the statues of slave-holders and war criminals in Britain's towns and cities, this way of locating the country's imperial archive in this 'military heartland' has escaped notice, reflecting the way that the armed forces seem to be exempt from public scrutiny.

Rural relations

The title of the first chapter, 'Khaki country', is intended to evoke the multiple dimensions of the army's presence in Wiltshire without diminishing the significance of their operations elsewhere in the UK and further afield. It begins with a descriptive account of the landscape of Salisbury Plain, pointing out the signs and symbols of military occupation today. Drawing on one of the few historical accounts of the Plain's transformation from the 1890s onwards, it explains how the War Office and associated bodies managed to justify occupying so much land over such a long period. Today the ruins of the 'ghost village' of Imber, evacuated in 1943, have been reduced to a tourist attraction. But the story of local resistance to its forced abandonment, although futile, was a crucial factor in convincing the Ministry of Defence to take the environment more seriously.

Since the Plain has been recognised as a precious ecological site, thanks partly to the absence of the industrial farming that has become the norm in almost all comparable rural areas, the Ministry of Defence has embraced a new role as a leading partner in nature conservation. Critics have called the army's claim that it is protecting the environment, rather than damaging it, military 'greenwash', a term that we amend to 'camouwash'. Chapter 1 ends with a brief tour of the camps of Larkhill, Bulford and the garrison town of Tidworth, constructed in the early years of the twentieth century at the peak of Britain's imperial power.

The second chapter begins in Station Road in the commercial heart of Tidworth, an ideal spot for navigating the question of how to tell who is military and who is not. The population of this garrison town, estimated to be just under twenty thousand in 2024, has almost doubled within the last two decades (approximately nine thousand in the 2011 Census), mainly due to the impact of the Army Basing Programme. Public spaces, such as shopping areas and leisure spaces, where residents and soldiers mingled in and out of uniform, were especially valuable for exploring local views on how the town was changing.

Officially the media department at Army HQ had decided not to support our project by granting access for interviews, but this did not prevent us from talking to a wide range of individuals living and working in the area. This included councillors at local and county level who represented the communities on the eastern periphery of the Plain.

Throughout the book we have tried to avoid the word 'civilian', except as the occasional technical term to designate those who are not in the army. As this chapter shows, there might be places that are off limit to members of the public but in many areas of life there is no neat binary that operates within this contact zone. The term 'civilian' can be misleading too, not least because it does not always correspond to the status of those who are attached to the armed forces.

Spouses and offspring of serving soldiers are technically civilians, whether they live in segregated housing or off the base entirely. Although they may benefit from certain discounts and other privileges, their lifestyle and experience of army life are likely to be very different from those of people with no contact. There are many categories of people who could be considered casualties of the military way of life too, regardless of recent reforms. Since this is a relatively small community, we have taken steps to protect people's identity, although some of the people who consented to participate in the project may remain identifiable.[8]

The local sport centre, built as a joint facility for soldiers and the public, is an important institution in Tidworth. There we met a number of people who live in the area, including some who could remember how much this small rural town had changed within their lifetimes.[9] But the chapter also includes a bus ride with an elderly Gurkha veteran, sharing his disappointment that few of the locals want to engage with him, either in public or in social situations. A Ghanaian-born pastor married to a serving female soldier offers his account of the racism he experiences in his job as a cab driver, describing the solace that he finds in caring for his congregation.

Different ethnic communities within the army's multinational workforce find similar forms of solidarity and connection in their respective faith-based communities. Yet, in spite of the British Army's professed commitment to equality and diversity, there are no mosques, gurdwaras, synagogues or temples in any of the camps and garrisons on the Plain. A discussion with school students brings home the way that children bear the brunt of the army lifestyle in ways that can override differences of class, ethnicity or faith.

The third chapter, 'Military sprawl', continues to introduce indi- viduals who inhabit this strange environment. The wife of an army officer reflects on her position within the institution as well as her relationship to the environment. Her perspective is one of several that draw attention to the army's strict social hierarchy, and the way it is replicated in the size and style of service family housing. But, while many members of the resident army community live outside the boundaries of the training area, military needs and priorities are routinely kept separate from political debates about rural housing, infrastructure, planning, crime, road safety and other regional issues.

In Ludgershall, a small town on the edge of the training area, conversations with local councillors reveal the pros and cons of 'Army Basing' for the area. The expansion of the military commu- nity has inevitably had uneven effects. The construction of new housing estates led to increased traffic congestion on country roads but there have also been new shops and businesses appearing in the high street. These discussions address the question of whether the planned integration between military and civilian communities will ever be truly attained.

Military methods

The next section is more focused on the political and policy-related aspects of life on the new 'super garrison'. Under the heading of 'The cost' it explores the impact of these policy changes at a local level, drawing on a conversation with the CEO of Aspire Defence, the company contracted to manage the redevelopment of the garrison over 35 years. This discussion is less about the financial implications of the intended reforms than the underlying forces that have driven them. Noting how the military way of doing things is often at odds with the democratic procedures followed by publicly funded civilian institutions, Chapter 4 investigates the quality of the new housing, the operation of a new joint NHS–military health centre and the challenges for schoolteachers who are expected to accommodate fluctuating numbers of service children.

Chapter 5, on the 'khaki economy', tackles the elusive question of whether it is possible to assess the economic benefits brought by the army presence. It examines various recent developments – a business enterprise centre, for example – that have been established by the local council partly to provide opportunities for veterans and military spouses to start their own businesses. This type of innovation recognises the fact that the army lifestyle disadvantages partners and spouses, not least because soldiers are expected to move at regular intervals, often with their families in tow. It also acknowledges that the many military veterans who chose to stay in the area require support in finding new forms of employment.

The discussion then turns to regional defence spending across the country, and especially the involvement of major arms companies. Drawing attention to the fact that the amount invested in defence and security in the wider south-west region is considerably higher than elsewhere in the UK, it points out that the rapid expansion of the arms industry – in partnership with industry, academia and local authorities – is largely taking place out of sight. It ends by questioning the effect of the military discounts offered to military personnel for goods and services, which were increased in response to public support for the armed forces during the Afghanistan war. It is not clear whether these discounts are supposed to integrate the military community into the local economy by supporting local businesses, or whether these privileges simply create an invidious distinction between military and non-military residents.

Chapter 6 begins and ends with scenes from Armed Forces Day, celebrated in two different Wiltshire towns in 2018 and 2019. As public events, they provide important opportunities for the army to manage what is known internally as the 'pipeline'. Military recruitment is referred to as 'inflow', while veterans (a term that signifies anyone who leaves after starting their contract, no matter how short their service) are classed as 'outflow'. In recent years, in line with other public institutions, the army has been subjected to regular cuts while struggling to maintain full capacity. In addition, a chronic recruitment crisis at one end of the pipeline has been compounded by the problem of retention at the other.[10]

Salisbury Plain is an appropriate place to examine this question because statistics show that recruitment in schools and colleges adjacent to military bases is likely to be more successful than in areas where the organisation has no contact with the public. Remembering that the UK is an outlier among its allies because of its practice of recruiting 16- and 17-year-olds, we ask how young people and their families feel about the presence of uniformed soldiers in schools. The chapter then turns to the 'outflow' and life after military service, PTSD and the role of military charities. It ends with a moment in a Quaker Meeting House which offers a space to reflect on the alternatives to the forms of war preparation provided by the local Armed Forces Day celebration.

Land rights

The third section of the book, which looks at some of the consequences of the army's occupation of the Plain, considers the legacy of military violence that can be found in rural places. Chapter 7 begins by reminding readers that the centenary of the First World War was marked with particular reverence in Wiltshire, as the Plain had been used in those years as a training area for thousands of troops, including many from Australia, Canada and New Zealand.

A brief sketch of a local Remembrance service in November 2018 is followed by a description of some of the military cemeteries that can be found locally. These secluded sites offer more evidence of the way that military geographies have shaped the area. But at the same time the chapter notes local concern over the belated, and often insufficient, recognition of the contribution of Gurkha and Commonwealth troops, both in local and official national narratives.

The focus then moves to Tedworth House, which now serves as a memorial to the waste of human lives and precious resources incurred as a result of the 9/11 wars. In 2011 the building was transformed into a state-of-the-art rehabilitation centre by the charity Help for Heroes, but responsibility for maintaining it reverted to the Ministry of Defence as public support waned, especially since the start of the pandemic.

The theme of veteran care and the commemorative history of war continues with a discussion of Operation Nightingale, a joint project with Wessex Archaeology in which veterans are invited to take part in archaeological research as a form of rehabilitation. This returns us to the ecological questions raised in the early sections of the book, as Chapter 8 looks more closely at the Ministry of Defence's partnership with various agencies responsible for conservation and heritage. The experience of farming on the Plain reveals a complex set of arrangements for sharing space, placing the landlord's concern for the environment in a rather different light.

The issue of public access to ancient rights of way, whether on foot or wheels, and the dangers of living close to a live firing range raise questions about the British military's conduct in its training areas in other parts of the world. The chapter ends by recalling the fate of the evacuated village of Imber, a reminder that the term 'civilian' invariably means collateral damage as opposed to merely non-military.

The Covid-19 pandemic offered a new dimension to this research since it drew attention to the military's role in national emergencies. Leaving to one side issues of loyalty, pride and patriotism often expressed by those connected to the armed forces, it was an opportunity to find out whether inhabitants of towns and villages on or near the training area felt protected as a result of living so close to so diers, who were categorised as key workers. Yet while the pandemi was a crisis that affected the entire population, there were othe events that suggested more sinister forms of danger nearby.

In March 2018, the attempted poisoning of the Russian spy Sergei Skripal, and his daughter, Yulia Skripal, drew global attention to the military laboratory at Porton Down, situated just outside Salisbury where the attack took place. The fact that this facility was associated with experiments in military 'secret science' dating back to the post-1945 era did little to reassure local residents that they might be safer living so close to the scene of the crime.

While we have focused on the reorganisation and refurbishment of the Ministry of Defence estate, it is important not to lose sight of those facilities that are deployed for purposes other than defence. The housing of vulnerable asylum seekers in disused military bases is not unprecedented in post-1945 UK history, but today the decrepit state of the buildings and their isolated locations raise questions about basic human rights. Once again, the fact that so many refugees are themselves casualties of war waged elsewhere – often in conflicts in which the UK armed forces are or have been involved – is integral to the wider military geographies that this book explores.

The time and place of war

In short, *England's Military Heartland* is a study of place, a glimpse of life lived next to and within the perimeter of a British Army 'super garrison' in a relatively remote region of south-west England. The ecologically precious area of chalk grassland is more likely to be associated with pagan rituals and traffic jams than with armed violence, but the environment of Salisbury Plain is steeped in the memory of more than a century of warfare, reaching back to the zenith of the British Empire.

This portrait of a militarised zone has encountered many obstacles, whether administrative, methodological or conceptual: how to convey the strangeness of a place which is at once a protected habitat for the vulnerable marsh fritillary butterfly and a site for testing the UK's first high-powered, long-range laser-directed energy weapon?[11]

dress this challenge, we return repeatedly to the
.e, specifically the timeline of war. Western think-
rests on the assumption that long periods of peace are
y intense periods of violent conflict.[12] This has always
eading and western-centric view of world history, and,
in the final section, even the UK Ministry of Defence has
ed it. The 2021 defence review announced that 'The notion
and peace as binary states has given way to a continuum of
ct, requiring us to prepare our forces for more persistent global
gement and constant campaigning, moving seamlessly from
rating to war fighting'.[13]

The legendary airfield Greenham Common, where the Welsh group 'Women for life on earth' first established the women's peace camp in 1981, has since reverted to a popular spot for bird-watching. Although it is sporadically commemorated in books, films and exhibitions, that unprecedented mobilisation against the siting of 96 cruise missiles by the US government is inevitably recalled with nostalgia. Yet it is a mistake to imagine that the world is a safer place now than it was then.

Accepting that lethal conflict is a permanent feature of what is still called international relations means acknowledging the fact that war preparation is continually under way in the most unlikely places. In 1980 the artist Peter Kennard created an image that challenged the apparent incongruity of rural England becoming a launchpad for US nuclear weapons. Entitled *Haywain with Cruise Missiles*, it depicts a stack of the deadly rockets in the centre of one of Constable's most celebrated landscape paintings. Today the artwork remains as potent as ever. Its power to rupture the superficially tranquil veneer of rural England has been recently restored, thanks to a major exhibition of Kennard's work in London as we go to press.

The prospect of state militaries actually deploying nuclear weapons has increased, not diminished. In early 2024 the Pentagon announced that it planned to station nuclear warheads three times the strength of the Hiroshima bomb at RAF Lakenheath in Suffolk, while global defence spending, already at record levels, continues to climb.[14]

By now the rural location of these sites of war preparation ought not to be a surprise, and the fact that we don't see them is precisely the reason why it is crucial not to overlook them. By drawing attention to this particular place, this book interrogates the costs and consequences for society as a whole of maintaining a professional military workforce, one that is part of a conception of national security that threatens the continuation of life on Earth.

Part I

The place

1

Khaki country

The presence of the British Army on Salisbury Plain is not obvious at first, or at least not unless you are actively looking. Observant motorists and their passengers heading south-west along the A303 would have spotted a road sign to 'Army Headquarters' as they unwittingly bypassed Andover. Those alert to military signage would have noticed the red-ringed sign to Boscombe Down at the exit to Amesbury and Salisbury, just before Solstice Park, and, as they looked over at the logos boasting burgers and pizza galore, they might have been struck by an artwork, designed by Charlotte Monelon, made from a recycled army helicopter.

After the excitement of Stonehenge, the grassland becomes arguably bleak, the only colour provided by the faded red and white traffic cones that line the verge. The featureless fields on either side of the road are sometimes punctuated by camper vans parked on public byways, with incongruous roadside merchants, their stalls flaunting union jacks, selling tea, burgers and strawberries over twelve months of the year. For the eagle-eyed, however, the signs are mounting. Occasionally the vibrating chug of a twin-bladed Chinook can be heard overhead, or a curl of smoke might emerge from distant artillery practice. Army trucks or even convoys are not uncommon, and the number of radio stations dedicated to a military clientele start to fill the airwaves: either BFBS – the Forces Station – or the Gurkha equivalent which caters to Nepali-speaking listeners.

These indicative sights and sounds become more obvious when you turn off the A303 to the right, following signs to the Stonehenge

1.1 The view of Stonehenge from the A303, with helicopter on the horizon.

Visitors Centre. Anyone who ventures away from the main road soon realises that this is no ordinary stretch of countryside. As the Wiltshire native Jonathan Meades observes: 'The plain is Britain's only steppe'.[1] Whether you stay in your car or decide to walk, you are well and truly within the Salisbury Plain Training Area, measuring approximately 38,000 hectares (94,000 acres), comprising one-ninth of the county of Wiltshire. It stretches from Warminster and Westbury in the west to the garrisons of Perham Down and Tidworth in the east.

At this point it is very hard to miss the uneasy cohabitation of military training, outdoor recreation and agriculture. On one side there is a rutted, gravelled track along the edge of Area 15, an impact zone for artillery practice. On the left is arable land, rented out to local farmers. A mess of tyre tracks marks the wide verge that runs parallel to the access road, evidence of the quad biking that is a popular pastime across the Plain. Next to that is a strip of grass flattened by the regular passage of horses' hooves.

Mounted sentry points – or vedettes in military jargon – appear at regular intervals along the side of the road. These were abandoned for a number of years because of funding cuts, but then it was recognised that these structures had a useful function as observation points from which to spot members of the public who might have strayed into dangerous territory. During live firing practice, perhaps one of the annual training exercises with US or other national military partners, the wire fencing is festooned with red flags to show that civilian access is forbidden. Otherwise it would be easy to imagine that the only hazard for intrepid hikers might be losing a sense of direction in such a wide, open space. In 2023–24 the charity Standing with Giants worked with the Ministry of Defence on its 'Respect the Range' campaign to inform and educate the public about the dangers of accessing military land. In July 2024 a series of 10-foot metal silhouettes, some modelled on soldiers from 5 Rifles, which trains on the Plain, were installed on the western section of the training area.[2]

The red flags and sinister vedettes evoke the real danger presented by unexploded shells or live firing, both of which are intrinsic to military training. They are also a reminder of the fraught question of public access to footpaths and other rights of way that were established well before the army's occupation of the Plain at the end of the nineteenth century. The Military Lands Act (1892) gave the War Office the right to purchase public and private land for military training, stipulating that a footpath could be blocked or diverted if it 'crosses or runs inconveniently or dangerously near to any land leased under this Act'. At the same time it recognised that an alternative footpath must be provided with the consent of the local parish clergy and a signed statement by two justices, testifying that the diversion was convenient for the public.[3]

Today the information relating to public safety varies from a clipped list of Do's and Don'ts on the Ministry of Defence website to a slightly more user-friendly approach to sharing the Plain, the outcome of many decades of negotiation with environmentalists, residents, ramblers, archaeologists and other interested parties. The history of this relationship with the public is the key to understanding how the British Army has been able to camouflage its presence across such a wide expanse of southern England. But the real question is: how did the Ministry of Defence manage to take over so much land in the first place?

Room for manoeuvre

In his detailed account of the armed forces' incursion into the region, entitled *Plain Soldiering*, N.D.G James describes how fundamental changes began to take place in the organisation and administration of the British Army during the latter half of the nineteenth century following public concern 'regarding the blunders and inefficiency that had come to light during the Crimean War'.[4] However, military historians to this day debate the tortuous process of reforming the army during the Victorian era following the carnage of the Napoleonic Wars.

The system through which officers purchased commissions, the brutal forms of 'recruitment', punishment and abandonment that ordinary soldiers experienced, and the question of training inexperienced men of all social classes to staff colonial garrisons in different continents, all of these phenomena were influenced by the prevailing attitudes of the public towards the British Army.

In addition to these changes in the military's organisation, there were also new expectations regarding what soldiers were required to do. As the British Empire continued to be expanded through an interminable succession of 'small wars', James wrote in 1987, 'increasing demands were made on the armed forces to assist in the maintenance of law and order, to deal with organised resistance to British rule and to meet any form of aggression'.[5]

Nearer home, the renowned prowess of the Prussian military and deteriorating relationships with the French pressured the British government to question its traditional reliance on the navy to deal with the defence of the country's borders and to develop a modernised army, equipped with the latest forms of weaponry. And after the defeat of the British by the Boers at Majuba Hill in 1881, military leaders were obliged to acknowledge the need to train in open country.

The combination of reforms to the recruitment and training of soldiers and innovations in weapons technology meant that there was a pressing need for more space to practise large formation exercises. The earliest large-scale manoeuvres, as they were called, were held in several areas deemed suitable, including the heathland around Aldershot, Hampshire, in 1871 and 1892, Salisbury Plain in 1872 and Dartmoor in 1873. Apart from obtaining permission from landowners beforehand, arrangements had to be made for the erection of temporary buildings, as well as creating private roads and ensuring water supplies.

To regulate these complex matters, the Military Manoeuvres Act was passed in 1897. The first exercises held on and near Salisbury Plain took place from 1 to 8 September 1898, culminating in a Review where more than fifty thousand soldiers gathered to form the 'greatest military assembly since 1871'. It took over two and a half hours for the troops to march past the saluting base.

By this time the War Office had recognised that Salisbury Plain was eminently suitable for a permanent training ground, and plans were laid to purchase large tracts of land. It was considered a good location because it was largely unenclosed, mostly consisting of 'light soil over chalk', which meant it dried out quickly after rain and was easily passable by horse and horse-drawn transport. Most footpaths were essentially sheep tracks, and the land was not regarded as agriculturally significant.

According to the Wiltshire Landscape Character Assessment, which documents the historical development of the region, the Plain was sparsely populated until the late eighteenth and early nineteenth centuries when a few farms were established. This meant that it already provided a large expanse of open space suitable for large-scale military manoeuvres and, furthermore, it was relatively cheap.[6]

In January 1897 the local paper, the *Salisbury and Winchester Journal*, reported that an area measuring 40,000 acres, or 60 square miles, was being purchased by the government to serve as a manoeuvring ground for cavalry as well as infantry, and to provide a rifle range for artillery practice. While the size of properties varied from a few acres to several thousand, 45 parcels of land in Wiltshire were bought by the government between 1897 and the end of December 1899.

According to James's account of the acquisition of landed estates, the Secretary of State 'made it clear that wholesale disturbance of agricultural population should be avoided'. Former landowners would be able to retain their houses with land in the immediate vicinity and they would retain rights to hunting, fishing and even shooting. Farmers would be entitled to retain better areas for cultivation, while any vacant land could be rented to smallholders or village craftspeople.

One of these properties, and the most significant in the long term, was the Tedworth Estate, measuring 6,618 acres and costing £95,000. Belonging to Sir John William Kelk Bt, it contained 13 farms, 8 farmhouses, 107 cottages and the Ram Hotel in North Tidworth. It was this parcel of land that would form the basis of Tidworth garrison founded in 1905. The purchase also included Tedworth House, a mansion of some renown built by Thomas Assheton Smith II in 1828–30 and maintained in good condition.

At the time of the sale the secretary of state made a statement to the effect that Tedworth House would not be allowed to fall into disrepair, and that the plan was to find a suitable buyer. It was clearly a matter of concern, one that the government was quick to anticipate lest it provided grounds for opposing the whole enterprise. However, in the main, local landowners were supportive of the scheme to turn over a large proportion of the Plain to the armed forces. In February 1897 Sir Henry Malet of Wilbury Park, Newton, wrote to the *Salisbury Journal* to indicate his approval:

> A few residents no doubt will have to be expropriated, but there can be no fear that they will be liberally compensated. As regards the district at large nothing but good can result. There will be a revival of movement and prosperity all around it. The markets will be stimulated, small cultivators of fruit and vegetables and poultry owners will benefit immensely, and the decaying villages and farms on Salisbury Plain will ere long, participate in the general improvement … I for one rejoice that Salisbury Plain is likely to realise its manifest destiny as the training ground of the British Army.[7]

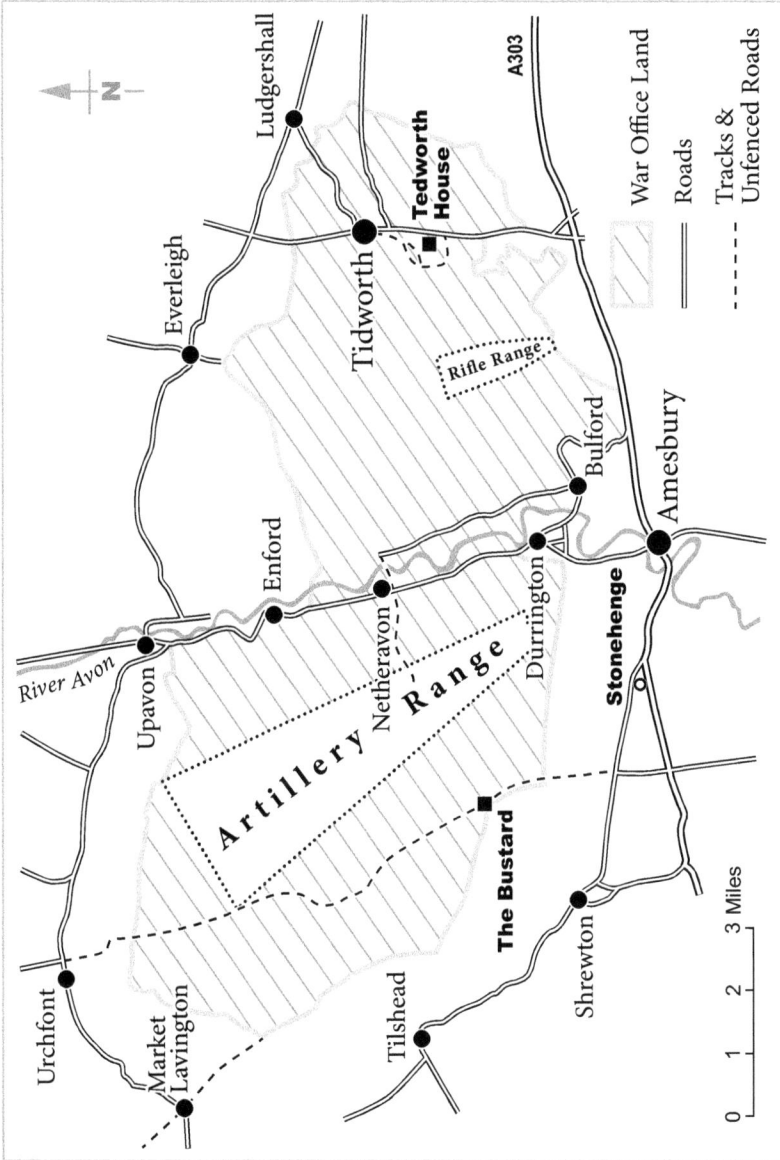

1.2 Initial acquisition of land by War Office (1899).

Ludgershall

Everleigh

Tidworth

Tedworth House

Rifle Range

A303

Bulford

Amesbury

Enford

Netheravon

Durrington

Stonehenge

River Avon

Upavon

Artillery Range

The Bustard

Urchfont

Market Lavington

Tilshead

Shrewton

N

War Office Land

Roads

Tracks & Unfenced Roads

0   1   2   3 Miles

While trumpeting his enthusiasm for the forced purchase of large sections of the Plain, Sir Henry's letter anticipated some local resistance. The first five years saw rapid expansion of the training area, and by 1902 over 40,000 acres had been acquired. A War Office and Defence Land Agent was appointed to supervise the running of the estate, which grew by 1,500 acres over the following decade.

Mimic warfare

It is hard to estimate how people might have felt about the military occupation of so much pastoral land, but recent archaeological work has uncovered that, far from being empty or derelict, the Plain was much more intensively farmed than originally thought.[8] Although the local human population was very small, the whole area of the Plain was used. Situated on its southern edge, the medieval city of Salisbury maintained its commercial and industrial dominance from the 1200s to the mid-1500s on the back of, among other things, the wool trade. Wool and cloth were also exported to many countries in mainland Europe and elsewhere through the port in Southampton. Even though these trades went into decline from the middle of the sixteenth century, sheep farming persisted as the mainstay of many farming communities scattered around the region.

The Wiltshire Horned Sheep grazed across the Plain in the summer months and were used to fertilise arable soils in the winter. From the early 1700s farmers had discovered that if they burned turf and spread the ashes on the ground – a process called 'burnbaking' or 'burn-beaking' – they could slowly convert grassland into arable soil. And in the valleys water meadows were also important to the farming economy.[9]

These local economies and pre-industrial farming ecologies were inevitably disrupted by the government's enclosure of such a large area. Inhabitants were also somewhat dismayed to see their horizon transformed by the military presence, as this quotation from 'Round About Wiltshire', a local guide written by A.G. Bradley, indicates in 1907:

As we pass above Milston with its little church ... the corrugated iron town of Bulford on the Plain beyond, comes painfully within range, and Sidbury Hill and other more distant heights about Tedworth ... seem to look even at this distance, as if worn by the tramp of horse and men and seared by the smoke of mimic warfare. But this is treason, for I can imagine no spot in all this island anything like so favourable for summering and exercising our hardly raised and none too numerous defenders ... Here we have a country dry and firm like the South African velt [*sic*] or the Manitoba prairies.[10]

In 1913 another local historian, Ella Noyes, ended the preface to her ruminative guidebook, *Salisbury Plain, Its Stones, Cathedral, Villages and Folk*, by saying, 'I have hardly touched upon the fact – unhappy from all except, perhaps, from a practical point of view – that the eastern part of the Plain has been adopted of late years as a military training ground, but it cannot be ignored.'[11]

In some ways, she continued, there is less change than might be thought. The sheer expanse of the Plain meant that 'the camps scattered here and there, from April to September – and even a permanent settlement such as Bulford Camp – are soon lost and forgotten in its immensity'. A fold in the downs might hide a whole contingent of men, while the sight of the cavalry at exercise is 'even picturesque to see'. By alluding to the intrusive aspects of the army's presence, Noyes managed to signify a grudging acceptance.

The 'dust and disturbance of passing troops and military traffic' might be offset by the 'sweetness and peace' brought by the autumn rains, while the season of firing practice 'which prohibits free wandering on the downs in the military area at certain hours of the day' could be easily forgotten as soon as it was over. In the final sentence of her preface, Noyes made her own feelings clear: 'The western and southern part of the Plain remain free from invasion'. Perhaps, in the months preceding the outbreak of war the following year, she was already anticipating the inevitable expansion.

In the decade following the end of the 1914–18 war, Noyes's fears were realised. The total area of the Plain purchased between 1920 and 1930 amounted to some 14,850 acres, most of which lay to the west of the existing estate. On 27 September 1927, for example, an area of 935 acres, comprising the parishes of Imber and West

Lavington, was added. This was the forerunner to numerous acquisitions which were ultimately to provide land for the School of Infantry at Warminster and what became known as the Imber ranges. During and after the Second World War purchases of land declined to such an extent that from 1 April 1940 to 31 March 1983 the net increase was only 1,537 acres, bringing the site up to 37,105 hectares as a whole.

Collateral damage

The Plain looks quite different depending on the season and time of day. On a hazy afternoon in spring it might appear almost lunar; the land swoops and falls as far as the eye can see, carpeted by yellow-green grasses and dusted by a purplish haze of the viper's bugloss and sainfoin prized by local beekeepers.[12] Meanwhile the grassy expanse is interrupted by incongruous squares of tall conifer plantations, originally planted during the Cold War to mimic the landscape of East Germany. It would be impossible now to subtract the ecological history of the Plain from an account of its transformation through military usage, yet, until recently, much of the evidence of ceaseless war preparation was concealed from public view.

In 2012 the Royal Geographical Society produced a guide to 'military environmentalism', a joint project with the Institute of British Geographers which brought this phenomenon to light. 'Discover prehistoric sites and rare species preserved on Salisbury Plain' it begins, enticing readers with the prospect of natural and historic wonders spiced with military glamour: 'An ocean of grassland and a sweep of big sky. Ancient monuments loom out of the mist; camouflaged soldiers crouch in the undergrowth.'[13] The author Marianna Dudley, a researcher focusing on UK Defence Estate, explains:

> As an environmental historian, I am interested in the gradual 'greening' of the military and its increase in environmental awareness over the twentieth century. I hope you enjoy the wonderful scenery and beautiful fresh air of this area as you learn more about military environmentalism.

The booklet offers a walking tour that begins at the village of Tilshead, a spot that offers a perfect starting point for exploring this strange territory. 'The extremes of Salisbury Plain sit side by side.

Use this spectacular landscape to stretch your legs, blow away the cobwebs and fire the imagination.' On the next page there is a warning: 'This walk takes place in an active military training area so you might see or hear soldiers on training exercises. Don't be afraid of them, but neither should you interrupt their training activities.'

The trail begins at a Neolithic long barrow, which appears as a raised pathway lined by tall trees. At the south-western end of the mound it is possible to see tree graffiti, or arborglyphs, carved by American GIs during the Second World War. One features a lifesize profile of a woman. Her hair is set in fashionable victory rolls and her dress has a low-cut V-neck, as if she was just heading off to the dancehall. Her shoulders have widened as the tree has grown over the years.

The next section introduces the geological makeup of Salisbury Plain, explaining why this is such an extraordinary environment. According to Dudley, 'Archaeologists regard Salisbury Plain as a "fossilised" landscape because it has been protected from decades of farming by the presence of the military.' Salisbury Plain comprises 40 per cent of the entire area of chalk grassland left in the UK, which partially explains why half of the wider military training area is now protected as a Site of Special Scientific Interest, a Special Area of Conservation and a Special Protection Area.[14]

The tour then leads to what appears to be a deserted housing estate on the side of Copehill Down. First built in 1978, this site constitutes one of the army's largest urban training grounds, commonly known as Fighting-in-Built-up-Areas. Covering over 70 acres, the site is routinely adapted to suit different geopolitical scenarios from East Germany and West Belfast to Basra and Bagram. Dudley describes seeing 'adobe desert dwellings built with Arabic signage on the walls' on the day she was permitted to visit.

'Washing was hanging on lines, there was also the wreckage of a helicopter and fake blood spattered in the dirt. You may find this level of detail surprising, but the military go to great lengths to create realistic battle conditions, even if the grassy plain has to stand in for dry desert.' Just a few miles away, she continues, a new Fighting-in-Built-up-Areas site was built that recreated 'typical Afghani

1.3 Copehill Down, a Fighting-in-Built-up-Areas training village on Salisbury Plain.

compounds' using a hundred shipping containers with removable hoardings.

Commenting on the project on BBC News in 2012, a senior officer told journalists, 'We cannot replicate Afghanistan on Salisbury Plain. But we can put in place adequate infrastructure to enable essential tactics, tools and techniques to be rehearsed, practised and perfected.' Wiltshire Council approved the plans on condition that the 50 'simplified structures' located at 27 sites were removed by the end of 2015.[15]

In 2016 a more substantial training facility would be added to this assortment of 'fake' environments when a dozen buildings were demolished to make way for a new 'modern, multi-purpose training camp'.[16] Costing £2.4 million, a complex of 11 building shells or 'stone tents' was built at the New Zealand Farm Camp to replicate 'a terrorist or refugee camp'. This was the 'biggest single invest-ment' in a training facility in the area since the 1980s. According to senior military figures, the investment would allow the army to 'pre-pare in a realistic and challenging environment': the site's 'diverse training features' provided a 'broad variety of challenging exercise scenarios'.

To the north of Copehill Down lies another outdated Fighting-in-Built-up-Areas site, the so-called abandoned village of Imber, requisi-tioned by the Ministry of Defence in 1943 for the purposes of training with assurances that this was a temporary measure. As Dudley explains, 'Villagers left under the impression that they would be able to return to their homes when peace resumed'. In fact this never happened, despite concerted protest from former residents and activ-ist groups. Today it is accessible only on certain public holidays when the church of St Giles is opened for visitors. In addition, once a year, hundreds of visitors are driven to the Imber in a style that accentuates the nostalgic aspects of the village: 'The Imberbus ser-vice uses, among other buses, classic red London double-deckers, complete with conductors using Gibson A14 ticket machines as seen on London Transport buses until the early 1990s.'[17]

The church itself has been maintained, although a sign at the edge of the graveyard warns visitors not to leave the path in case of unexploded bombs. The rest of the village was allowed to fall into disrepair after the army took over. The guide offers a rationale that might sound logical today, but skips the depth of feeling aroused by this betrayal. 'The village was retained for training,' it explains, 'and remains in use today as our Armed Forces prepare for operations.'

In order to look more critically at the phrase 'retained for train-ing' we need to turn to an eyewitness account written in 1947. This describes the state of the village in the immediate postwar period:

> At the approach to the village, the outpost trees were gaunt and bare, stripped of all their foliage as by a tornado. They were bleached skel-etons of trees. We were on a real battlefield ... The useless telephone wires once connecting Imber with the exchange in Warminster, hung in tangles from the cracked poles. The first farm-house was empty, its rooftiles missing, the next windowless, with rabbits fleeing through

its drunken doorway. For rabbits had taken over possession of Imber. There were droves of them, sweeping across the roadways and gardens, like game on the plains of Kenya.[18]

The author, an environmental activist called Monica Hutchings, had visited the place on two previous occasions before 1939, finding it a well-kept and lively village despite being a little on the remote side. Hutchings's opinion of the army's careless treatment of Imber after the war reflected her frustration that there was a serious housing shortage in the south-west, and that this destruction was simply needless.

> Some of the damage appeared wilful and nothing to do with the ravages of time or nature, or even the whistling of shells overhead. For Imber was not and never had been a target in itself, or the scene of a hand-to-hand-battle school. It was just that it was in the area used for War Office exercises.[19]

It seemed like another world, she wrote, 'but we remembered that it was a world at the mercy of missiles that went just a little astray, and worse still at the mercy of marauding hordes of rabbits from their undisturbed breeding grounds. How little the Army understand about food production.' Noting that, had the boundaries been moved by just a mile, Imber would have been outside the area and therefore still flourishing and productive, Hutchings continued, 'With all the barren parts of the Plain as a battle-school, we could not understand why it should be found necessary to sacrifice a thriving village, and why the boundaries had not been drawn to exclude Imber'.

From the tone of Hutchings's writing it is clear that the army was seen as far more than the occasional nuisance and inconvenience that Ella Noyes had described in 1913. By 1947 it was regarded as a careless interloper. Worse still was the attitude of the War Office, which remained intransigent in the face of a national campaign to restore the village. 'Owing to the size and range of modern weapons,' Hutchings railed, they would not give it back. Her response was to travel the perilous road back to the now forbidden zone, accompanied by a film-maker and cameraman who secretly shot almost an hour of footage. Extracts were used in her film *New Face of Britain*, but, as she later wrote, 'it was only a part of the theme of the film – this usurping of homes and agricultural land by the military'.

Hutchings's testimony on the fate of Imber provides just one example of the opposition encountered by the postwar government, which stood accused of reneging on the firm promise to return public land and buildings after hostilities ended. Today, while the ruins of Imber survive as a memorial to a different geopolitical era, there is nothing anachronistic about them in our age of perpetual war. The gaping windows and torn roofs stand as testimony that the word 'civilian' ought never to be used to designate a simplistic 'non-combatant' status. Civilians are those whose lives are merely collateral damage in the practice of modern warfare.

Accidental environmentalism

While the material presence of outdated training facilities provides a haunting spectacle, the Royal Geographical Society tour guide is keen to direct attention to the benefits incurred by constant military use of the Plain, most of which were, initially at least, a by-product rather than a deliberate contribution. The first item that appears to have thrived on the army's presence is a minute, translucent creature popularly known as the 'Fairy Shrimp', otherwise classified as *Chirocephalus diaphanus*. As Marianna Dudley explains,

> Fairy Shrimp are no bigger than your little fingernail. They live in puddles and ditches and are one of only a few species able to undergo cryptobiosis, which is a state of torpor in which they shut down to survive extreme droughts and temperatures. This means their eggs can survive up to 15 years, even when their pools dry out, and hatch when water returns. Historically, the shrimp were dispersed in puddles around the plain by the hooves of grazing cattle. But cultivation of this area declined in the nineteenth century and the shrimp's survival was under threat. It was even protected under Schedule 5 of the Wildlife and Countryside Protection Act of 1981.

The puddles created in tank tracks have inadvertently created an ideal habitat, and for this reason the species has been hailed as a symbol of the 'accidental environmentalism' that has resulted from the army's longstanding occupation of the Plain.[20] The emphasis on conservation entailed in justifying the British Army's use of this apparently unproductive terrain helps to explain why contemporary military bases and training grounds seem to evade scrutiny as sites of ongoing war preparation.[21]

Another example of this phenomenon is provided by the distinctive clumps of trees that also define this landscape. 'The military planted the trees for training purposes,' asserts Dudley, 'but they have also become habitat for a variety of species'. Some of these patches of woodland have been planted by defence estate managers, while older maps indicate that others predate the military era. Trees are useful for windbreaks or preventing soil erosion, for example, as well as recreational pursuits such as fox-hunting. Now they offer shelter for troops on exercise as well as acting as landmarks in the open countryside. As Dudley remarks, before introducing a section on the cultural significance of the Plain in literature and folklore, 'this kind of empty, open space is really rare in southern England so you can understand why the military wanted to use it …'.

Khaki conservation

Driving across what appears to be open country from the vantage point of the A303 it can be hard to believe that this apparently undeveloped region bears any relation to violent military conflicts conducted far away. At the same time it is important to remember that the area falls within the local authority jurisdiction, making it subject to all manner of restrictions, obligations and compromises. With the exception of planning for live training exercises, the Ministry of Defence remains hostage to civilian directives, especially those that apply to landscape and biodiversity protection. How on earth did this happen?

The accidental 'military environmentalism' described by the Royal Geographical Society promotes the benefits of military land use for land and environmental management, and it is a term often used to justify the military's right to maintain ownership of large sections of national territories.[22] Rachel Woodward, who has been scrutinising this phenomenon over more than two decades, has dismissed military environmentalism as 'greenwash' because it seeks to disguise the fundamentally destructive nature of contemporary militarism and is instrumental in controlling vast territories without impediment.[23]

In her critique of what she terms 'khaki conservation' she borrowed the phrase 'crater-as-habitat' from Patrick Wright's path-breaking study of the military occupation of the Dorset coast: *The Village that Died for England*, first published in 1996. Writing in the context of the proliferation of US, French and British military bases in the second half of the twentieth century, Coates, Pearson, Dudley and Cole have argued that this claim became an 'attempt to wrap the ongoing (and growing) project of American militarisation in a new ecological cloak'.[24]

In the UK it is hard to comprehend this embrace of environmental objectives without noting the widespread civilian protests against military damage of Salisbury Plain in the 1960s and 1970s. In his introduction to the first edition of *The Buildings of England: Wiltshire*, published in 1963, the famous architectural historian Nikolaus Pevsner described the impact on rural Wiltshire – where he had a second home – with barely contained anger.

> Wiltshire would be as wonderful as it must have been in Hardy's, in Hudson's and in Jefferies's days, if the army, and more recently the air force, had not got hold of it. As it is, the army is up in Salisbury Plain with towns of barracks and genteel soldiers' housing and with all the mess of tin huts and tank tracks, and the air force is down in the northern plain with the mess of the airfields and the noise of the planes.[25]

The deserted village of Imber was to play a significant role in this transformation. While former residents had been allowed to visit periodically, if only to weep over the ruins of their former homes, by 1960 the services on the Saturday nearest to St Giles's Day had become an annual pilgrimage. Even this controlled right of access would shortly be terminated, however, partly because the church was pronounced unsafe. In his history of the campaign to restore the place to its rightful inhabitants – *Little Imber on the Down* – Rex Sawyer describes the anger that remained long after the village had been cleared.[26]

> By the end of 1960 the battle lines, if not formally drawn, had at least been pencilled in. Villagers, still smarting under the refusal of the

authorities to allow them to return to Imber, were now further embittered by the threatened removal of their church, a potent symbol of their hopes for reinstatement. Farmers, notably Sydney Dean, were anxious to return to the land their families had tended for centuries. All that was needed was a catalyst to bring things to a head. This was provided by the War Office and was not so much a spark as a slow burning fuse.

The military authorities had been pressing the Ministry of Transport to make a Draft Order prohibiting the public rights of way in the Imber Range Area, and a temporary order had been in place since 1951. In December 1960 the Defence of the Realm Act, which had permitted authorities to close highways during the war years, ceased to operate, but it was clear that the War Office intended to block public access on a permanent basis.

The following month Amesbury Rural District Council agreed to submit a formal objection to the government. Led by Councillor Austin Underwood, a campaign was assembled in order to demand a public inquiry, and a demonstration was announced for 22 January, with the intention of delivering a symbolic notice to the army to quit. The first protest march was an astonishing spectacle.

> Various estimates recorded vehicles in excess of 350 cars and a similar number of vans crawling bumper to bumper through a landscape invaded by scrubland, across the mud-churned tracks to Imber, stopping momentarily to offer lifts to the hundreds of foot travellers. Motorcycles, scooters and pedal cycles wove between the slower vehicles skidding on the greasy surface. A three-mile queue moved turgidly forward past fields criss-crossed with tank and lorry tracks, derelict buildings and triangular notices along the verges warning 'TO LEAVE THE ROAD IS DANGEROUS' and 'THERE ARE MISSILES THAT CAN KILL'.

Although most of the protesters were local, and at least two hundred had a strong connection to Imber itself, many came from as far as London, Liverpool, Sussex and the Midlands. But it was not just the unexpected crowds that would make the War Department take notice. Underwood was an experienced campaigner and knew how to solicit media attention. Mimicking the eviction order given to residents of Imber twenty years earlier, he nailed a 'Notice to Quit' sign on the side of the Bell Inn. The text of the poster read: 'We, the people, hereby serve notice on the War Department to vacate and deliver up to the County of Wiltshire the Parish of Imber'.

In front of military officials disguised in civilian dress, he urged the assembled crowd: 'Isn't it wonderful! Here are the army vehicles, the people in control at the War Office and they are powerless. Here we are, together with them, back in Imber. Visit the church and the remains of what was Imber. Reclaim your heritage!'

Underwood's rousing words ended with a direct challenge: 'If the stones cannot cry out, then the men must cry out. I will be one and there will be hundreds and thousands more ...' He was followed by other speakers, equally passionate. Among them was Monica Hutchings, who recounted her admiration for Imber's fertile soil. 'Let the army use land on which nothing will grow,' she exclaimed, 'the services own one seventh of the whole acreage of this one county. I think it is too much.'[27]

The rally ended with a unanimous vote:

> To keep open all rights of way in the Imber area and strenuously oppose any move to close them
> To re-establish the farms and agricultural life of Imber
> To re-establish Imber as a civil and ecclesiastical parish.

Underwood's militant campaign would continue for the next few months, although he never again managed to draw such a large crowd. The War Department – which was subsumed into the newly created Ministry of Defence in 1964 – was rattled, however, and began to take notice, especially as similar demands to release military lands were being expressed in other parts of the country.[28] In October 1970 Edward Heath, newly elected Conservative Prime Minister, announced that he had asked Lord Carrington, the Defence Secretary, to conduct a review of the armed services' land holdings with a view to finding areas that could be released, especially in national parks and coastal areas.[29] This led to the formation of the Defence Lands Committee, headed by Lord Nugent of Guilford.[30]

The Nugent Committee produced a report in 1973 which laid the groundwork for better co-operation between the government, environmental statutory bodies, county councils, and civilian groups like the Ramblers.[31] The Ministry of Defence – usually referred to as the MoD – appointed its first conservation officer, based at Westdown Camp near Tilshead, with a brief to organise and integrate those relationships. Any hopes of restoring any meaningful rights of access to the former inhabitants of Imber were finally laid to rest, however. The Nugent Report recommended that the village would remain closed to the public except for relatives visiting the churchyard and that the ecclesiastical authorities should be invited to consider whether the annual services should be continued.

Despite the intransigence over the future of Imber, the report marked a complete change in tactics regarding the way in which the Ministry of Defence was able to justify its occupation of so much land. According to Dudley, 'Mentioning in particular the success of rare birds nesting on SPTA as an example of the inadvertent conservation occurring across military landholdings, Nugent foresaw that if the army was to continue to use land for training, it would have to justify its presence by recognising and meeting its duty as a holder of some of the richest lands in the country in terms of wildlife, heritage and natural beauty.'[32]

This landmark report signalled that, instead of symbolising the confiscation of rural England from its indigenous inhabitants, the army might be seen as rightful custodians of the land. In his detailed account of the campaigns to eject the army from the Dorset coastal village of Tyneham and adjacent heathland, Patrick Wright draws out the political implications of this compact.

> Seen from a distance, the army's conversion to conservation raises questions about the ecological cause, and the lengths to which its activists are prepared to go in their eagerness to place a limit on environmental transgression – preferring tanks to the limitless principles of private property and the individual's right to choose.[33]

Alert to what we might now call the 'optics' of listening to environmentalists after the Nugent report was published, the Ministry of Defence began to grant more access to particular sites for the purposes of conservation studies. In 1976 a small publication, entitled *Sanctuary*, was launched, with the aim of documenting biodiversity and sustainability projects across the military defence estate.[34] In 1992 this same magazine published an article about the surprising presence of the fairy shrimp, and the idea of the shell-crater-as-habitat became an incontrovertible fact.

Today *Sanctuary* is an annual publication, nearly a hundred pages long, and over the years it has gained a positive reputation for its focus on military conservation efforts. The naturalist and broadcaster Chris Packham provided the foreword to the 2017 edition, for example, congratulating the Ministry of Defence for proper management and protection of its estate. 'You see,' he wrote, 'I approve of their lack of access, their level of protection in our over-crowded, over-trampled age and I am reassured that they remain properly protected and managed with the natural environment in mind.'[35]

Packham, who is President of the Board of Directors of the world-famous Hawk Conservancy Trust located just off the A303 west of Andover, singled out *Sanctuary*'s focus on the 'considerable and successful' efforts of Ministry of Defence staff and partners working overseas, giving special mention to 'the potentially positive aspects of the reactivation of military training in Belize, a country with significant but imperilled natural resources'.

> Likewise in Laikipia – Kenya, where a training exercise helped con-solidate economic security in a region fraught with conflict and dif-ficulties. Conservation management and sustainable building in the Falklands also exemplify the expanding and flourishing stewardship of the Defence Estates, not only at home but all over the world.
> Top work! I salute you!
> (If civilians are allowed to do that!)[36]

To this date the Imber Conservation Group, one of the founding members of the military conservation effort, has a regular feature in the magazine, providing updates on items like the spawning suc-cesses of the common toad, the flowering of the viper's bugloss in spring, the wall brown butterflies and the growing winchat populations.[37]

In this way *Sanctuary* has operated as a valve for both local resi-dents and military communities, encouraging them to appreciate nature and outdoor recreation on the UK's military estates. This is a tactical strategy in which integration is promoted, allowing the military to continue its activities while carefully managing ecosystems around and inside its training areas. In fact *Sanctuary* is at pains to emphasise the difficult balance that is struck between conservation and military training needs, which remain paramount in the management of the defence estate. However, in addition to justifying the military presence as an environmental asset for the country, *Sanctuary* has also managed to adapt its brief to address the rapidly accumulating evidence that climate change has serious implications for global and regional security.

In 2013 the Intergovernmental Panel on Climate Change released its Fifth Assessment Report in which it offered peer-reviewed research about the role of human activities in contributing to climate change, largely through the release of polluting gases from burning fossil fuels. As reluctant governments were grudgingly forced to address the scientific evidence, national militaries were put on notice that they had an important role to play. In response *Sanctuary* shifted from a chronicle of conservation successes and archaeological finds – especially those that demonstrate the Ministry of Defence's willingness to engage with the outside world – to a corporate tool that fitted a more overtly political agenda.

That same year the banner on the front cover changed from 'Conservation Magazine' to 'Sustainability Magazine'. More ominously, the logos of 'industry partners' from Wessex Archaeology, Veolia and Sodexo to QinetiQ adorned the inside pages. QinetiQ is a multinational defence contractor based at Farnborough in Hampshire. It currently operates the military aircraft testing site at RAF Boscombe Down on the south-eastern edge of Amesbury. This arrangement was part of a multi-million-pound deal that also included plans to modernise air ranges at MoD Aberporth, Wales, and MoD Hebrides, Scotland. In 2023 the UK government signed a further £80 million, ten-year industry partnership with QinetiQ to instigate 'Team Pegasus'. This is intended to 'enhance the UK's ability to provide its military platforms and systems with the data needed to keep them safe and effective'.[38]

In the fiftieth anniversary edition, published in 2021, an editorial explained how the magazine had evolved since its inception in the 1970s.

> While *Sanctuary* continues to feature more traditional articles relating to environmental and heritage conservation, recreation and access, there has been a significant increase in sustainability content over the last decade. The magazine highlights topics such as the sustainable management of the MOD's built asset and procurement processes as well as responses to climate change.[39]

As we shall see later, these kinds of environmental arguments effectively conceal the fact that military activities are fundamentally unsustainable. Militaries are also major polluters and biodiversity often exists adjacent to, or even interdependent with, deathly toxicity.[40] As Adrian Parr points out in his book *Hijacking Sustainability*, the concept remains the subject of fierce debate, not least because there is little agreement on what it actually means in any given context.[41]

Rather than dismissing military environmentalism as 'greenwash', as Woodward argued so persuasively two decades ago, we suggest that the word 'camouwash' might be more appropriate in the light of this latest brand of institutional piety. The Ministry of Defence is able to conceal the British military's complicity in contributing to global climate change behind a thicket of phrases such as 'carbon sequestration', 'sustainable construction projects', 'stakeholder engagement forums' and 'nature capital'.

Although we return to these questions towards the end of this book, the Plain itself tells a different story about the longer impact of military occupation over time. From the First World War chalk carvings to the blasted tank hulks, to the mock Afghan village, to the rutted tank tracks, the topography of Salisbury Plain Training Area offers evidence of historic violence on almost unimaginable scale. Following this survey of the distinctive horizon of grassland, scrub and woodland for signs of invasion, it is now time to enter the built environment to encounter the sedimentation of 120 years of military history in bricks and cement.

National heritage

If you were planning to head across the Plain as a way to avoid the A303, it would be a good idea to consult a map. Most of the larger roads run from north to south connecting the larger towns and cities – Salisbury, Marlborough, Devizes – and some minor routes follow the path of meandering rivers like the Avon. Travelling east from Tilshead, in the direction of Tidworth, you would first need to drive south before turning on to the Packway, an old road that was rebuilt by the army at the end of the nineteenth century.

Taking this route across the Plain would ensure that contact with the modern British Army was unavoidable. While Tidworth, the focus of this book, is the largest town on the eastern side of the Salisbury Plain Training Area, the 'super garrison' encompasses a sprawling conglomeration of camps and training facilities that suggest significant investment in defence infrastructure as well as a highly securitised environment typical of all military bases. Even without a tour guide, the indelible signs of Britain's involvement in war-fighting in many parts of the world can be read off these built-up areas too, revealing a very different story about national heritage from the one offered by Stonehenge a few miles to the south.

The Packway sets off across a bare expanse of Plain towards the garrison town of Larkhill, one of the earliest camps to be established. Originally named Lark Hill because it was the highest point in the parish of Durrington, it is now famous as the home of the Royal School of Artillery. In 1898 the empty expanse of the designated training area allowed the army to experiment with new forms of shooting technology at sufficient distance from human habitation.

As a result the firing ranges that were established in this section of the Plain proved invaluable for troops, including cavalry regiments, based at Aldershot, the official army headquarters in neighbouring Hampshire. Until then soldiers had been required to travel to Okehampton for commensurable access to space and remoteness, although the weather in Devon was judged to be less favourable. By 1906 there were several camp sites on the Plain providing accommodation for visitors, one of which was to become the permanent garrison of Larkhill.

This is one example of the practical and logistical factors governing the spread of military facilities across Salisbury Plain in the early 1900s. Larkhill was also an early centre for army aviation after amateur flying enthusiasts demonstrated their skills on a rented area of land near Stonehenge. In *Plain Soldiering*, James describes how, in 1911, No. 2 Company of the Air Battalion Royal Engineers was established at Larkhill, the first flying unit of the armed forces to use aeroplanes as opposed to hot-air balloons.

This evolved into No. 3 Squadron, Royal Flying Corps, in May 1912, the first RFC to use aeroplanes.[42] In July of that year, however, Captain Eustace Loraine and Staff Sergeant Richard Wilson were killed in the RFC's first fatal accident. Today their deaths are commemorated by a stone memorial, known as Airman's Cross, which sits at the entrance to the Stonehenge Visitors Centre. The accompanying plaque reminds tourists drawn to prehistory that the area also happens to be the 'cradle of British military aviation'.

In 1914 the aerodrome was closed and transformed into garrison accommodation. In fact the outbreak of war provides one of the founding narratives of the military settlement on Salisbury Plain. In addition to the hundreds of young English recruits who required instant accommodation under canvas, the arrival of large contingents of troops from Canada, Newfoundland, New Zealand and Australia from October 1914 onwards necessitated the rapid construction of temporary settlements. In 1917 these were described as 'wooden and tin hutted camps – some huts on brick supports about two to three feet high'.[43] Many of these survived until the 1950s or later when they were replaced by permanent barracks and administrative buildings. Traces of this history survive in many forms, from the military cemetery and monuments to street names, earthworks and other forms of memorialisation.

Driving into Larkhill now it would be impossible to mistake this as an ordinary rural community. Barbed wire tops the metal fencing around the garrison and a security notice marks the terror threat as 'heightened'. A little further, the stark red-brick rectangle of the Garrison Church of St Alban the Martyr comes into view. This was built in 1937 to replace the corrugated iron building that was hastily erected in Christmas 1915 to serve the spiritual needs of the Commonwealth troops. Today everything on the right-hand side of the road falls within the UNESCO World Heritage site. In every direction, however, there are reminders of British military history, sometimes predating the army's use of the Plain.

As you continue along the Packway, for example, you pass through a neighbourhood called Strangways, named after Brigadier General T. Fox Strangways who perished at the Battle of Inkerman during the Crimean War.[44] But not all cues point to the past. On the other side of the road there is a large new housing estate providing accommodation for service families relocating from Germany. This is tangible evidence that the government's decision to close some of the military bases in Europe represented significant investment nearer home.

On leaving Larkhill, the Packway passes the outskirts of Durrington, an ancient village just over two miles north of Stonehenge. Famous today for the archaeological finds at Durrington Walls and Woodhenge, the parish was transformed by the military expansion at Larkhill and its population has grown considerably as a result. After crossing the River Avon, the main road continues through Bulford camp. At the end of the 1900s Bulford was a small farming village within an estate owned by a Miss Seymour. More than a thousand acres of land, which included the village, was sold to the War Office in two sales completed in 1898 and 1900.[45]

Here there is further evidence of the Commonwealth troops hastily assembled in 1914. The modern Canadian Estate, with street names like Quebec and Toronto Road, commemorates Britain's historic relationship with its older Commonwealth of white settler nations and their contribution to the First World War war effort. Directly opposite is a cluster of nearly three hundred new-builds, another development mandated by the Army Basing Programme. Its modern streets are named after First World War battles at Cambrai, Messines and Ypres.

Bulford camp, which was developed as a permanent settlement between the wars, is hard to navigate because there is no obvious centre. Sections housing different regiments are ringed with high security fences. It would be easy to miss the signpost, but this is also the location for Bulford military court, situated inside Kiwi barracks. Here soldiers are court-martialled for a range of offences within military law; proceedings take place in a context that is largely impenetrable to civilian inquiry.[46] Those who are convicted are sent to the Military Corrective Training Centre in Colchester, Essex.

As you find your way through the maze of barracks and housing estates you might notice the sign to Gaza Road which abruptly brings the contemporary history of colonial warfare directly into the heart of England. Then Tidworth Road leads to open country again, criss-crossed with white chalk tracks, with rifle ranges visible in the distance. The uniformly spaced and enclosed fields are labelled from A to F – Alpha to Foxtrot – and marked with signs warning against unauthorised entry. Rectangles of cement and gravel mark points where troops crouch to aim at their targets in the distance. After a short while a giant outline of a bird becomes visible on Beacon Hill to your right. This is a Kiwi, carved into the chalk landscape by Commonwealth troops from New Zealand in 1919.

As the road curves into the garrison of Tidworth, the first purpose-built army buildings come into view. The town was originally two villages – North Tidworth and South Tidworth – and the Wiltshire–Hampshire border ran between them until county boundaries were redrawn in 1992. The barracks and army lines were constructed on the former Tedworth estate in the first decade of the 1900s, and the town that developed from this foundation provides one of the best examples of military place-making in the country. In order to transport men, equipment and building materials, a system of railway lines was constructed across the Plain. It ran through the heart of Tidworth garrison for many years until it was dismantled, leaving barely a trace. However, the red-brick walls of the Victorian barracks survive as testimony to British colonial power at its zenith, casting a peculiar shadow over this part of the world.

In many ways Tidworth's built environment can be approached as a heritage centre, much like a theme park designed to acquaint the visitor with distant geographies. Names of roads and buildings act as mnemonics, summoning legends of military prowess, bloodshed and honour that no British schoolchildren would ever be asked to learn today. Sandwiched between The Mall and Bazaar Road, the Grade 2 listed barrack blocks still bear their original names over their front elevation: Aliwal, Assaye, Candahar, Mootan, Bhurtpore, Delhi, Jellalabad, Lucknow.

Behind them runs a minor throughway linking both new and old administrative buildings, identified by a mundane sign that reads Grand Trunk Road. In every direction there are road names derived from British imperial expansion into South Asia: Plassey, Meerut, Lahore, Lowa, Nainital, Baroda, Agra, Jasna, Jamrud. The mis-spelling in the word 'Nepaul' is not so much a hint of illiteracy as a sign of the long relationship between the British Army and its Gurkha workforce.

There are buildings too that demand attention, as they speak of social history as well as a fusion of local and military culture. The A338, also known as Pennings Road, runs through the town, passing Tidworth Garrison Theatre as it links the barracks to the commercial centre. An earlier incarnation was built in 1909 next to the barracks, on the corners of Bazaar and Lowa Road in order to provide entertainment for troops.[47] Over time it became famous for hosting national and international stars such as Norman Wisdom and James Cagney. Tony Pickernell, former manager of the theatre and grandson of its first manager, once described it to us as the 'bee's-knees of theatres out in the suburbs'.

In 2013 a larger replacement was built 'outside the wire' and is now managed on behalf of the Defence Infrastructure Organisation by Aspire Defence, the private sector initiative tasked with the development of the 'super garrison'. The theatre is used for hosting garrison and defence industry events and, in theory, is accessible to members of the public. The corporate red-brick and glass frontage of the theatre makes quite an impression in this small town.

As in Larkhill and Bulford, the design, layout and street signage of 'married quarters', designated today as 'service family accommodation', have their own stories to reveal. In James's account of the Tidworth's early development he recounts the fact that the original sets of housing – two rows of 24 units assigned to each barrack block – were built one in front of the other rather than in a longer terrace. 'They were known locally as "Merthyr Tydfils,"' he wrote, 'presumably since it was thought that they bore some resemblance to the rows of houses to be seen in some Welsh mining areas'.[48] By 1984 most of these were either demolished or derelict.

Driving round one of the new estates designed for soldiers of different ranks and their families, it is clear that, while architectural and environmental standards have improved considerably, military narratives play an important role in maintaining Tidworth's civic identity. The pattern of naming buildings and roads after historic battles seems just as important today as it has been in the past. Over many decades planners have been able to draw from an inexhaustible sourcebook with little sense of the political implications of their choices. Thus the 'crimson thread' of heroism, sacrifice, terror and slaughter runs through Tidworth garrison and its adjoining camps, marking the whole of the training area as occupied territory.[49]

Just as the aftermath of the Crimean War prompted reform of a sclerotic and corrupt institution, so Britain's most recent wars have resulted in a concerted attempt to alter the political, social and cultural profile of military labour in response to public dismay about what all those grim sacrifices were for. Yet, as time goes by, it becomes harder to gauge the impact of these latest measures, some of which were aimed at integrating the armed forces into a disintegrating welfare state.

While the prospect of military training summons images of guns, tanks and bodies dressed in khaki, it is the sprawling infrastructure of the military base that remains almost impossible to visualise.

Camouflaged in a benign rural setting, tucked away behind the world-famous megaliths of Stonehenge, Tidworth is a spectacular example of an overlooked military outpost: at once an anachronistic monument to imperial history yet also a laboratory for understanding what it is like to live in such close proximity to the British Army today.

Contact zones

Station Road in Tidworth may, at first glance, look like any other high street in a small English town. On one side there is a large supermarket with its own car park, and on the other a string of cafés, shops, salons and restaurants. It does not look like the commercial heart of an important military base, a zone where ordinary citizens are often indistinguishable from soldiers. In fact it is the kind of street where it is entirely unremarkable for an armoured vehicle to stop at the zebra crossing, or where you might find yourself drinking your morning coffee next to men and women just returned from the firing ranges. It therefore provides a perfect opportunity for glimpsing what it might be like to cohabit with the British Army in the most mundane settings.

Cynthia Enloe – whose book *Bananas, Beaches, and Bases: Making Feminist Sense of International Politics*, published in 1990, inspired a generation of anti-militarist scholars and activists – has long warned that routine exposure can render the sights and sounds of the army's presence an unremarkable, and uncontested, fact of national life.[1] Yet there have been few concerted attempts to study a military base in order to test this proposition in the context of the UK. Perhaps this is because it is extremely hard to get close enough in order to draw any useful conclusions, especially since most researchers are deterred from gaining access to military personnel. But it is also true that focusing on the army in order to assess its impact on – as well as its relationship to – the surrounding civilian communities is the wrong way to go about it.

2.1 Everyday scene in a garrison town.

The US anthropologist Zoë Wool has suggested more recently that, by focusing attention on the scale of everyday life in a situation where the armed forces interact with the public, it becomes untenable to assert that there is a strict separation 'between a military world and a broader sociocultural one'.[2] The clientele of the businesses in Station Road certainly suggests that even those who are not 'in' the army may have increasingly blurred relationships with the military institution. And as we have already observed, even in unremarkable places, 'military geographies are everywhere. But often you have to know where to look.'[3]

Chef's Delight Café offers a range of dishes from the standard English breakfast and toasted sandwiches to falafel and curry with rice. It is popular too, which means you are guaranteed an informative chat at any time of day. On one table a group of uniformed soldiers are comparing training schedules for the Iron Man triathlon and the Fan Dance challenge.[4] The familiar figure of cab driver Fraser can be spotted next to the steamed-up windows. Originally from Scotland, like many veterans he settled in the area after leaving the forces in the 1990s.

One of the top talking points locally was an empty plot of land next door which was slated for commercial development. There had been a great deal of debate on social media about this space, especially in anticipation of the thousands of new residents who were about to descend, thanks to the new Army Basing policy. Locals had hoped to see a Primark or some other store that would help to make the town less isolated (and, perhaps, less dominated by the military presence). Town and county councillors had tried to inject some realism by responding that Station Road wouldn't have the footfall for that kind of shop. It had eventually been decided that it would become a DIY depot, a decision greeted with mixed feelings.

Some people had expressed a need for more affordable local housing, and this was increasing tensions too. They had hoped for more flats for non-military residents, complaining that their needs were being forgotten in the rush to prepare for the influx of families from Germany. Others argued that there was no denying that the army had brought a lot of benefits to Tidworth. At least now there was a proper supermarket since a large branch of Tesco had opened on Station Road in 2007.

Older inhabitants were conscious of how much the high street had changed over the decades, voicing opinions that would not be unusual in any rural English town. Elizabeth, who was in her eighties, was born in a neighbouring village and had stayed in the area all her life. Her parents had married in 1939 just before her father joined up, as so many local men did. During the war Elizabeth and her mother were housed in a Nissan hut, which was a typical model of army housing at the time. On his return her father left the army and the family moved into council housing in Tidworth.

When we met in the café Elizabeth was discussing the transformation of the town with her friend Ellen, who was also local. 'Station

Road has changed so much since the 1950s,' she conceded. 'There used to be a lovely shoe store, a fish shop, milk delivered to the front door: everything you needed. And it was a flourishing place. Now it's just cafés and you can walk around all day without seeing someone you know.'

'There's housing going up everywhere,' observed Ellen, who was trying to think of the pros and cons of living alongside the army. 'So now, the problem about living in a military area is the lack of GPs and the difficulty of getting appointments. Cross Plain surgery has closed down now too which is worrying.' Ellen had lived in many different garrison areas with her husband, who had been in the army. They had moved back to Tidworth on his retirement. 'It has always been very easy to meet soldiers around here,' she said, 'not that there's anything wrong with that, obviously I married one!' But being surrounded by so many young men was not always a good thing. 'There are often drunken soldiers in Amesbury,' she said, 'which does put you off going out there on a Saturday night.' In 2017 the Channel 4 programme 999 *What's Your Emergency?* explored the impact of large numbers of soldiers in Wiltshire. That episode was called 'Squaddies'.

The disappearance of the fish shop may have coincided with the diminishing access to GP services, but there had been notable new additions too. Some of these could be attributed to the history of colonial warfare, catering to a clientele whose presence could be explained only through a knowledge of military history. At the top of Station Road next to the bus stop and the empty plot of land a small shop boasts a large orange and black sign that reads 'Gurkha Variety Store: Spices – Fresh Meat & Vegetables – Off Licence'. Just above the door a smaller sign announces 'Nepalese, Asian, Caribbean, Fijian and African food products including grocery, frozen food, fresh vegetables and meat products for all your needs under one roof'.

The business was started in 2010 by four former Gurkha soldiers and their wives, whose families had been entangled with the British Army for eight generations, both in Nepal and in the UK. Launched with the support of local business initiative Plain Action and Community First, the shop supplied many imported food

2.2 Shop in Tidworth, established in 2010 by Gurkha veterans and their families.

products – including spices, noodles and frozen food – that were hard to find locally. It was certainly welcomed by the Commonwealth soldiers and their families, especially as it offered services for arranging money transfer, mortgages and overseas travel.

Station Road also hosts a string of generic outlets like Domino's Pizza and Subway, and other types of retail business that are ubiquitous in many high streets across the UK. There is more than one charity shop, a kebab shop, a curry house, a tanning parlour, a tattoo parlour, a nail salon and a music store called Garrison Guitars. Tesco took care of everything else. A sign advertising a discount for military staff and their families was displayed in many a shop window. There were also some businesses that could make sense only in a place like this.

Before the pandemic, Pothead & Panface, at the western end of Station Road where it continues into Lahore Road, was a good example. This was a curious café, furnished with red American diner-style chairs and surfaces made from (what looked like) repurposed wooden crates, adorned with Bob Marley Flags. Soldiers could often be seen huddled over mugs overflowing with whipped cream. More intriguingly, a notice in the window advertised an 'Authentic German Menu' in large orange letters, a gesture towards those families who had recently been relocated in Wiltshire.

It turned out that the owners were veterans who had been given a start-up loan of £18,000 by X-Forces Enterprise in order to open the business and begin their post-military life.[5] Forced to move in 2021 when their lease was not renewed, they relaunched as a mobile burger van, and were listed on Tripadvisor as one of the most popular outlets during the pandemic. Meanwhile their prime location in Station Road is now filled by an establishment with a more utilitarian name: 'Bar, Soldier, Beer'.

To draw attention to these kinds of interactions and commercial enterprises in Station Road is not to say that Tidworth is a flourishing town that is simply occupied by the army. As we have seen, it did not exist as a single entity before the garrison was built in the grounds of the original Tedworth estate in 1905. Nor is it the case that public tolerance of the army presence has happened organically without any form of intervention. Within living memory at least, Tidworth's inexorable transformation by the army has been managed and overseen by committees of local representatives who have attempted to maintain something like a balance. Over more than a century, however, this proximity has produced something quite unique.

While there are plenty of residents who are distinctly 'army', many of the people shopping in Station Road are not wearing uniform. However, they might still be connected to the organisation in a variety of roles: veterans, spouses and their children, admin and support workers, cleaners and other service providers. Catherine Lutz describes this category as 'civilians in camouflage' which is a useful way of complicating our understanding of the word 'civilian'.[6] In conventional usage it's a technical term designating non-military status. In reality it is not so cut and dried.

Military fitness

Tidworth Leisure Centre is tucked away at the top of Ordnance Road, behind the buildings that line Station Road. Designed to offer a number of services that are accessible to the whole population, it represents an early, somewhat experimental, attempt to foster integration. It is operated by Aspire Defence, the company that manages Project Allenby Connaught in partnership with Wiltshire Council and Army Library Services.

In October 2022 it was reopened after substantial renovation and currently boasts two fitness centres, one for the public and the other for military use; tennis and squash courts; a six-lane 25-metre pool, with splash and learner pools, a flume and viewing areas. All the facilities are open to the public, although some are reserved for soldiers at certain time of day. Its success as a shared amenity has meant that it has subsequently been replicated in the garrison towns Colchester and Aldershot, both of which had experienced substantial redevelopment.

In many ways the leisure centre is unusual, not least in that it exists to serve the population of a relatively small rural town. But it is not intended just to keep the locals fit. It also houses a public library, located on one side of the centre's main entrance. On the other is the HIVE information hub, a standard feature of all army bases. Next to that is a crèche and pre-school. From the exterior there is little to indicate that the leisure centre was primarily built for the military's benefit, although sharp-eyed observers might notice the seasonal plastic poppies and camouflage netting draped over the railings outside. Once you step inside the main entrance, however, it becomes clear that this is no ordinary sport centre.

On any given day mothers will be arriving with small children, excited to get into their swimming costumes for an Aqualete class. Meanwhile, groups of soldiers pass through the turnstiles on their way to the gym, wearing customised sports kit with their regimental symbols embossed on front and back. If a door is left open by mistake, you might catch a glimpse of military scuba gear. The army swimming sessions are staffed exclusively by military lifeguards, and closed to the public, whereas for the swimming sessions open to the wider public military and non-military lifeguards work side by side.

Inside the centre's small café, young women sit companionably drinking tea next to sleeping babies. Occasionally a soldier will come in, moving briskly with unmistakable military gait. He or she might be a parent, accompanying a child to get a snack.

On Friday afternoons the leisure centre tends to be quiet because so many soldiers return home for the weekend. The groups of Nepali women hired as cleaners come in early that day in their Sodexo uniforms, often expressing concern they might disturb people with their vacuum cleaners. 'Don't worry,' laughed a gym employee on one occasion, 'they've all gone home. Let's hope World War Three doesn't ever start on a Friday afternoon. Otherwise we're done for.'

Not everyone has been happy with the shared facilities. Before this programme of refurbishment in 2021–22, some non-military users were complaining that the changing rooms leading into the swimming pool were very basic; one or two even suggested that the centre compared unfavourably with new leisure centres in big towns and cities. 'It's just a shame the outside looks so ugly, it's a shame really it's not got a bit more glass or whatever, that's the side of it that looks a little bit ugly.' There was also a lot of grumbling that the pool was unusually cold. This was because the water has to be maintained at a specific temperature for the army fitness tests that are regularly conducted there.

Military families had their gripes too. There were no discounts, for example, although a Forces defence card grants some free swims to service children. The garrison and the council acknowledge that this has generated some annoyance, but the centre has to gain revenue and would not be commercially viable unless it offset free or reduced cost membership by renting out the centre to big clubs. Unlike the Aldershot centre, which hosted the UK Olympics team in 2012, Tidworth is just not close enough to London to attract corporate clients.

The centre manager Matt assured us that the communication between the military and other users was harmonious. He had grown up in Durrington, just north of Larkhill camp, and knew from experience how deep the divide could be. When he was young, the army kids looked down on him and his friends as being 'rough' and, 'to be honest, we thought they were rough too'. When he was offered the position, he jumped at the challenge to break down barriers – although this was not always straightforward: 'I mean we often get arguments between the soldiers wanting to lift weights to heavy metal music and women who want pop music playing while they use the running machine. This is a common issue. But it's mostly OK.'

Tidworth Town Council has been delighted with the results, viewing the leisure centre as added proof that the military presence could provide solid benefits. According to one councillor, 'I think one of the biggest things that the civilian population gain from the army, certainly, over the last ten years since they've become more settled is, we've got facilities that we can use that a big city would like to use. So, we do gain a lot by the military, really. Yes, there's a lot of things the military has brought that we can use, that normally would never, ever be here.'

In addition to being manager, Matt had also been working on developing sports activities that did not rely on active support from either the military or the council. While Tidworth enjoyed its showcase sports centre, other garrisons had nothing that was remotely comparable. Larkhill, for example, just a few miles to the west, was notorious for its lack of amenities. The garrison commander told a Larkhill Community Partnership meeting that the town was seriously under-resourced in terms of both leisure facilities and shops, 'a bit like Aldershot in the 1950s'. It seemed that the Ministry of Defence did not routinely build this sort of infrastructure into its planning as it expected it to be provided by other dispensers of public funds.

By way of response Matt had started a new venture called STAR (Stonehenge Triathlon and Road) in Durrington with an ex-army friend who had settled in the area. Their aim was to be inspirational and inclusive, and to serve the whole community, whether army or not, from the age of 14 upwards. Offering cycling and swimming, track and cross-country running, the club is staffed by a range of coaches who are dedicated to working with individuals at all levels.

Much smaller than the Tidworth facility, it was still a bonus for those who were not connected to the army, and open to those who were simply keen to socialise while taking exercise. It also provided a form of escape for those who wanted to 'get away from the green', whether army or not. However, not all those well-meaning initiatives have been successful in bringing the disparate community together. For some people, especially those who were neither army nor long-term residents, Salisbury Plain could be a lonely place, as we learned from some of the individuals, like Bhakta Limbu, who shared their stories with us.

Socialising in the suburbs

Bhakta Limbu, a Gurkha veteran in his early seventies, left his wife with a few other women in his small rented apartment and stepped out of the building. As always, a cap was perched on the top of his tall frame; he was wearing a faded jacket over checked shirt and walked on worn black leather shoes. After tea with a Nepali friend at Delight Café, he crossed Station Road and hurried towards the Tesco superstore where he withdrew £500 from the cashpoint. Quickly pocketing the cash, he continued to the bus stop at the top of the main shopping street. He was heading to a Gurkha shop in Andover where he would arrange for the money to be transferred to his sons in eastern Nepal.

There were actually two Gurkha stores closer to his home in Tidworth, but he preferred to use the money-transfer facility in Andover which was run by an acquaintance. This monthly ritual presented another chance to socialise too, since he often felt isolated in the garrison. Despite the gradual rise in population, the Nepali community in Tidworth was still in its formative years, and, contrary to popular assumptions, was certainly not as close-knit as some of the older veterans hoped it would be.

Like many other Gurkhas above working age, Bhakta had found himself in Britain as a result of the decision in May 2009 to offer UK residency to all veterans with a minimum service of four years, an outcome of the Gurkha Justice Campaign fronted by the actor Joanna Lumley.[7] Now Gurkha veterans of all ages are eligible to live in the UK, and tens of thousands of former soldiers and their spouses who had been living in the mountains of Nepal started packing their bags.

At first Bhakta had resisted the temptation to emigrate but, over time, news spread that many veterans, including some older than himself, were able to save their welfare benefits and remit the spare pounds to their families struggling financially in Nepal. In 2012, following a costly visa process, he arrived in England with his wife. Now they survived on the bare minimum in order to save every penny to send home.

The digital notice board at the bus station announced that the bus from Salisbury, bound for Andover, was due in ten minutes, but it rolled up more than half an hour late. Buses rarely arrived on time here, and the drivers had informed him that there were two main reasons for this. One was the long-standing problem of the increasing volume of traffic on Salisbury's medieval streets. The other was the congestion in and around Tidworth due to the recent increase in the size of the population.

Bhakta climbed the stairs to the upper deck and, frustrated to see his favourite seat at the front was occupied, reluctantly sat further down. He smiled at a child sitting across the aisle, but his mother told the boy to turn away. After a group of noisy school students boarded at the Wellington Academy bus stop he noticed a fellow Nepali, dressed in a hi-vis waistcoat. He called out, and the man accepted his invitation to sit next to him. He turned out to be a fellow veteran, now working as a private security guard on local building sites for army housing. They chatted about various topics and gossiped about the Nepali community; for both men this might be the extent of any meaningful social interaction with strangers that day.

The elderly veteran's sense of isolation was not self-imposed, and it was not from lack of trying that he was unable to make friends in the area. He had expected a bit more appreciation in Tidworth, given its military connections. He had even thought that the British people were going to welcome him – and other Gurkha veterans – with open arms, as Lumley had famously declared they would in her victory speech in front of Parliament.

He soon came to realise that his contribution to the British Empire did not count for anything. On the contrary, he was perceived as an unwanted foreigner, treated no differently from the asylum seekers who were so hated by the newspapers. Since then he had heard that larger Gurkha settlements, like Aldershot, had encountered open hostility from majority white residents. Luckily Bhakta had not experienced direct discrimination in Tidworth, but he did not feel accepted, even though he had made every effort to learn the language, and new cultures and customs, and to mix with everybody. During the first few months he even tried shaking hands with people in Tidworth town centre, as well as residents of his building. But few would stop to have a chat with him, let alone invite him to visit their homes.

Men of a certain age

Bhakta's experiences were in sharp contrast with many other army veterans of his age, especially those who felt welcomed into spaces designed to ease their loneliness. Every Monday to Wednesday, precisely at 9 am, Mike Giles opens the small gates of a garage owned by the Ludgershall Youth Club. Soon he is joined by others who open the double doors of a wooden shed and proceed to get out their woodwork. Leader of the group, Mike is skilled in the trade, and knows how to operate and fix the machines. Amid the noise of the power tools, hammering and sawing, his long beard is soon covered in sawdust. The men chat while they cut up larger pieces of wood and carve toys that can be sold at the Easter market. Before packing up at 1 pm, they take breaks in a smaller shed where some of the wives join them, helping to prepare tea and coffee. The atmosphere is relaxed and friendly, although one topic keeps coming up: the decline of their town over the years.

A short, stout man in his early seventies, Mike is a proud army veteran. Having enlisted at the age of 15, he served for 28 years, doing tours of duty in many countries and conflict zones, including Northern Ireland and Bahrain. He has mostly good memories and suffered neither mental trauma nor physical injury as he did not engage in direct combat anywhere; he worked in the supplies or logistics division of his regiment. He was posted to Tidworth in 1987 and retired two years later, living in the area ever since. After engaging in local politics over many years, he was elected Mayor of Ludgershall in 2016.

'Being the mayor of a small and insignificant town means I have plenty of free time, but hardly any resources to do the things you want to do.' He uses every opportunity to support the residents of the town, many of whom are army veterans past working age, often with health and other problems including social isolation. In 2013 the charity Age UK published research that showed that rural communities were ageing faster than other parts of the UK with approximately half of the rural population aged over 45, compared with 36 per cent in major urban areas.[8] In its report it specifically called on the government to prioritise the chronic problem of loneliness.

It was Mike who came up with the idea of starting a branch of Men's Shed. This is a charity originating in Australia that supports social clubs for older men with the aim of reducing their social isolation and promoting craftsmanship, mainly in carpentry. There are approximately five hundred Sheds across the UK, and in 2016 Mike raised £5,000 with the help of his friend Chris Williams, also a local councillor. Together with Jamie Balls, then garrison commander, they launched the Tidworth and Ludgershall Men's Shed, an event that Mike considered 'a highlight of my life'. In 2019 they had 22 registered members who paid a monthly fee of £1, and at least half of them attended every week.

Within a year they had 'mended roofs, built a hide for children to enjoy wildlife, and put up some engraved wooden signposts'. Mike was especially proud of the positive impact made in the life of a traumatised Iraq veteran who had enraged his neighbours because he couldn't control his dog. 'But when we built a nice fence around his house, the dog could not get out. His drinking habit seems to have improved as well, and now his neighbours don't hate him as much.' But overall the main goal is to keep themselves busy and to foster conversations and friendships so that they do not feel isolated at home. Nor is this the only network available to them.

One of the largest senior clubs in the area connecting Ludgershall, Tidworth, Amesbury and Andover is the Friday Club, which meets every week in Ludgershall Town Hall. Approximately 30 to 40 people, many of them veterans and their partners, attend regularly. Pete, a leader of the group, explains: 'Like Men's Shed, this is a self-funded charity. We hold different activities here not only to provide fun for the participants, but also to raise money. Our town council is poor, so we have to pay the rent for this hall as well.'

Activities include bingo, quizzes, raffles and knitting. Sometimes participants are invited to play their instruments or share other talents for entertainment. The hall is usually humming with the sound of conversation. Tea and biscuits are available for a small price, and second-hand books are on sale. Downstairs, volunteers open the library; some participants go there to return or borrow books.

A significant fact about the Friday Club – as well as Men's Shed and other similar initiatives – is that the members are predominantly white. The standard position is that people of any ethnicity, nationality, religion or age are welcome in these social clubs; there is certainly no formal exclusion. In practice, however, it is different. The organisers do not see this as a problem, nor do local authorities. But members of minority ethnic communities do not feel welcome in these groups, as Bhakta found out the hard way.

He had joined Friday Club on the recommendation of an acquaintance and was eager to take part in the conversations and entertainment. One morning he drew pictures of Lord Buddha and Mount Everest in order to introduce the club to his native country. He played a popular folk tune on his flute, which he had brought from Nepal. But he was surprised by the reaction:

> People simply stared at me. I accept that some of them probably did not understand my accent, and just smiled at me. Gradually, standing in front of them and talking about my country, I began to feel like a clown – a clown quite unsuccessful at making everyone laugh. Also, people did not show much interest in speaking with me, even when I

sat close to them and tried to start a conversation. Finally, I gave up and stopped going there.

This was a common experience among younger people too, whether from Nepal or from Commonwealth countries. When asked about racism and social exclusion, the standard reply from army welfare workers, local councillors or charities was that 'foreign soldiers and veterans generally take care of themselves'. There was little acknowledgement that this too was a social problem, something to be tackled proactively, rather than by blaming minorities for 'sticking to their own groups'.

Weekly worship

In the context of casual racism from white residents, faith-based communities can offer an alternative sanctuary. Kofi first arrived in London from Ghana in 2003, on a visitor visa, and moved to Tidworth in 2012 when his soldier wife, Afua, was transferred from the Royal Tanks to the Fusiliers Regiment and posted to the area. His faith had given him a sense of belonging in this often unwelcome place, shaping his identity and sense of self-worth. Trained as a pastor in his home country, he started a Ghanaian Pentecostal church in Andover in 2013 and another in Trowbridge, Wiltshire, in 2018. His day job was driving a taxi.

The services are held in community halls, and each has a membership of approximately 30 families although the numbers inevitably fluctuate. Sundays are very hectic for him: 'I give a sermon in Trowbridge between 10 am and 12 noon, and drive for nearly an hour to Andover and conduct another sermon there between 2 pm and 4 pm.' His religious leadership goes beyond caring for the souls of his church members, although he finds the experience of preaching, and the congregation's recitation of the liturgy and singing of hymns, to be 'almost therapeutic'. He also helps them with the arduous work of filling out UK visa application forms and searching for reliable immigration lawyers.

Surveys indicate that people connected to the military are more religious than the general public. According to a 2018 report by the

Forces Net, citing the Ministry of Defence, 69 per cent of the regular members of the British Armed Forces declared themselves to be Christians, alongside approximately 28 per cent who stated that they had no faith. This showed a significantly higher level of adherence to Christianity among the military than among the rest of the population in England, Scotland and Wales, only 50.6 per cent of whom declared themselves to be Christian.[9]

Three years later, the percentage had dropped to 62.4 per cent for UK regular forces, with 69.7 per cent of the reservists identifying as Christians, which indicates that the numbers of younger soldiers declaring themselves to have no religion was growing in line with the rest of society.[10]

Military policy continues to be centred on Christian practices and traditions, which have been difficult to question.[11] The Plain hosts a number of historic churches, some of which predate the military occupation, but Tidworth garrison itself did not have its own church until one Reverend W.S. Jaffray, a Presbyterian padre working for the army in Tidworth, wrote to the War Office on 14 July 1908 to ask if it could provide one.[12] The first garrison church in Tidworth, St Andrew's Church, was opened for worship in January 1909.

St Andrew's closed in 1964 when a larger religious site, the Garrison Church of St Andrew and St Mark, was created as a combined place of worship for the Methodist Church, Church of Scotland and Free Churches.[13] This, too, shut down in 1985 and interdenominational services were held at St Michael's Garrison Church which was built by the army, initially for the Church of England, in 1912. The Roman Catholic Church of St Patrick and St George is believed to have been built around the same time and continues to serve Catholic members of the military to this day. As in other parts of the UK, there has been a significant decline in church membership in the garrison churches of Tidworth, and the pastors are keen to increase the number of their followers.

The data on religious affiliation are not disaggregated in terms of nationality and ethnicity, although it is likely that the number of minority ethnic soldiers who identify as Christian remains statistically significant.[14] Yet most prefer to join separate congregations, often exclusive to a specific denomination, which gather in church buildings, schools or community halls. These religious gatherings not only serve their individual spiritual needs but also enhance their collective sense of identity. The legendary Fijian choirs are often asked to perform at festivals and regularly tour the country. Meanwhile, although Buddhists, Hindus, Muslims and 'Other Religions' collectively account for approaching two per cent of the forces, there is not a single temple, monastery, mosque or synagogue to support minority faith communities in any of the garrisons on Salisbury Plain.

In 2018 there were plans to open a Hindu temple in Tidworth with support from the garrison and town council. This was touted as an important religious infrastructure that would provide a source of identity and community for Nepalis, a building that would draw other Hindu worshippers from nearby with the added benefit of contributing to the local economy. Unfortunately, however, nothing came of the project as some of the most active and enthusiastic proponents either retired or were transferred, and the fledgling Nepali community in Tidworth was not in a position to pay for the construction and upkeep.

There were also significant internal issues, including caste, which accounted for the lack of momentum. These factors were harder to gauge from the outside, but stemmed from the history of ethnic politics in Nepal, where many members of the middle castes, including Gurkhas, object to the historical weaponisation of the Hindu religion to subjugate and marginalise certain castes and ethnic groups.[15] As a result of these tensions the Gurkhas have not managed to open any Hindu sites in the UK, although they built a large Buddhist monastery in Aldershot in 2015, launched by the Dalai Lama himself.[16]

In spite of this it is the Hindu festivities that attract the biggest crowds. The Tidworth Nepali community hosts some activities through the year, including film nights, a summer barbecue and festive gatherings, advertised through its Facebook page and the Nepali radio programme on Castledown Radio. By far the biggest celebration is the Hindu festival of Dashain which takes place in September to October and runs over fifteen days. The longest holiday in Nepal as well as in the Brigade of Gurkhas, Dashain differs from other national faith-based celebrations in involving minimal religious activity. Some Gurkhas may perform certain rituals at home; those who are more devout may travel to other parts of England to worship at a Hindu temple. But Dashain is very much a secular gathering that has huge social and cultural significance, whether in Nepal or throughout the diaspora, including this corner of Wiltshire.

Nothing to do

It is perhaps in the school lunch room that the boundaries between who is 'army' and who is not – regardless of nationality or faith – are the most consistently challenged, eroded and overcome. Teenagers tend to have more pressing concerns, particularly when it comes to deciding how to spend their time outside school hours. As in many small rural towns, isolation and boredom are common among younger people as well. At Avon Valley College in Durrington, a group of 15-year-olds chorused that there was absolutely nothing to do in the area. 'Yeah, I just sit in my room on camp most of the time,' complained one girl. 'I mean, we can always go into Salisbury or Amesbury for the day but there's not much to do and Southampton is much more fun.'

Some members of this friendship group had been in Wiltshire only for a short while. Sara's family was from the Midlands. They had been told they were moving again next year, but she couldn't remember where they were being sent. Julia's family had been relocated to Wiltshire from Germany two years ago. She had loved life in Germany – there was so much to do and she really felt like she was part of something. She had trouble catching up with schoolwork when she arrived in the UK because the schooling was so different. Her dad had quite a few years left to serve. 'Germany's all closing down now,' she said in a forlorn voice.

It is a common stereotype that highly mobile service families avoid developing relationships with more settled non-military families, and vice versa. By contrast, this group of young women all agreed that you couldn't choose friendships on the basis of whether people were in the army or not. Even though you might cry when they leave, you just coped, and you could always keep in touch on social media. Their easy-going sociality seemed to contradict stories of insular military communities drawing comfort only from each other.

'But it's harder for people like me who are from other countries,' said Julia. 'It's really expensive to go back and if we want relatives to come and visit us we have to sponsor them and it's really hard because we have to pay for everything.'

She motioned towards another girl in their group, 'See, it's the same as with Soneeya. She's from Nepal but it's the same thing. And neither of our countries have direct flights to them.' She rolled her eyes: 'It's 23 hours to Fiji via South Korea!' Another girl in the group piped up to say, 'And me? I'm just English!' which for some reason made everyone laugh.

These young 'civilians in camouflage' were clearly adept at finding ways to negotiate social and cultural differences within the confines of the school gates. But the evidence explored elsewhere in this chapter suggests that forms of isolation and exclusion in this rural community can be exacerbated by divisions between those who are habituated to army life and those who are not. In the next chapter we return to the question of housing, conscious of the ways in which the lines between inside and outside are further complicated by the strict hierarchies maintained within the institution itself.

Military sprawl

Perham Down lies due east of Tidworth and is within the same parish, having been purchased by the War Office as part of the Tedworth estate in 1898. Its history illustrates the way that the larger garrisons expanded beyond their original boundaries, swallowing ancient villages and creating new places in the process. Home to 22 and 26 Engineer Regiments, Swinton Barracks (named after Major-General Ernest Swinton KBE, CB, DSO, the 'originator' of the tank) now loom over the base. An illuminated sign placed in front of the razor-wire fence at the entrance advises visitors that they will have to submit to an ID check before being granted entry. The security level is routinely set to 'heightened'.

Claire had offered to take us to Warren Hill, a ridge to the south of Perham Down, and was aware that she was running late as she rushed home after her weekly yoga class. It was taught by a fellow army officer's wife in one of those outlying Wiltshire villages with flint stone houses and a winterbourne stream typical of the chalk downland. Since she lived in Perham Down she always enjoyed the chance to socialise with friends afterwards.

Warren Hill and the paddocks in the valley below it are part of the 'dry' training area that incorporates the eastern third of the Plain. This is where soldiers carry out training activities that involve guns and tanks, but not the use of live fire. The public are permitted to use this section, although they can sometimes be diverted or turned back by a training exercise. The view from the hilltop promised an ideal vantage point and Claire was the perfect guide.

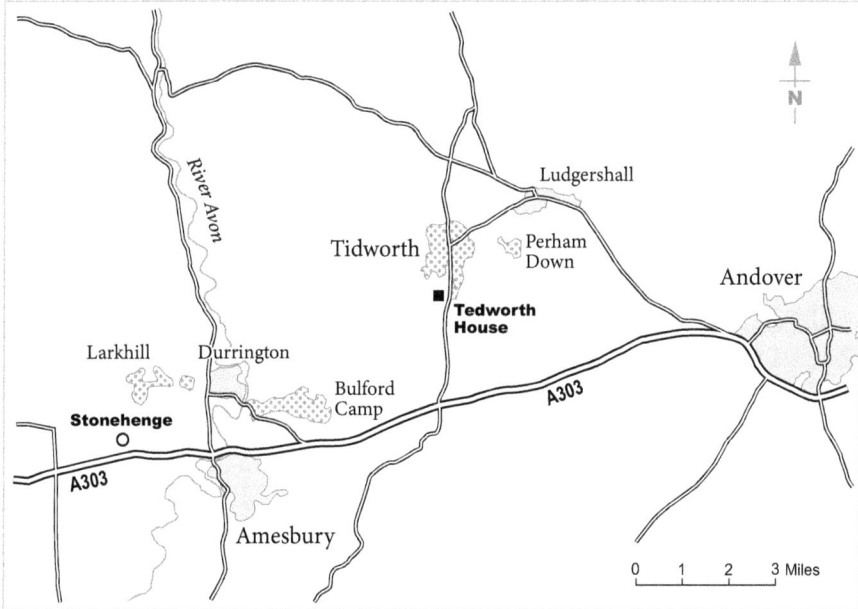

3.1 Garrisons on the east side of the Salisbury Plain Training Area. Tidworth is approximately 3.5 miles north of the A303 which runs east to west along the bottom of the map

Before setting off she had given us a sense of her immediate neighbourhood. The service family housing estates in Perham Down are 'outside the wire' which means that Claire can get to her house without crossing any military checkpoints. The block where she lives with her family, known as the 'officers' patch', is a quiet circle of detached and semi-detached homes facing a central lawn, shielded from the main road by a curtain of sycamores. She feels secure enough to allow her children to play out on the green or in the surrounding woods, unsupervised for hours at a time, and doesn't even bother to check that doors and windows are locked.

Despite this sense of community Claire is able to point to graduations of status and accompanying privileges that are not immediately visible to an outsider. On the other side of the road there is a row of detached houses, often referred to locally as mushrooms because of their squat appearance and rounded grey roofs. They are slightly smaller than the detached houses on Claire's side, because, even (or especially) within the officer class, the number of bedrooms and bathrooms is determined by rank rather than family size, and the 'mushrooms' are for the majors. For the higher ranks domestic servants are provided along with the house, and there is an expectation that the occupants will entertain frequently.

The film *Military Wives* (2019), directed by Peter Cattaneo and starring Kristin Scott Thomas, captured aspects of this reality in well-researched detail, showing how the wives were expected to observe the strict hierarchies of rank and seniority inside the institution. And the testimony of those, like Claire, who are expected to navigate this strange culture on a daily basis, helps to convey what it feels like to inhabit a place like this.

A bird's-eye view

As we reached the main road Claire explained that there was no crossing point and we would have to listen out for cars and run as quickly as possible. She reassured us that, before her children started school, she used to do this with a double buggy as well as the dog. At her signal, we sprinted across the road and made our way through the trees on the other side to reach a sunlit clearing surrounded by grassy hills.

The previous week she had been turned back from her walk because a Chinook was landing here. Sometimes there might be tanks manoeuvring, much to her children's delight. Today it was quiet, and the dog was happy to be let off the lead, gambolling up the steep slope. Claire went in front, seemingly with little effort, and, as we paused to catch our breath, a patchwork of fields unfolded in the distance. We continued to climb until we had a 360-degree view of the landscape that made the effort entirely worthwhile.

Earlier she had joked that she deliberately tried to know as little as possible about what her husband did for a living for fear of becoming too 'army'. But she admitted that a lot of knowledge had seeped in by osmosis; and it was easy to spot the signs of army activity, however nondescript. She pointed to a rectangle of bare chalk next to the village – ground exposed by tanks on manoeuvre. She dismissed a passing helicopter as 'not military' on account of its size. Directly below us, we noticed a small building with a tidy lawn in front. This was used for fitness tests.

At our feet there was a conspicuous pile of stones that turned out to have no military significance at all. It had been made by a local couple who had started a ritual of carrying a stone each time they climbed the hill as a form of protest about litter and fly-tipping, a gesture that was intended to convey respect and care for the neighbourhood and surrounding countryside. This couple lived in former army housing, a dour 1980s terraced block behind some trees, and now the only civilian properties in the village. In contrast to the uniform rows of service homes, at least these had been embellished with individual touches such as conservatories and front porches.

Around the back of Swinton Barracks, almost out of view, was an area of Service Family Accommodation reserved for the regular soldiers, known as Other Ranks. This had been recently renovated as part of a comprehensive upgrade, known as Project Allenby Connaught, which was launched in 2006. From this distance, their flat frontages looked like a row of white sails descending down the hill. According to Claire, however, despite their rejuvenated appearance they were probably quite damp inside, 'like all army housing'. Her well-qualified observation encapsulated something of the fraught politics of the current defence estate in Tidworth and its surrounding camps.

From the hilltop it was possible to see the complex mass of buildings inside the wire, and therefore not accessible to the public. Two red-brick officers' messes built in the 1970s partially obscured the new single-living accommodation block built by the company Aspire Defence, which was in charge of the new project. While the deplorable condition of 'married quarters' had been receiving most of the media attention, the state of housing for unmarried soldiers had proved equally shocking. The situation was briefly exposed in 2018 when a review carried out by the Defence Safety Association was leaked. Commissioned after a series of fires at a number of bases, including the Aliwal barracks in Tidworth, the study concluded that cuts to funding have led to an 'unacceptable degradation'.[1]

The report revealed that 373 fires had been logged across the three services in 2017–18, prompting fear of 'a Grenfell Tower-style catastrophe'.[2] Responding to findings that highlighted 'faulty equipment' and 'broken or unserviceable infrastructure', the Tory MP Johnny Mercer, a former army officer and a member of the Commons Defence Committee at the time, told the *Sun* newspaper: 'Animals would not be housed in such dangerous conditions. It is disgraceful how ministers talk up our armed forces at every opportunity, and yet, away from the spotlight, ask our most loyal public servants to endure totally unacceptable and lethal living environments.' And this was not the first time that the appalling state of army living quarters had become a political issue.

From camps to conurbations

While, as we have seen, the architectural historian Nikolaus Pevsner disparaged the presence of the army on the Plain in the 1960s as 'towns of barracks and genteel soldiers' housing and with all the mess of tin huts and tank tracks', the cultural critic Jonathan Meades, writing in 2022, was more specific in his account of subsequent development:

> Things haven't improved. The insipid neo-Georgianism of the barracks, housing, churches and messes of the 1920s and 1930s, designed by the War Office architect W.A. Ross, was evidently a source of inspiration to successive generations of military architects who have competed to outdo one another in dullness.[3]

This tendency to follow the more dismal trends of the day was particularly evident from Meades's architectural survey of army living quarters.

> Every fashion in low-rise social housing – whether garden suburb, bogus 'vernacular', system-built instant failure, pseudo-Victorian terraces, Poundburyish set design (the 'Canadian Estate' at Bulford) – has been meekly essayed in the sure knowledge that the hutches will never be anything more than temporary accommodation: the Professionals move on after two years.

It is very rare to find such forthright criticism of the contemporary military presence tucked away in the English outback. Yet Meades's catalogue of architectural mediocrity also offers a useful sense of the timeline of the occupation. He was withering in his verdict on the 'dispiriting' inoffensiveness of the camps today. As for the wider impact of soldiers over the Plain itself, he was equally unsparing, referring to it as 'blight'. However, another planning term that might help to capture the inevitable transformation of the built environment by this voracious military organisation is 'sprawl'.[4]

Sprawl is a value-laden word that usually describes the processes leading up to, and consequences of, the construction of new housing estates springing up on the edge of cities, towns and villages, often blurring the boundaries between previously distinct places. In the context of southern England, sprawl is usually applied to the post-war practice of urban development and planning that urbanised vast tracts of the whole region. Andover, barely twenty minutes' drive from Tidworth, provides a good example. Once a rural market town, it was a candidate for the massive programme of planning reform enshrined in the New Towns Act of 1946.

In the 1950s urban planners and local government officials scoured the south of England in order to relocate those displaced by slum clearance as well as the Blitz. In the early 1960s Andover was finally identified as an 'overspill town' and plans were drawn up to increase the population from 17,000 to 47,000 by 1982, with nine thousand new homes. At the end of the century the town was again designated as a major development area; a new round of house-building anticipated the population growing by an additional ten thousand.

Although the expansion of Andover has mainly affected its north-eastern edge, that is, on the opposite side from Salisbury Plain, its relative proximity to the training area has helped cement its identity as an 'army town'.[5] At several points in recent history the availability of new privately owned housing stock in Andover has proved a bonus for the Ministry of Defence when it needed to ease the pressure on its own supply. In 2010 the town's military identity was further strengthened when a new HQ for the Army's Land Forces opened there at a cost of £44 million.

While 'sprawl' captures the sense of housing estates pushing the boundaries of urban areas into the surrounding fields and villages, the concept has rarely been applied to military bases, either in the past or in the present day. Yet there are two ways in which it is useful here. First, it can describe in fairly literal terms the construction of new buildings on land already designated as defence estate, continuing to this day under the Salisbury Plain Masterplan. Second, 'sprawl' is a fitting concept to help understand the encroachment of the army into the adjacent areas, driven in part by its insatiable need for accommodation.

Tin towns

When the permanent barracks in Tidworth garrison were being completed in the first years of the 1900s, semi-permanent and makeshift camps were proliferating across the rest of the Plain. Over time some of these camps became distinct conurbations as the housing and welfare needs of personnel and their families became more pressing. The garrisons of Tidworth, Perham Down, Bulford and Larkhill saw the emergence of churches, shops, the odd pub and housing for military dependants, and each place took on a distinct identity of its own, despite absorbing some existing settlements and in some cases becoming almost contiguous.

Mary, a Tidworth resident in her late eighties, was able to provide many details about this process. As a child she had lived in a small cottage in the village of South Tidworth which, at the time, fell under the jurisdiction of Hampshire Council. She went to the local village school which drew children from both South Tidworth and the neighbouring village of North Tidworth, which was in the county of Wiltshire.

Although the two villages were adjacent, North and South Tidworth were considered to be places of different social status. Historically the residents of South Tidworth had been the upstairs servants of Tedworth House before the estate was sold to the army in 1897. Those from North Tidworth were employed to do the harder and dirtier work downstairs. They were also employed at the famous Ram Inn, established in 1848, where coach horses were changed, as well as in the small shops and businesses that served travellers before they set out across Salisbury Plain.

No such opportunities for work existed in South Tidworth until the army turned up. The only time the children came together in solidarity was on their annual sports day when they competed against pupils from the local garrison school. 'If you wanted to be nasty about another child you would pointedly say "Oh they're from North Tidworth, you know?"' said Mary.

As Mary jokingly referred to herself as being from genteel South Tidworth, her family's presence in the village dated back only to the construction of the first army buildings. Her grandfather, who had been in the Royal Engineers and fought in the Boer War, had developed a chronic lung condition whilst fighting in South Africa and had been advised to move to a more temperate climate. After he left the army he had moved with his wife down to Tidworth from the North West in order to help build the new garrison.

The initial building work started in 1902, with the isolation hospital, sewage works and cemetery the first projects to be completed. By 1904, ten houses – called Clarendon Terrace – were erected on the Grand Trunk Road, along with the eight barrack buildings that provided the centrepiece for the new garrison. One of these was converted to a larger hospital as an afterthought, since the original one was not suitable for treating routine injuries and maternity cases.[6] Meanwhile a 'tin town' consisting of corrugated iron huts had gone up at Brimstone Bottom between North Tidworth and the village of Ludgershall to house the builders and their families. Significant building work continued until 1913, made possible by widespread public support for the army in the period leading up to the outbreak of war.

Mary was also connected to the military through her father, a soldier in the Yorkshire Light Infantry who met her mother when he was posted to Tidworth. Mary herself was born not in the village but in colonial Burma where her father was posted until the outbreak of the Second World War. Mary and her mother were sent back to England before the Japanese invaded.

After her parents separated, Mary returned to South Tidworth with her mother in time to observe the new period of intense building work that marked the postwar years. Three new housing estates effectively merged South and North Tidworth so that by the 1970s they had become one town. In 1992 the county borders were redrawn as part of reforms to local government, and the whole of Tidworth was included within the county of Wiltshire. Mary, meantime, had spent many years teaching in the British military school in Cyprus, before being evacuated – for the second time in her life – when civil war erupted there, and returning to Tidworth to look after her mother in the final years of her life. She now stayed in the same house, adorning the walls with paintings of Cyprus.

The doubled-edged meaning of military sprawl as a surreptitious process that entails blurring civil–military boundaries, as well as building tied-housing estates in rural places, captures the way in which consecutive wars have had an impact on communities outside the boundaries of this incongruous military outpost. The apparent cohesiveness of Tidworth as a functioning modern garrison today conceals not only its complex class history but also the porous boundary between what is strictly military and what is not. Its relationship to neighbouring towns such as Andover, Amesbury and Ludgershall also exemplifies this inexorable process.

In 1968 the army purchased 132 houses in Andover – nearly a third of all houses built or under construction in the town that year – for families who were returning home after the British withdrawal from Aden. Those families would have been integrated – to some extent at least – into the surrounding community but this purchase was significant for another reason as well.

Before 1960 the military pay structure had deterred non-commissioned officers and 'Other Ranks' from saddling themselves with a wife and children whose needs detracted from the serious business of training and fighting.[7] Until then the wellbeing of the families of those who did marry had largely been left to the various charitable organisations, some of which had been founded in the late Victorian era.[8]

When the British Army finally accepted that rank-and-file soldiers were entitled to marry while still in service, there was a grudging recognition that the welfare of army families was partly the responsibility of the army itself – whether this took the form of tied accommodation or moral support during deployment or bereavement. Once the question of army salaries had been resolved, allowing young soldiers to support a family, the levels of investment required to meet their housing needs would have been phenomenal. In 1968 the availability of newly built housing estates in Andover must have seemed like a fortunate coincidence.

In more recent times, during the army housing crisis that came to light as troops were deployed in Iraq and Afghanistan, families were once again moved into commercial units in Andover's Augusta Park development. These had been purchased by the Ministry of Defence while the army's decrepit housing stock in Bulford was refurbished and rebuilt.[9] While this may have been a practical solution to a short-term problem, it will have diminished the availability of housing options for local residents. It also had the effect of creating enclaves of army families within zones of social housing and privately owned properties. In another recent example, in order to find enough accommodation for families being relocated from Germany, the Ministry had purchased one hundred units in a new commercial housing development on the edge of Tidworth garrison.[10]

Leaving aside any questions of security, the impact of the military workforce overflowing into public housing estates is in stark contrast to the rigid stratification of conventional army accommodation, both old and new. Although there have been attempts to create integrated communities where army families live alongside members of the public – not to mention mixed-rank neighbourhoods – these experiments are said to go against the grain of institutional culture. As Claire had explained during our guided tour of the officers' patch, regardless of what their children felt, soldiers and their spouses have repeatedly made it clear that they preferred to live in service-only estates that were segregated according to rank – a reaction she described as 'part and parcel of army life'.

Over the next few years deliberations over whether to allocate housing on the basis of family size rather than rank were met with organised protest by army spouses who told the defence select committee that 'for officers and their family members, who had made personal and financial sacrifices for ten or twenty years, this was utter betrayal'.[11] The prospect of officers' families having to downsize their living accommodation and move to regular service housing, while those with more children would be entitled to the more spacious properties designed for their superiors, was simply unacceptable.

In spite of this opposition the policy change was announced in early 2024. The response was immediate. Just a few days after receiving threats of resignation from officers, who complained that this would totally undermine the organisational hierarchy, the Ministry of Defence decided to pause the policy, a move that the former Armed Forces minister Mark Francois described as a 'welcome victory for common sense over bureaucracy'.[12]

Bridging the gap

In the mid-1960s, when the local councillor Chris Williams had joined the army, military bases were relatively accessible to the public. This included accommodation for families too, as we saw from the purchase of homes in Andover in 1968. Chris could remember a different time when there was no barbed wire round the camps and no high-security checkpoints warning members of the public to Keep Out.

This situation changed overnight when, in 1972, the Official IRA discharged a car bomb outside the Parachute Regiment's HQ in Aldershot as retribution for Bloody Sunday. From this point all military staff, buildings and compounds were seen as possible targets and were therefore off-limits to the public. As a further precaution army uniforms were rarely seen in public, outside ceremonial occasions at least, and the issues facing service families were rarely discussed in the media. It was not until the armed forces were embroiled in Iraq and Afghanistan that the profile of the military in public life began to change.

From the early 1980s, after leaving the army, Chris Williams had devoted his life to acting as a bridge between the garrisons and surrounding populations across the Plain. As Wiltshire councillor for

Ludgershall and Perham Down, he was committed to building a mutually supportive relationship across the divide. This was a sense of duty that he shared with other veterans who served on parish and county councils. Like Mary, Chris attributed his energetic support for the local community, and particularly its growing service family component, to his familiarity with the area.

Perched on the edge of this sprawling military complex, Ludgershall, a small historic settlement with its own castle, once designated a 'rotten borough', provides a useful case study because its population includes a wide variety of people, both with and without connections to the army. Until 2007 it was classified as a village but managed to acquire town status in anticipation of the planned extension of army housing. Chris, town council chairman at the time, worked hard to make this change. 'Ludgershall is growing and will get bigger over the years regardless of the economic conditions,' he told the local paper. 'I don't want to have to rely on Tidworth for information about what is happening in this area – if we hadn't done this Tidworth would have taken us over.'[13]

Ludgershall had been forced to adapt to the transformation of this eastern corner of the Plain. In fact the village had been saved from extinction by the War Office, according to the *Andover Advertiser*, reporting on the dramatic incursion of the army in 1902. As T.S. Crawford writes in *Wiltshire and the Great War: Training the Empire's Soldiers*, 'In 1901 the population [of Ludgershall] was 576. In 1911 this had almost doubled to 1,117. Amesbury, Andover and Devizes also prospered from the military presence, and Tidworth and Bulford grew into small army towns.'[14]

The rapid revival of fortunes in towns like Ludgershall can be traced to the army's expertise in creating new infrastructure for transport and logistics. The original military encampments on the Plain had relied heavily on the rapid construction of railways, for example. As documented in *Plain Soldiering*, before the army arrived, most of the routes across the Plain were simply well-trodden pathways, marked by signposts or boundary markers. Hard roads and metal rails were urgently needed in order to transport men and equipment, just as they were in the colonies and other war zones.[15]

By the end of the century different train companies were competing to establish new branch lines across the whole of central and southern England. Ludgershall was a strategic location for the War Office because it had already been integrated into the national rail network. The line connecting southern England to the Midlands had been built in 1882, predating the arrival of the troops by more than a decade.

Some railway lines were significant in terms of military history, as Dixon relates in her history of the town. King George arrived in Ludgershall by train in 1914 to pay a royal visit to the Australian Commonwealth troops based at Perham Down. During the Second World War demoralised French troops passed through Ludgershall into Tidworth on their way back from Dunkirk in 1940. It was reported that many of them piled their guns up in the shape of a pyramid in Tidworth barracks and vowed to never to fight again.[16]

But apart from the supply tracks in Ludgershall, which offer an intriguing symbol of industrial heritage in an otherwise rural district, these iron rails across the Plain have long been dismantled and most of the evidence had been removed by 1986.[17] Detailed historical accounts indicate that many of these sites in and around the main garrison at Tidworth were repurposed as the whole area acquired an immense strategic value in the First and Second World War, particularly those areas under American control. Technological changes too demanded constant revision of designated spaces. In the 1970s Ludgershall station was used as a vehicle depot for the Royal Army Ordnance Corps, although those facilities later moved out to a more remote part of the Plain closer to the artillery training.

Today, while the material history of this military-industrial transport network is fascinating in its own right – not least showing how experience gained in foreign wars had an imprint on the English landscape – a number of those apparently abandoned spaces have acquired fresh significance in the light of the current expansion. In planning terms they are designated as brownfield sites, which now offer strategic locations for further encroachment.

Us and them

In 2019 a new housing estate for service families was completed on land formerly occupied by Corunna Barracks, incorporating an old railway supply line that once ran from Ludgershall station to the Plain. Comprising 242 new homes for a mix of officers and other ranks, the Corunna estate was one of three new projects carried out by the construction firm Lovells, as part of the £250 million accelerated homebuilding programme in the garrisons of Tidworth, Bulford and Larkhill.

The Corunna estate provides a good example of potential friction, not least because of the initial dispute over its location. When the Defence Infrastructure Organisation first selected Ludgershall as a suitable place to build accommodation for the new arrivals, it identified a site at some distance from the town. Had the estate been built there without further consultation, the inhabitants, recently transplanted from German bases, would have found themselves marooned on an island between Perham Down, Tidworth and Ludgershall. Although the distances between them are walkable, the location would have made it harder for the spouses and children to feel integrated into any one place, let alone part of the community in Ludgershall, which technically sits outside the training area.

Mike Giles, the town mayor, whose commitment to the community was described in the previous chapter, was unhappy about this initial decision. A long-time resident of Ludgershall, where he ended his army career after 28 years of service, he was adamant that 'We didn't want to create a, sort of, them and us situation.' When planning was under way for the proposed housing site, Mayor Giles and other members of the town council approached the Defence Infrastructure Organisation to suggest that the families already being displaced from their homes in Germany should have the opportunity to be part of Ludgershall and not isolated in the fields that separated the town from the village of Perham Down.

As a result, the decision was made to move the planned estate to Corunna barracks, a former Second World War ordnance depot slightly closer to the town's western perimeter. However, this concession, which was intended to benefit all concerned, aggravated local people's unease about how the new housing development would impact on their lives.

Residents were especially alarmed because the increase in population would undoubtedly put more pressure on a local transport infrastructure that was already felt to be straining at the seams. This was partly due to the chronic underfunding of buses in rural areas, as well as the nationwide increase in private car ownership. Acute traffic jams in Tidworth during spring of that year created particular anxiety and frustration.

Two local Facebook groups were bristling with complaints about driving and parking difficulties. One contributor, who worked inside the garrison at Tidworth, posted that it had taken them thirty minutes instead of three to get to work one day. In another discussion forum about construction work around Tidworth's Station Road, a local resident directed a scathing commentary at the local mayor. Accusing Wiltshire Council of delusions of grandeur, they complained that bad planning decisions were turning a small Wiltshire village into a gigantic car park.

The combination of pricey bus fares, exorbitant taxi charges and narrow, winding roads highlighted the disadvantages of increasing the population in a rural district with relatively few retail outfits and amenities. This did not bode well for families accustomed to a better standard of living in Germany.

Websites intended to prepare the new arrivals debated the pros and cons of offering subsidies to allow people to keep their cars.[18] Many prospective residents turned to social media sites to find alternative ways of getting about, whether by bus or taxi. They were shocked to find out that a fifteen-minute cab journey to the garrison towns and villages of Tidworth, Bulford and Larkhill from mainland railway stations in Andover, Grateley and Salisbury would cost between £25 and £40.

'Our culture'

Families relocating from Germany began moving into their new homes from the second week of July through to the end of August

2019. On some days there were as many as 30 container lorries arriving on site. Chris confirmed that the operation was handled very effectively, co-ordinated both by Army HQ and locally by the garrison in Tidworth. It had apparently taken place with little or no disruption to the town, and local people had barely noticed the increased traffic.

The influx of new neighbours was generally thought to be excellent news. For one thing shopkeepers and facilities such as hairdressers had noticed an increase in trade. Chris was enthusiastic about the greater sense of community as a result of so many young families moving to the area. 'The immediate thing is that if you drive through Ludgershall round about a quarter to nine, what you see is lots of young mums with their children going to the school ... And then you go into this new coffee shop and you walk in there in the morning and there's young visitors or young mums or whatever, having a coffee and chatting away.'

An affable man in his early seventies, Chris was an important public figure in Wiltshire, and particularly in Ludgershall where he had owned a home with his wife since the early 1980s. Like many of those active in local politics, he was a military veteran, although the community he represented included a wide variety of people, both with and without connections to the army. 'Let's be honest,' he told us when we met in a café that had recently opened in town, 'the whole of Wiltshire is a military county and people like to retire here and live here. So, there's a good percentage have got a military connection or are ex-forces or their father or somebody would have worked for the army in some way or another.'

Chris's optimism echoed Mayor Giles's confidence that the town would benefit from the new population. 'You only have to go to a remembrance parade to see how the people of Ludgershall treat soldiers.' The town's formal embrace of their military neighbours was evident from the installation of commemorative street furniture and other forms of decoration marking the centenary of the First World War. Three years earlier the council had given 26 Engineers the freedom of the town, which entitled them to march ceremonially through the main streets; this also offered the regimental sergeant major the right to sit on the council meetings, albeit without the ability to cast a vote.

Chris described these local fusions of the military and the civilian as 'our culture', adding that the visible signs of the army presence in this rural setting made him nostalgic for the times he drove a Chieftain tank and 'rolled around the place'. The sight of people in uniform, military vehicles and barbed wire and the sound of Chinook helicopters, whose flight path happened to be directly above his family home, made him feel connected to these memories well after his retirement. However, he was also alert to the perils of getting the balance wrong and had reservations about plans for further commercial development in Ludgershall, not least the intractable problem of traffic.

In 2020 permission had been granted to construct another new housing estate on the outskirts of Ludgershall, this time on ground once occupied by the former Defence Medical Equipment Depot, which had supplied medical equipment and supplies to the armed forces until its closure in 2005.[19] The proposed development, with a gross value of £108 million, was led by Lovell Partnership in collaboration with Homes England, and promised 413 houses for sale on the open market, 25 per cent of which would be affordable. Chris was not impressed. 'To be quite honest,' he pointed out in his mild Liverpudlian tones, 'the last thing we need are more houses now in Ludgershall.' His priority was to increase the number of shops and leisure facilities in the town to meet the needs of existing residents.

Wearing his county councillor hat, he had been actively working on encouraging businesses to occupy this same site, but ultimately this effort had been unsuccessful and the housing development, called Drummond Park, was scheduled to begin the following year. In the meantime he had identified another promising location, this time owned by Wiltshire Council. He was lobbying for a retail outlet, perhaps an Aldi, or, alternatively, a soft play area for the children of the new estate.

Both of these plans represented his hopes of bringing the military community into greater contact with surrounding neighbourhoods, with amenities and outlets that catered for everyone. 'Hopefully

3.2 Street furniture in Ludgershall, 2018.

one day we will pull all the wire down and we can live as we should be,' he sighed. 'I don't know if it will ever happen these days – most people just don't think of it. They have more important things to think about.'

This conversation took place in a new tearoom that Chris had described as a local 'good news story' when it first opened on Ludgershall High Street. The interior was lavishly furnished: velvet armchairs with plush floral pillows, framed vintage silhouettes and an array of Art Deco teapots, porcelain cups and saucers, and lace doilies. The owner had previously run a tailoring shop on Station Road in Tidworth, providing uniform alteration, formal mess dress and medal-mounting for the local military population. This connection, and its associated glamour, was not absent from her new venture too. Jordan Wylie, a famous veteran and self-styled adventurer who had written about his experiences with Somali pirates during his time working in maritime security, cut the ribbon at the tearoom's inauguration.

'But there's a lot of people you meet who have moved into the area and things like that,' Chris continued, 'and you learn new things from them and all that as well, so it's a good mixture, a good cross-section.' He attributed the success of the tearoom to the massive increase in Ludgershall's population as a result of the influx of army families.

In many ways local public figures like Chris Williams and Mike Giles were best placed to field these worries about the expansion. As veterans themselves, they had deep knowledge of life inside the military as well as on its doorstep. Moreover, in their role as councillors they had the backing of Wiltshire Council which had been an early trial for a programme of co-operation between a local authority and the Ministry of Defence. In 2006, under the rubric of the Military Civilian Integration Partnership, the council undertook to work with the Ministry of Defence in order to address the welfare of military personnel, their families and veterans living within the region.

This initiative, which we examine in greater detail in the next chapter, was devised under a Labour government at a time when the armed forces, already enmired in Iraq, were being deployed to Helmand province under the auspices of the NATO-led International

Security Assistance Force. In addition to public unease about the war, relations between government and military leadership were under such strain that the then prime minister, Gordon Brown, was obliged to act.[20] In 2007 he convened a cross-party committee to address public perceptions of the military profession. A report entitled *National Recognition of Our Armed Forces* was published the following year.[21]

The document acknowledged that the army, in particular, had become increasingly separate over the preceding years, and that, with the passing of the generation who had served in the Second World War, fewer people understood the nature of military work. The report recommended a number of measures to increase the visibility of soldiers in public, ranging from military parades and appearances at sporting events to recruiting in schools and other educational establishments. Brown also inaugurated an annual Armed Forces Day in order to encourage members of the public to say 'thank you'.

The combination of these various attempts to reform not just the image of the profession but also the conditions of military service has had far-reaching consequences. In the next section we look at some of the ways in which these changes have impacted on the lives and prospects of those living in and adjacent to the Salisbury Plain 'super garrison'.

Part II

The cost

4

Relocation, relocation, relocation

Kate is feeling exhausted when she arrives at the Beeches Family Centre at 10.45 am, and the Mercians' coffee morning is in full swing. She squeezes through the café door with her young baby in his carrier in one hand and reaches out with her other to wrestle her two-year-old inside. The warmth that comes with being among friends washes over her as she hears their welcoming voices, punctuated by occasional bursts of laughter coming from one corner or another.

The centre is a curious space that appears to be part of the fortified military base in Bulford Camp but is in fact accessible via open gates as you approach from the main road. As well as housing the local army support centre, accessible to all service families, it hosts an under-fives day nursery and runs coffee mornings, drop-in clinics and social events that are open to the whole community. Inevitably, very few non-military people make use of these facilities, but for many of the younger women who live locally due to their husbands' work they can provide a lifeline.

Kate lets her two-year-old run off to play while she waits for her coffee. Beeches is an informal café, with hot plates and microwaves in the place of a real kitchen, but these mornings had been a lifeline for many of the women who attended. Even with the terrible weather outside, the room is busy, with thirty or so other wives sitting around circular tables, many feeding babies while they sip their drinks. This ethos of community and togetherness was something that she really liked about the coffee mornings. Being surrounded by so many women in a similar boat was a great source of comfort when she first moved to the Plain with her husband.

She had met him when he was already in the process of enlisting, and they had thought long and hard about it might mean for her if they were to get married. Talking about it never really prepared her for the reality; there were so many things about the military way of life that you just couldn't fathom before you joined. But now living on an army base seemed so routine and ordinary that Kate barely thought about it any more.

Jessica also looked forward to this weekly social event. She had found that becoming habituated to the patterns and restrictions of army culture made it harder to stay in touch with civilian friends. For one thing she felt that they did not understand the stresses and tensions involved in being a military spouse.

Joining a new community where people lived in relatively close-knit communities was not without problems, though. Jessica sometimes felt isolated when her husband was not around. Not having any children of her own, she couldn't go to the mums' and tots' group, and even felt out of place at the coffee morning because most of the other women had toddlers in tow. She looked over at Lucy and thought how much easier it was for her to make friends because she had a baby. But that wasn't the only factor that was potentially divisive.

Lucy was known for being outspoken, and she enjoyed the chance to have a moan. This was her husband's third posting, and the family's first time living outside Liverpool. Salisbury Plain had been a bit of a shock to the system as the social life was so poor, but this coffee morning was one of the few social events where everyone was welcoming, despite being attached to different regiments. But Lucy felt that officers were stuck up and tended to treat the lower ranks like dirt. And this extended to officers' wives: you would never see them at the Beeches coffee morning. In fact you rarely met them socially as even their housing was segregated.

Claire, whom we met in Chapter 2, had been quite frank about internal hierarchies among the spouses. We had witnessed an awkward exchange during our walk when she encountered the wife of a sergeant major in her husband's regiment. While she was apologetic at the time, Claire had also pointed out that even the officers received differential treatment in their 'patch' in Perham Down. At that time the higher the rank, the bigger the house, and those near the top even had extra space for live-in servants. But it was not just the marked distinctions in the size of family accommodation that Lucy minded.

She felt that the lower-rank housing was very poor and badly maintained too. Her own house had suffered badly from damp, and been earmarked for treatment, but they were still waiting. The battle against mould was one not even the combined forces of the UK defence sector seemed able to win.

Terms and conditions

A wooden sign that greeted the young women converging in Beeches Family Centre said 'Army wife, toughest job in the army!'. This may have been a wry inside joke, but it was one that wore thin rather quickly. For most of them it was a blunt statement of fact that the challenges involved in being a military spouse were considered trivial compared to the rigorous demands of their soldier partners' profession. But it was also true that the government had been coming under increasing pressure to recognise the plight of military families as a crucial factor in defence planning.

Future historians may be better placed to analyse the long-term impact of the wars in Iraq and Afghanistan on improving the conditions of military labour. Viewed within a longer historical perspective, the reforms and restructuring initiated in the first two decades of the twenty-first century might be more usefully seen as a moment in a cyclical pattern of change stretching back to the Napoleonic Wars, if not further.[1] The simple fact is that waging war has always drained the nation's economy, and standing armies can turn out to be expensive luxuries in countries that pride themselves on being democratic.

In more recent times adjustments to the terms under which the armed forces are recruited, maintained and rewarded have depended on many factors: the rationale for the conflicts (or threats) in question, the state of the economy, the weather of public opinion, the authority of military leadership, the rate of military fatalities and anything that happens to raise the profile of an organisation whose employees are said to 'put their lives on the line'. As outlined in the Introduction, the Armed Forces Covenant, launched in 2011, entailed their commitment to reforming the sector. But it was not the first attempt to recognise the scale of neglect.

The Military Civilian Integration Partnership launched in Wiltshire in 2006 represented a significant step forward in terms of an official recognition of the problems and privations of service life. Running alongside the experimental partnership between local and central government, there has also been a significant programme of reform aimed at modernising the outdated military estate. The rural garrisons of Tidworth, Bulford, Perham Down and Larkhill might be invisible from the A303, shielded by the mystical aura of Stonehenge, but their partial transformation over the past twenty years represents a massive investment in defence infrastructure.

Allan Thomson is the Chief Executive of Aspire Defence Ltd and, through the company's subsidiary business Aspire Defence Services, oversees Project Allenby Connaught across Salisbury Plain and at Aldershot. This is a 35-year private finance initiative launched in 2006, the same year that saw the inauguration of the Military Civilian Integration Partnership in Wiltshire. Since then, Aspire Defence has been managing a £1.45 billion construction project in Tidworth, Bulford Camp, Larkhill, Perham Down and Warminster.

In the early stages this entailed building or refurbishing 562 buildings, demolishing 497 others, and maintaining support services such as cleaning, storage and waste disposal, and transport, at a total cost of £8 billion. The private finance initiative was also contracted to boost employment for army personnel and civilians in Wiltshire and Aldershot, historically the official 'home' of the British Army.

A veteran himself, Allan had been an important voice in discussions about modernising service life and certainly had the appropriate experience to manage such a large project. He enlisted in 1989 and was originally an engineer in the Royal Corps of Electronic and

Mechanical Engineers, spending most of the first ten years working with the Royal Marines in Germany. As he moved up the ranks, he told us, he became involved in equipment acquisition and communication, and even ran the army budget for a few years. In 2011 and 2012 he did two tours in Afghanistan as the Head of Equipment Acquisition and Support before taking a defence infrastructure job and becoming involved in Army Basing. In his final post he was engaged in what he called 'the land acquisition business'.

> And then I realised I had to get out before I was 50, I wasn't going to become a general, I didn't think, so I thought I'll take the pension and get a second career and just was applying for jobs and managed to get this one. So that's the story, an engineer by background but now involved in infrastructure.

The concept of reorganising disparate army bases across the UK into a small number of larger garrisons seemed an obvious way to consolidate resources, tackle the housing problem and introduce some radically different ways of organising army family life. The problems were legendary: 'In the late nineties everyone knew that the accommodation in the army and the housing was appalling, the way the soldiers lived and so on, and what I call SLA, single living accommodation, lots of men in multiple occupancy rooms, no en-suite, you know, or power showers and so on.' The concept of reorganising disparate army bases spread across the UK into a small number of larger garrisons seemed an obvious way to consolidate resources, tackle the housing problem and introduce some radically different ways of organising army family life.

With reorganisation into fewer and larger bases, Allan thought that 'people could have job security, the kids could sit in schools, and not get moved around all the time and not have to go to boarding school like my kids did. So it was always the sort of long-term plan and slowly but surely that has happened, with a lot of investment.' He was keen to remind us that these changes mostly started under a Labour government, while, as he pointed out, the Tories have subsequently claimed all the credit.

Project Allenby Connaught was radical: only half of the existing Tidworth estate was retained – mostly the churches and older

4.1 Aspire Defence was set up to deliver Project Allenby Connaught for the Defence Infrastructure Organisation.

buildings that were in reasonable condition. The remainder was either demolished and replaced, or significantly refurbished.

> Tidworth was almost completely flattened in terms of accommodation for the soldiers because they were located in old Indian Army type blocks. We kept a very small number of them for heritage reasons, but they've been converted to offices, and otherwise we've built, I don't know the number, but a large number of 40-man blocks, individual bedrooms with en-suite bathrooms and wet rooms for the soldiers.

Allan was quite proud of the success of the first seven years of the project, but there was a lot more to do. Besides, plans were already being laid for the Army Basing Programme, and by 2016 the project had been expanded to provide more infrastructure for the troops and their families relocating from Germany.

Locked doors and tight lips

In the meantime the Military Civilian Integration Partnership was weighing up the disparate challenges presented by the large number of bases in the South West. In 2006 the total number employed by the Ministry of Defence was estimated to be 81,000 people, around 1.6 per cent of the region's total population. Three years later, Wiltshire Council published the results of its first scoping exercise, commissioned by the South West of England Regional Development Agency.[2] Recalling Jonathan Meades's remarks about the 'dispiriting' blight of the garrison towns on Salisbury Plain, it is little surprise to learn that more than a century had passed between the founding of Tidworth garrison in 1905 and this effort to calculate the economic and social significance of the military presence in this part of the country.

The fact that some of the statistics had never been collected before was in itself an indication of the historical gap that existed between the local authority and the Ministry of Defence in London. In addi-tion the British Army was not accustomed to handing out informa-tion to civilians without a green light from above, which, during the hectic days of deployment in two major war zones simultaneously, was not always forthcoming. Wiltshire council's research team, led by a former marine biologist with the help of a retired detective and RAF veteran, were routinely greeted by locked doors and tight lips as they sought information about costs, numbers and details of the military way of life. Nevertheless they managed to compile a sub-stantial account that provided a benchmark for future research.

A second objective of the research, anticipating significant restruc-turing of the armed forces, was to assess the potential impact of these changes on Wiltshire, which had the largest concentration of mili-tary personnel of all the counties in the region. In fact the garrisons on Salisbury Plain had already been officially identified as the site of a 'super garrison' in the Defence Estate Development Plan of 2008.[3]

One of the researchers' first findings was the distinctive demo-graphic profile of military communities. Army garrison areas across the South West region were populated predominantly by young men, often with young families attached. Further research by the Military Civilian Integration Partnership team in 2012 examined the impli-cations of the 'dominance of males' in the area, with the greatest numbers in the 21–25 and 26–30 age brackets.[4] While this was not an unexpected result, it raised a number of issues concerning social welfare that might have been overlooked.

A related finding was the lack of 'a targeted programme of sexual health services for the military community'; another was the relative lack of specialised support for couples undergoing relationship difficulties as a result of the particular strains of married life in the military – including the pressures of separation as a result of deployments. As a result NHS Wiltshire began to work with the military to provide a programme including testing, screening, treatment, partner notification, safer relationships and contraception.[5]

In addition to providing figures for soldiers and staff, the survey also estimated the number of dependants – who, like the active service members, were mostly concentrated in Wiltshire. The January 2012 School Census found that 8 per cent of the pupils attending Wiltshire's maintained schools and academies were from service families, two-thirds of whom were in primary school. Young families with a relatively high number of children created a high demand for childcare as well as for schools, doctors and dentists. This was a factor that could cause resentment among the local civilian population who might be already on waiting lists to register with a doctor.

National scandal

Following the audit there was a flurry of research inquiring into the fluctuating levels of financial support provided to Wiltshire's military communities by statutory agencies, the voluntary sector and the military itself. A further study by Wiltshire Council, for example, investigated rising levels of deprivation following the 2008 financial crash, with a particular focus on the Salisbury Community Area, Tidworth and Ludgershall.[6] These reports were in part prompted by revelations of the inadequate conditions endured by single soldiers as well as service families – a state of affairs that came to the attention of the national media only because of the rising numbers of military deaths and serious injuries in military operations in Iraq and Afghanistan.

It was housing that always grabbed the headlines. In 2007, for example, the *Telegraph* published a story that revealed the shocking state of service family homes in Wiltshire. One woman they inter-viewed was Hannelette van Zyl, 25, the wife of a Royal Engineer serving in Afghanistan, and a mother of two. She described what it was like living in her three-bedroom Ministry of Defence house in Bulford: 'Down the hill from us most of the places are boarded up because of vandalism and all sorts of nonsense going on … It looks tacky and horrible. If we go in through the front door the paint on the door and on the walls is peeling. The woodwork is falling apart really.'[7]

Nor was it just family accommodation that was derelict. The previous month an all-party committee of MPs had branded much of the troop accommodation in Britain 'disgraceful', attributing the worrying problems with morale and retention to the crisis in army housing. The Salisbury MP, Robert Key, the senior member of the Commons Defence Committee, amplified the message that many soldiers living in army accommodation in south Wiltshire garrisons would be better off in tents in Afghanistan, as their quarters were 'completely unacceptable'.[8] One block in Larkhill was so bad it had been described by military bosses as 'unfit for human habitation' and had been left empty and unused. Mr Key said he had seen the block and it is 'one of the worst in the whole of the UK'.

Shortly after these reports, the *Telegraph* claimed in another arti-cle that army families called a special housing helpline more than four hundred thousand times in the previous year – equivalent to nine calls per property. A comment by Sir Menzies Campbell, then leader of the Liberal Democrats, indicates how political this issue had become: 'It is a national scandal. When people are risking their lives for their country in Iraq and Afghanistan the least they can expect is decent housing. Instead they are provided with shabby accommodation that will take years to fix.'[9]

While the research commissioned by the Military Civilian Integration Partnership was taking place at a local level, mostly away from public scrutiny, successive governments were jostling to rationalise the whole framework of military-related employment. In 2010 a Strategic Defence Review conducted by the coalition government recommended a comprehensive analysis of terms and conditions of military service, based on the principle of the Armed Force Covenant which would be published the following year. But it also framed the case for reorganising military bases within the UK as a radical cost-cutting exercise. In November 2011 the Ministry of Defence announced that the plan to relocate twenty thousand soldiers would save £250 million per year.[10] This was welcomed by the Chief of the General Staff, General Sir Peter Wall, who said that the relocations would allow the army to 'reinforce vital links with local communities in the UK'.[11]

A key part of the reorganisation strategy was a plan for long-term accommodation of a workforce that was to be predominantly based in the UK, reducing the need to uproot service families every few years.[12] The armed forces would continue to offer subsidised housing for single soldiers and service families, but they would also encourage members of the armed forces to take greater responsibility for their own housing.

This scheme claimed to offer greater choice and flexibility for armed forces personnel – whether single or with family – by offering them the choice of renting privately, or buying a home with financial assistance from the Ministry of Defence. In due course unmarried couples would be entitled to service housing on equal terms with married counterparts.[13] A more significant reform, announced in 2024, was that accommodation would be offered on the basis of need rather than rank, as in the old system. But as we saw in the previous chapter, this would turn out to be hugely controversial just at a time when the armed forces were struggling to retain staff, particularly among army officers.[14]

Out on a limb

Despite these overdue reforms, the question of sub-standard army housing throughout the country remains an acute source of embarrassment for governments and defence ministers in particular, with leaking roofs, dangerous levels of dampness and endemic mould periodically receiving media attention. It has also emerged that maintenance is contracted out to impersonal and inefficient companies.

In 2022, for example, a new scandal erupted when it emerged that the Ministry had been forced to apologise to service families, not just for the appalling state of their homes but for the chaos and disruption caused by the government's mismanagement. In addition to unresponsive pleas for help with loss of hot water or heating, it turned out that nearly a third of military homes required repair, despite maintenance contracts worth £650 million having been awarded to contractors six months earlier.[15]

We were curious to find out whether the standard of the three new estates planned for the families relocated from Germany under the Army Basing Project would be any different. Apart from the Corunna estate in Ludgershall, which, as we saw, had 242 houses, there were two other developments in the neighbouring garrisons of Bulford and Larkhill.

Sandra was the Community Relations Manager for Lovell Homes, the developer contracted to build the new housing. In September 2019 she agreed to show us the new developments, and, as we drove, she reflected on the visible changes to the area. 'I think Larkhill and Bulford feel a little more out on a limb, as it were, but certainly Ludgershall and Tidworth and Perham Down, it's all very well serviced now. It still needs a little bit of love. But like I say, I think with more and more people coming it can't help but have a positive impact, I think, I hope.'

Sandra's slightly nervous optimism was in part a response to our comments on the indisputably bleak aspect of the new housing estates, especially those 'out on a limb' sites far from useful amenities and surrounded by acres of open country. The social and cultural aspects of life in this austere setting did not appear to have been included in the calculations, unless that was what was meant by 'a little bit of love'. It was clear that these remote new developments were the result of political decisions made at the highest level, and Salisbury Plain was an important testing ground.

The Plumer estate was just a short drive from Beeches Family Centre in Bulford. The building work had progressed quickly: although the builders had broken ground only in November 2017, by July the following year the work had already been completed.

4.2 Lovells construction billboard advertising the new estates for army families.

This was primarily due to the two-part segregated building system, a typically Scandinavian model of using a pre-assembled timber frame which can be brought to the site and installed relatively fast. The brick 'envelope' is then built around the frame.

The new housing was designed to resemble the adjacent Canadian estate, but with a few adjustments. For example, on each of the new sites there are three bungalows purpose-built for adapted living, marking a break from earlier attempts to modify existing properties for people with disabilities, which had never been particularly successful.

Early in the process, the Army Families Federation, an independent organisation that represents the views and needs of army families to senior commanders and government, had raised concerns that the prospective inhabitants were dreading leaving their homes in Germany for what awaited them in England.[16]

This was reflected in a Facebook group to which we were directed. One new resident warned others that 'People will be in for a big shock ... it's nothing like Germany at all, the new houses are so tiny'. Accustomed to bigger houses, well-developed infrastructure and better public services that offered more comprehensive support and welfare, some were also worrying about how they would cope with living in such a rural area.

But Sandra was optimistic. 'For the most part, the people that we've spoken to are really pleased to be in new properties because they've come out of very old, dilapidated stock, from flats that are rundown, mould on walls, really, really tired, unloved properties. As they've moved into clean, fresh, modern homes and that I think has definitely soothed – sweetened – the bitter pill.'

As incoming residents settled into their homes, however, the cracks began to appear. On the Facebook page families shared complaints about damp, mould and leaking pipes, problems common to new housing being left unaddressed over time. As with many new-builds, a time lag between the houses being rapidly built and then eventually occupied meant that homes were not being tested for problems quickly enough. As a result any defects had been left to get worse. Given that Lovell was responsible only for fixing problems that arose within the first 12 months, there was potential for further trouble down the line.

One of the advantages of living in a close-knit community is that children are routinely allowed to play unsupervised in the street. But a resident noted on the Facebook group that 'this may be a military environment and it feels acceptable for this sort of behaviour but let's not forget that we still get a lot of civilian traffic passing through the estate that may not be aware of the relaxed approach to child safety'. These concerns shed light on some of the tensions that can arise in a residential service neighbourhood that is not sealed off from the rest of the town or village.

Neither Lovell's PR skills nor its construction team could fix one particular problem. Stories began to emerge of paranormal activity in the new homes after one resident posted that she was convinced she had seen the ghost of a young girl in a white dress roaming from room to room. Others claimed to have caught their children talking to someone in an empty room, while another woman told the Facebook group that

> When we first moved in I could never sleep. I always felt like I was being watched. The doorbell would ring and no one there. Weird noises would set the dog off. My son saw a 'monster' in the kitchen window and I've seen a face. Random toys would go off in the middle of the night. I've done a cleanse since and nothing. We were built on an ancient burial ground so there's that.

The ancient burial ground to which she referred was a Saxon cemetery that was discovered in 2016 on the land earmarked for development. The archaeological remains on the site have since been excavated and recorded, as part of 'the MoD's continuing stewardship of the archaeology of Salisbury Plain'.[17] But although the bones have been removed and the ancient graves filled in, the ghosts of the people who were buried there are still said to haunt the new residents of the Plain.

Lives on the periphery

Further west along the Packway, the garrison of Larkhill camp has experienced the greatest impact of the expansion. The marked increase in the population has inevitably had repercussions for social services, notably health and education, which have historically received far less attention than the state of tied accommodation. The new Alanbrooke estate, with 450 new homes, was almost twice as large as the new estates in Bulford and Ludgershall, and a new primary school was built to accommodate the incoming children. In addition to specialist support for mental, sexual and other specialist health needs identified in the Military Civilian Integration Partnership research, routine healthcare for service families had also been flagged as an issue.

As a result, since November 2022 the town has a state-of-the-art health centre that illustrates the new compact made between the local authority, NHS, the Ministry of Defence and the garrison itself, in accordance with the Armed Forces Covenant. It is a large building, with two floors and a frame of structural steel jutting out over the entire front facing. It has been designed with an inclined, canopy-pitched roof to avoid disrupting the ancient ley lines that lead down to Stonehenge.[18] Its imposing architecture both creates shade from the sun and complies with government guidance about how to integrate security concerns into the design of accessible spaces.

These architectural considerations are particularly salient because, unusually, the centre is used by both soldiers and members of the public. It is the first joint military and NHS medical facility in the UK, built in collaboration with the Sarum Health Group of GPs. The NHS GP practice is on the left as you come in, while the Army Medical Centre is to the right.

The design of the mixed waiting area is light and airy, consisting of a central atrium with high ceiling and windows on three sides. Those in military uniform sit next to others wearing jeans and trainers on rows of padded wooden seats. Unlike in primary care centres in the rest of the UK, especially those in similar rural areas, the average age of the patients is low. Soldiers and young mothers with children visibly outnumber older residents awaiting their turn.

A practitioner enters the waiting room and calls out a woman's name, and she bundles up her reluctant son and leads him through a set of double doors into the NHS practice on the left. Moments later another doctor comes in from the right and a man in uniform gets up gingerly to make his way through to the Army Medical Centre.

A young Fijian family arrives through the front entrance and checks in at the civilian reception desk. The father is in uniform, and he is cradling an infant in his arms. His wife stands next to him, a bag full of nappies and other baby essentials slung over her shoulder. He explains to the receptionist that they have come for their daughter's six-week check. The mother and child are part of the wider military family, but they are classed as civilians in terms of access to services. They will turn left into the NHS practice.

It is not that the treatment differs but that the clientele is quite diverse in terms of medical issues presented. The army doctors focus on assessing and treating the kinds of problems that impact the lives and work of soldiers, in particular musculoskeletal injuries sustained during training. The GP practice offers the care needed by young families. Some of the more expensive equipment, such as scanners, belongs to the NHS and is shared between the two health centres.

When it comes to dental treatment, however, neither members of the public nor soldiers' families have the same access as those who are in the armed services.

The dental care provided to military personnel is vastly superior. On the top floor of this building there is a bespoke military dental practice, with capacity for 15 dental chairs. Soldiers must have a dental inspection every year as part of their fitness and wellbeing assessment, but this service is not available for spouses and children, who are required to make their own arrangements. As a result, access to adequate and affordable dental care is another issue for service families, as it is for the wider population.

Constant churn

Louise was the practice manager of a busy GP practice with surgeries in Ludgershall and Tidworth. 'We are used to high levels of churn being embedded in the military community,' she said, explaining that the turnover of registrations and deregistrations was a good indication of the transience of their patient base. She was addressing a group of military and civilian healthcare professionals at the April 2019 quarterly meeting of Wiltshire County Council's healthcare thematic group.

In fact her practice had been conducting a research project called 'Churn' for the previous four years which had indicated a 26 per cent increase in the number of patients between 2016 and 2019. Out of ten thousand registered patients, two thousand were part of this seemingly ever-increasing turnover. While such a figure was not unusual in larger cities, it was rare for rural areas to experience such a high rotation of patients. 'It creates a lot of work to have the military on your doorstop,' she pointed out, adding that this sort of administrative labour was not recognised at government level, or within the army.

The work involved tracking down and summarising people's medical records from across the world. This meant dealing with issues such as medications that have been prescribed elsewhere but are not provided routinely by the NHS, and keeping track of the numbers of patients who came from service families or were veterans. In 2019 the practice was in the throes of incorporating a much larger influx of service families as a result of Army Basing. This created another layer of administrative labour, not least because of the challenge of accessing sufficient public funds ahead of the influx so that it was equipped for the new arrivals.

Primary care practices in the area were bracing themselves for new registrations that would be in the thousands, but there is an eighteen-month lag between new registrations and increased NHS funding, and this was aggravated by the Ministry of Defence's inability to provide exact numbers for new arrivals in a timely fashion. This had created a lot of frustration, as it had in the education sector too.

In 2019 the primary care practices around Salisbury Plain were already starting to feel the pressure of increased patient numbers. In Tidworth, Castle GP Practice had recruited more GPs and nurses with a special grant. It had also spent £100,000 of the existing budget, taking a calculated risk about the numbers of people projected to register as patients. 'We have recorded a 5 per cent increase in registrations that came with the advance party from Germany,' reported Louise jokingly, 'and we think we are ready for the landing.'

Louise felt that they had needed to do a lot of work to manage people's expectations. She told the group about a recent case where a child needed to be prescribed medication for ADHD that was routinely prescribed in Germany but was not typically used in the UK without agreement from a consultant. Some medical products that had been free in Germany – infant paracetamol and topical eczema treatments for children, for instance – also had to be paid for in the UK. As a result incoming families had been warned to bring at least three months' supply of medication before arriving in Wiltshire.

The way in which schools and primary care facilities go about accessing the funds they need to provide an adequate service to local populations, and how much they get, is a problematic element in the situation. The complicated, and steadily diminishing, funding structures within the NHS and state education are at odds with the directive to give special privileges to soldiers, service families and veterans.

Louise was vocal about the issues at stake: 'There is no recognition for the kinds of challenges healthcare practices face in areas like this with a large military community ... Schools get the Service Pupil Premium, which is meant to provide extra support for service children, but we get nothing. And primary care is where they will usually hit with an issue!'

As Louise noted, schools with service children receive extra funding from the Department of Education, in the form of a Service Pupil Premium of £310 for each child per year. This fund, referred to as SPP, was meant to be used by the school to provide extra pastoral and academic support for service children, in acknowledgement of the particular challenges they face and also part of the commitment to delivering the Covenant. In schools with a small percentage of service pupils the SPP brings relatively few benefits, but when there is a higher proportion, the difference can be substantial.[19]

If there is a critical mass of service children, for instance, the SPP can generate enough funds to pay the salary of another member of staff, such as a trained counsellor. The school might also provide a specialised Learning Support Assistant for children who are struggling with catching up with work after moving schools, or organise a weekly pizza lunch for children whose parents are deployed. An Emotional Literacy Support Assistant can help with anxiety and anger issues, working one-to-one or in small groups.

Army oversights

The cacophony was deafening as the children assembled for their lunch hour. Some of them had their boots on the wrong way round and were looking forward to getting out to the playground, despite the bitter cold. As they waited impatiently for the sign to start their lunch, it was clear that they were well-trained to respond to hand gestures. Moira, the teaching assistant at this Church of England primary school, clapped her hands three times and raised one arm, and peace descended. She quickly explained that we were there to talk to them, encouraging them to answer our questions.

We began by asking one table how many had a parent in the army. Hands shot up: 'My daddy's a soldier!' one boy said, as he pulled the lid off his yogurt pot. A few nodded, mouths full. 'My mummy is a vegetarian!' said one girl importantly, while a chorus of voices informed us that, 'I like football' and 'I am going sledging after school'.

The following week we learned more about the military intake to the school as we were invited to attend the annual nativity play. Some of the parents filing into the village hall were wearing military uniform, but all were waiting anxiously for the children to enter in their roles as angels, donkeys and wise men. This was a school attended by a large number of service children in a village that has traditionally housed officer families who have chosen to buy their own property.

It was evident from the segregated seating choices of the parents, let alone their outfits, that there were significant socio-economic variations among the school intake. In 2012 service children accounted for some 46 per cent of all pupils in maintained schools living in Tidworth Community Area.[20] This is now changing, as more service families are choosing to ferry their children to schools in neighbouring villages.

This pattern of parents voting with their feet had led to complaints from some non-military families who were finding that local schools were now oversubscribed and there were no places for them. The research on the effects of military churn had also revealed that civilians employed by the Ministry of Defence were also missing out.

The resulting pressure on school places had become intermittently intense in the intervening years. But after the much-publicised launch of the Covenant in 2011, headteachers in and around the garrisons began to find that aggrieved service parents were citing this as a reason why their children should be accepted. As schools don't have any such obligation as a matter of law, and extra places cannot be conjured up overnight, this aggressive invocation of the Armed

Forces Covenant merely highlighted the delicate balance between structural disadvantage and special privilege.

The new forms of collaboration between public bodies and military organisations also highlighted one particular problem: the army's method of operation is often incompatible with the more measured pace of democratic institutions. A good example of this could be seen in preparing for large numbers of schoolchildren relocated from Germany.

Local authorities need at least nine months' notice in order to be able to budget for extra school places, and they also need solid proof that those spaces are needed. Military employees are usually given six months' notice to move, and this can lead to confusion about the exact numbers of children who might be expecting to attend school in the new location.

This was brought home to us when we were observing the twice-yearly Tidworth Area Community Partnership meeting in 2019, where headteachers were receiving an update on the progress being made with regard to rebasing and school places. The garrison commander was astonished to learn that there were ongoing issues with some schools being over- or undersubscribed.

One of the headteachers present had informed him that his school had received sixty extra pupils from military families the previous September with no advance warning. The garrison commander apologised and agreed that the garrison needed to do better, adding that this oversight might have had something to do with the general churn of personnel being moved across the UK. The mood in the room, however, showed that this excuse was not good enough.

While these logistical problems of relocating army families from Germany were providing huge headaches for educational staff in the area, they did not come out of the blue. The Army Basing plan was merely the latest example of the cycle of military churn, since Tidworth and Bulford had both increased in size during the previous few years as a result of the earlier Project Allenby Connaught. And it was not just a question of numbers and places; the need to change schools frequently affects the quality of education as well, despite the assistance provided by the Service Pupil Premium.[21]

In schools with large numbers of service pupils, the effects of constant relocation mean that many young people fall behind with their education, and those with complex learning difficulties are not identified quickly enough. It also creates problems for schools in ways that that go beyond the particular needs of service family children.[22]

Churn impacts a school's Ofsted results, which measure pupils' progress at two different stages of their schooling. Differences between the German and British education systems meant that some of the younger children were arriving with different levels of literacy. Added to this there were bureaucratic issues. Service children who had taken standardised tests when living in overseas bases – in Germany or Brunei, perhaps – could not have the results included in their progress report despite having gone through the same process as in the UK. This is because headteachers are required to carry out very thorough school-level analysis to track the progress of individual pupils in a way that identifies the progress made while they are attending a particular school. These data inevitably affect school ratings and are therefore important for the survival of the school.

At the same meeting headteachers commented that the army's inadequate approach to education could be seen in the way that it failed to account for how people actually made decisions as families. In Tidworth, instead of building two smaller schools near the new housing estates, one large new school was built with the result that it was too far for many parents to walk there with small children. The army had also asked for new school places in nearby Bulford, assuming that service families would send their children to schools in the towns where the soldier parent was posted, as opposed to where they had been housed with their families.

The aim of the original Military Civilian Integration Partnership between council and government department, formalised in 2006, was to 'enhance the economic and social benefits of the military population throughout the South West'. At the time – with the armed forces overstretched in two disastrous wars – there was scant empirical evidence measuring the impact of armed forces communities in any part of the region, let alone the county of Wiltshire which contained a high concentration.

In the next chapter we explore the question of the economy in and around the large military base on Salisbury Plain. After nearly two decades of accounting, it seems reasonable to ask whether there are indeed any benefits to the wider population living on or near a military base, and, if so, how they might be calculated.

5

The khaki economy

As we took in the view from the top of the hill, learning from Claire's expert eye how to make sense of this strange landscape, she talked about how much her daily walks meant to her. After she married, she gave up her career in the NHS and her one-bedroom flat in north London to follow her husband to his posting in Catterick garrison in Yorkshire. As soon as she arrived she started receiving invitations to tea in the homes of other officers' wives, and the cognitive dissonance generated by such a dramatic change in her lifestyle was intense.

She recalled being newly pregnant, sitting in a variety of immaculate living rooms and gazing out of the window at the windswept moor, politely sipping tea from a china cup and saucer while engaging in small talk. Meanwhile, inside her head she was screaming, 'What is wrong with you people? Don't you work?!' She felt like she had been transported back in time and recast as a 1950s housewife.

Nine years later Claire could say that there had been upsides as well as downsides to being an army wife, or 'following the drum' as she called it. This was an eighteenth-century expression for the motley troupe of female camp-followers – wives, mistresses, sex workers, laundresses – who used to trail after their military menfolk, sometimes even staying close to the battlefield itself, a practice immortalised in Thackeray's novel *Vanity Fair*, published in 1848. Until the 1960s very few of the rank-and-file soldiers were married, and, if they were, their quarters were hardly an inducement for young spouses.

In the 1980s the anthropologists Hilary Callan and Shirley Ardener were the first to identify the dynamics of the 'incorporated wife' in their historical investigation of the lives of women married to professional men: diplomats, businessmen, politicians or officers. Their work investigated the way in which these wives were expected to perform unpaid work for their husbands' employers.[1] The enduring currency of this phrase in the context of the upper echelons of the military emphasises the weighty role that officers' wives still play in upholding the morality and decorum of the institution.[2]

For ordinary soldiers it is little different, although much of this labour may be carried out in the domestic sphere where partners operate an invisible emotional support network. Cynthia Enloe has described the role of the 'Model Military Wife' as the ideal embodiment of compliance and resourcefulness, a figure that functions as the 'bedrock' of military culture, although still classified as a civilian.[3] And it is still an unwritten rule that the soldier's job comes first.

Over the years Claire and her young family had lived in six different homes, moving across the United Kingdom from Catterick in Yorkshire to Swindon on the other side of Wiltshire, and then to Salisbury Plain. She had to put her career on hold to accommodate these constant moves and was often alone for long periods when her husband was deployed. However, she recognised that she was able to raise three children as a stay-at-home parent which might not have been feasible had they been paying a mortgage or private rent.

Now accustomed to her role as an officer's wife, she was determined to strike a new balance between the injunction to behave like an 'incorporated wife' and the person she was outside of her husband's job. For the wives of soldiers in lower ranks the choices are far more limited. Yet the question of military partners – including, as we will see, husbands – having access to careers and meaningful employment lies at the heart of modern calculations about raising and retaining a military workforce, fit and primed for taking orders.

Be your own boss

One Friday afternoon Kofi's taxi is waiting for business outside Andover station. A train from London Waterloo pulls up at the station and he eyes the passengers as they exit. Frustratingly there is no call for his services yet again. Half an hour goes by before the next train and this time he spots a young man with khaki uniform and matching khaki rucksack walking towards the taxi rank. As Kofi is first in the queue, he sticks his head out of the window and smiles at him eagerly, but, on seeing that he is black, the man immediately turns his head away and moves to solicit the car behind. Its driver, who also happens to be white, points to Kofi's car, as is the rule – forcing the reluctant soldier to accept what's on offer.

There is an uneasy silence for about five or six minutes as the taxi speeds towards Bulford camp, taking the cross-country route via Tidworth at the man's insistence. As he negotiates the roundabouts leading out of Andover, the 42-year-old Kofi attempts to break the ice. His eyes focused on his phone, his passenger confirms that he is serving in the Signals Regiment. Kofi tells him, 'My wife is also a soldier in Tidworth; she is a chef at the Fusiliers.' The soldier grunts in acknowledgement but does not even look up. As the car begins to speed up along a straight stretch of road, he asks abruptly: 'What part of Africa are you from? Do you have good roads like this in your country?'

Kofi is used to such derogatory remarks. He offers his standard reply: 'I was born and bred in Accra, capital of Ghana. Actually my country is not as bad as it was after the British left in 1957. It's the economic powerhouse of West Africa now. The road system in my country is much better maintained than it is in this country, go and see for yourself!' His response silences the soldier, who does not thank him as he pays the fare and hurries into Kiwi barracks.

Kofi explained to us that, having arrived in London in 2003 on a visitor visa, he had moved to Tidworth in 2012, after his wife, Afua, who had enlisted in Ghana as a Commonwealth citizen, was posted here. In addition to the routine racism, he has had plenty of other problems to deal with. For one thing, his financial dependence on his wife, as well as his immigration status as a dependant, was humiliating. Then, as a military spouse, he found himself the primary carer for their young daughter. 'Afua went to Estonia on a tour of duty when our daughter was only seven months, and I had to not only take care of the infant, but also comfort her mother crying on the other end of the line.' He wished the army could have provided some kind of support, 'but there was nothing'.

The couple applied for a visa for her sister so that she could help out with childcare during Afua's absence – but she was twice refused entry into Britain. The assumption was always that relatives would overstay once they were legally in the country for a limited time.[4] Kofi is angry about the fact that their relatives are refused visas to help out, especially in the light of his wife's readiness to risk her life for Queen and country. He feels that 'no matter what we do, we do not – will never – belong to this country; if I could help it, I would return home tomorrow'. Desperate to make some money, he had bought a car and registered it as a taxi, spending a considerable part of their savings. His business is quite good – if he can work, that is. He explains: 'If Afua is home, I can work Friday night and Saturday. During the week, however, I always struggle to find childcare.'

This is a common problem for couples who are reliant on one salary. Sophie's husband is a soldier, often away on deployment, and the cost of childcare made it impossible for her to return to her previous job as an admin worker. As a result she started her own business from home. Pretty P Bows is a small, online enterprise that uses Facebook to sell bespoke, made-to-order children's hair bows. The bows themselves are exquisitely made in brightly coloured and glittery fabrics, embossed with images of animals and popular TV cartoon characters.

The headwear may be distinctly non-military but the business model Sophie is following is very much in tune with current defence policy. Across the country, councils and higher education institutions run schemes to help spouses of military personnel, and also those transitioning out of military careers, to start their own businesses. Start-up programmes include training in planning, market research, finance and networking. They often advertise themselves using the acronym BYOB, or Be Your Own Boss, an inside joke for those more accustomed to Bring Your Own Bullets or Build Your Own Base.

This level of support for business has increased incrementally over the past two decades, and is firmly established in Wiltshire, thanks to the closer collaboration brought about by the Military Civilian Integration Partnership. Wiltshire Council, in collaboration with Swindon Borough Council and the Federation of Small Businesses, provides funding, office space and support across the county through The Enterprise Network otherwise known as TEN.[5] Six dedicated centres – in Corsham, Salisbury, Ludgershall, Porton Down, Tisbury and Trowbridge – are run by Wiltshire Council employees officially employed to engage with the country's large military community.

Castledown Enterprise Centre, in Ludgershall, is a purpose-built business centre with 17 offices and space for light industrial manufacturing. It opened in 2012 and a year later its units were completely occupied. Of 43 companies registered there in 2019, two were directly involved in the defence sector: Rheinmetall BAE Systems Land Ltd, a joint venture between two large British and German arms companies that designs and builds military vehicles; and JWC International, a maritime cybersecurity training consultancy. Most of the other companies were small enterprises developed by local residents in the retail, construction, and education and training sectors, often directly related to military culture.

In a consumer market where dogs are the local pets of choice, for example, Devil Dood Direct is an outlet that sells numerous canine products, from chews to toys, garments and other accessories. The owner originally started the company out of her garage in Catterick garrison. When her husband was relocated to Wiltshire she rented a 550-square-foot unit in the Enterprise Centre where her business seems to have gone from strength to strength.

Mark, Director of the Flatcap Coffee Roasting Company, served in the army for 22 years before being medically discharged with complex PTSD.[6] Originally from Lancashire – hence the decision to call the company after the famous regional headgear of Lancashire and Yorkshire – he and his partner started the business with support from the charity Help for Heroes. The unit they occupy in Castledown is painted in the black, gold and white colours of the brand logo. Although ambivalent about his time in the military, he feels he is a good example of overcoming adversity.

Amanda is the manager of Castledown Enterprise Centre and was originally hired because of her connection to the military through the Reserve service, as well as having been self-employed. She has worked hard to develop and advertise the centre by working with military spouses and maintaining links to the garrison in Tidworth. Drinking coffee from an oversized mug decorated with the Flatcap Coffee branding, incorporating the union flag, she explains that the previous administrator was an army wife and she herself is in the process of hiring an apprentice who will develop links with the local military community.

Other businesses target the same market by offering training and financial support. A firm of accountants works with small businesses and employs a number of military spouses. It started as a two-desk office and went on to rent a whole unit. Southwest Health and Safety was founded by an ex-regular who settled in Wiltshire after leaving his regiment. The company provides health and safety training to other soldiers transitioning out of the armed forces.

Amanda thinks that military dependants and veterans are best able to tune in to the rhythms of these types of start-up businesses. They also work to a certain standard, she feels, that is reflective of the kinds of discipline associated with a military career. Not all spouses want to start their own businesses, though. The Forces Families Jobs website was set up to help partners of military personnel and those transitioning out of the military to find paid employment in the areas where they lived. Every employer who has signed the Armed Forces Covenant is registered on the site, and applicants can also ask for help with building CVs.

On the ground, however, there are many spouses who are frustrated by the lack of career prospects in Wiltshire. Emma, who was based in Larkhill, complained that 'There are hardly any jobs, and when they do become available it's jobs at Home Bargains and B&M Bargains. I don't think there are any jobs around here that would help in building a career.' According to Emma, the picture looked even more bleak for families recently relocated because of the massive gap between the wages paid in England and those they were used to in Germany.

The increased levels of encouragement and material support for military spouses are a relatively new phenomenon for an institution not known for its gender-awareness policies. Backed by the Army Families Federation, a charity that relies on its employees having first-hand experience of army life, the issue is closely connected to the military recruitment and retention crisis.[7] The fact that spouses are unable to pursue careers of their own, because of frequent moves and long periods of single parenting, is frequently cited as a major reason why people leave the armed forces. Added to the instability of army life, there are also limited opportunities for well-paid jobs in rural areas where bases are often located.

The average salary across Salisbury Plain hovers between £25,000 and £27,000 a year, which is below the national average and reflects both lower than average salaries in the military and the predominance of hourly paid and low-wage work in the county.[8] With tens of thousands of military dependants living in the South West of England, the question of spouses' life courses – beyond the careers of their serving family member – remains a pressing one for the overall stability of the military institution. But in the meantime, what about those who live near a base who have little or no connection to the army? Are there any financial benefits to be gleaned from proximity to such a specialised workforce?

Modern ways of living

One way to calculate the economic impact of a military community on a particular area is to examine what happens when the troops leave town. In 2016, in a belated attempt to 'update their defence estate' during a government-enforced period of austerity, the Ministry of Defence announced that 56 defence sites would be closed by 2040.[9] Union leaders reacted immediately to the news, calling the closures 'brutal'. Mark Serwotka, general secretary for the Public and Commercial Services Union, said: 'We are opposed to these closure plans that throw the future into doubt for thousands of staff.' Mike McCartney, national officer for Unite, told the BBC that 'In many instances the bases earmarked for closure are at the heart of their local communities providing a source of decent and secure employment'.[10]

One of these was MoD Caledonia, the naval base at Rosyth, just north of Edinburgh. Local media described the news as a 'kick in the teeth' and a 'death knell' for the town. A campaign to keep the base was backed by local communities and politicians, who hoped that the ensuing delay meant that there could be a change of direction from the Ministry. Older residents fondly recalled the time when the pubs were full of sailors and people could enjoy subsidised amenities like the swimming pool. However, despite Rosyth being given a 'stay of execution' in 2022 when the Ministry revised its 'disposal time-line' to 2026, the site is still in the process of being 'drawn down for closure' and the swimming pool remains closed.[11]

Needless to say, the Ministry defended its decision on the grounds of focusing both on national security and on the wellbeing of military families but it is worth dwelling briefly on the language used to justify this reduction of military bases in the UK. Just three years earlier, in 2019, the new Defence Secretary Tobias Ellwood had revealed a new five-year plan, arguing that 'The defence estate currently accounts for approximately 1.8% of the UK's land mass, with over 40% of the estate being over 50 years old. This does not support the future needs of the UK Armed Forces or represent the best value for the taxpayer.'[12]

In other words it was necessary to shrink the total area of land owned by the Ministry of Defence in order to invest more wisely in the sites that were left. One of the stated aims was to increase prosperity for the 'surrounding communities', whether this was in the construction business or from releasing sites that were in prime locations but surplus to Ministry requirements.[13]

In 2022 the final strategy paper published by the Tories reflected a need for a less cumbersome, more competitive and forward-looking style of estate management. 'New generations joining Defence will expect to see greater connectivity, energy efficiency, workspace flexibility and flexible working. The demographics of our military and civilian workforce will also change as we achieve our aim of a more diverse workforce, driving changes in the accommodation demand.'[14] Indeed, the terms of reference are almost unrecognisable from earlier government edicts, sounding more like an advertising pitch for a corporate military career than an attempt to sort out its bookkeeping:

> As we modernise the estate, we must adopt a master planning approach to the development on our establishments. In addition to delivering military capability, this will emphasise the importance of spaces, both built and natural, in fostering a sense of community and place, to enhance the wellbeing of our people and support modern ways of living. For example, as Service Personnel increasingly choose to live off-site, the need for on-site social facilities may grow.

The prevailing argument in these recent documents is that the military brings economic prosperity and jobs to the regions in which it is concentrated. But how does this 'khaki economy' work, and to what extent does the military presence brings prosperity to the 'surrounding communities'?

Company town?

This question takes us right back to the foundation of the original garrison in Tidworth. We saw that some neighbouring landowners positively welcomed the War Office's incursion on to the Plain, notably Sir Henry Malet who, in 1897, foresaw 'a revival of movement and prosperity' across the whole district. 'The markets will be stimulated,' he predicted joyfully, and 'small cultivators of fruit and vegetables and poultry owners will benefit immensely, and the decaying villages and farms on Salisbury Plain will ere long participate in the general improvement.'[15] But regardless of the benefits to local small-scale food producers in the early days, how might we begin to measure any financial benefits enjoyed today by those living in the environs of a large military base, beyond estimating the takings at nearby pubs or taxi firms?

As they prepared for the new arrivals, Wiltshire county councillors spoke enthusiastically about the projected local benefits of an

5.1 The khaki economy of an army town.

increased military population who would spend their salaries on retail, hospitality and leisure activities, as well as on council tax. Even in neighbouring Ludgershall, a town that was not officially within the boundaries of Ministry of Defence land, there was evidence that this might be the case. Councillor Chris Williams's anecdotal accounts of increased footfall in the shops and cafés following the construction of the Corunna estate nearby seemed to offer proof that the expansion was having a regenerative effect. But once again, how might this be measured over time, and how have other analysts estimated the economic benefits of living close to a military base?

In her book *Homefront*, an in-depth historical and ethnographic case study of the relationship between Fort Bragg, the military base, and Fayetteville, North Carolina, Catherine Lutz suggests that a US garrison might usefully be compared to a company town. This is a term associated with the history of settler colonialism, where a particular company, often working in an extractive industry such as mining or logging, might create and control economic opportunities to attract workers, supplying their social and cultural needs as the community expands. Since the army is a labour-intensive and hierarchical institution with a huge labour force that interacts with, but is also housed separately from, the rest of the population, the analogy of a company town might seem helpful.

The common-sense argument suggests that, although the US military is a non-profit state institution with certain tax exemptions for serving personnel, their dependants and veterans, there are inevitably material implications for everyone living around a base.[16] For non-military residents there are benefits to be had from providing retail and services on the edge of the establishment, although they remain dependent on the goodwill of the organisation both at local and at national level.

While this concept may have proved appropriate in the postwar era, Lutz claims that it is significantly less useful as a model today. Economic research actually shows that military spending creates fewer jobs per dollar than other forms of public spending and, furthermore, investment in military research and development drains scientific and engineering talent away from other sectors, leading to their underdevelopment compared with countries that spend less money on their militaries. By paying attention to the growing social and economic inequalities in Fayetteville in comparison to nearby cities, manifested in its expanse of poor housing and predominance of minimum-wage jobs, Lutz concludes that the majority of military wealth does not filter down to create a generalised prosperity.[17]

There are significant differences between the relevant military institutions in the UK and the USA – not least the absence of a national health service in the USA – and the concept of company town is even less helpful in analysing the economic impact of a sprawling base in a rural part of England. As we saw in earlier chapters, the majority of people living in Tidworth or Ludgershall, or indeed throughout the Salisbury Plain Training Area and adjacent towns and villages, do not actually work directly for the army or for the Ministry of Defence. While there has been little concern that the Ministry might pull out of Salisbury Plain altogether – it is patently too valuable a space for that – the military's uncooperative and internally focused organisational habits make it an unreliable neighbour.

Instead of adapting the analogy of a company town, we might see the British Army more usefully as the institutional equivalent of a parasite. Over many decades its fluctuating presence has been beneficial to the economic health of the area while also causing a high degree of uncertainty due to its insularity and very different mode of operating. This does not make it easy to calibrate the potential cost benefits of living next to a military base. Due to the army's dominating physical presence, however, and the large workforce with attendant spouses and children, the threat of pulling out can be acute.

The example of Rosyth illuminates the implications for a town when a longstanding naval base is facing closure. It is no different from an army base. The decision to withdraw 11,000 British troops from Germany by 2016, with the remaining 4,500 recalled by 2019, immediately prompted fears in Germany about the impact on local communities that had developed organically over seventy years of occupation.[18] For some, the pull-out was not expected for another 15 years and the revised timing came as a shock. British forces were estimated to contribute around £1.3 billion a year to the local economy and for some of the communities living adjacent to the bases the implications were alarming. In Bergen, for example, a third of the local economy depended on the UK forces.[19]

In one report, Rainer Prokop, the Mayor of Bergen, described the move as 'the most severe upheaval for us since the Second World War ... We don't know what the effect will be on business; a lot of them will be affected, it could be up to 40 per cent of them.' Nor was it simply a matter of economics. 'The British live among us,' he told a reporter. 'They are a part of everything here. They started out as an occupying force, but over time they became military partners, neighbours, friends and many started families here.'

There are also unknown challenges associated with expanding a base. When the plan to create a 'super garrison' on Salisbury Plain was announced, which entailed importing 4,300 personnel and their families within a relatively short period, the then leader of Wiltshire

Council, Jane Scott, was quite frank in anticipating difficulties. 'We learned the hard way,' she told a BBC journalist.

In the days before the Military Civilian Integration Partnership was set up, 'it wasn't working well' she admitted. 'Families would move away and schools would empty and we'd have no prior knowledge. Equally a hundred children might suddenly arrive.' But it wasn't just about the mismatch between democratic methods of planning and military rationality. There were also financial implications for local government arising from the formal commitment to increase support for armed forces communities. Yet until the Military Civilian Integration Partnership audit there was little in-depth research into the economic impact of maintaining an army base in a particular location.

It is estimated that the approximately 56,000 direct military and defence civil service jobs at the military sites in the South West, together with the military-related population, contribute around £2 billion GVA to the regional economy, just over 2 per cent of the regional total, and support an additional 24,000 indirect jobs.

In 2020 Oxford Economics published a document funded by the Ministry of Defence detailing research on the wider value of the British Army.[20] The report, which included sections on domestic defence, global influence and economic prosperity, was aimed at highlighting the benefits, at both a national and a local level. Citing the existence of 58 primary bases 'throughout the breadth of the UK', the report stated that the sheer numbers of personnel located on these bases meant that they 'can represent an extremely important source of spending and income for the surrounding local communities'.[21] But the methodology for calculating the financial benefit derived from the army's presence – otherwise known as the 'khaki pound' – was limited because it was impossible to know what would have happened if there had been no base.

The main example used in the Oxford report was Catterick garrison in the district of Richmondshire, Yorkshire, the centre for training infantry and Gurkha soldiers, home to 6,400 army personnel and 530 civil servants. The report asserted that spending by base personnel supported almost two thousand jobs in the local area, the impact of which was felt in 'consumer-facing sectors such as retail and wholesale, accommodation and food services, and arts and entertainment'. This was estimated to contribute £66 million to local GVA.[22]

Further calculations suggested that, by adding these two thousand jobs to the 6,900 posts permanently based at the garrison, the base supports almost 30 per cent of all jobs in Richmondshire, either directly or through what the authors term 'induced multiplier effects'. This data are accompanied by brightly coloured diagrams showing the estimated co-relation between wages and expenditure in the area.

A more immediate illustration of the commercial life of a garrison town was provided by a feature on Tidworth's branch of Tesco published in *The Grocer* in 2023. The store manager Emily Turner was interviewed outside the shop, which had been selected as the journal's 'store of the month' in its long-running mystery shopper survey.[23] Asked what distinguished Tidworth Tesco, she replied: 'It's quite a unique set-up in terms of customer base. And it's a very close-knit community, so a lot of our spouses work for the military and we have colleagues who are in the army too.'

She went on to explain what this meant for their trading patterns, which were clearly unlike those in more urban environments: 'Where other stores might see a typical weekend spike in trade, we find a lot of our customer base are in the area during the week and go home to their families at the weekend.' Trade would also be drastically affected when large numbers of soldiers were sent away on exercises and then returned all at once. 'Some weeks we might be really quiet, and some weeks you've got eight thousand soldiers coming home and they all need to do their shopping. It's a very unique setting.'

In order to cope with these fluctuations in trade Turner revealed that she worked closely with 'our armed forces network. We do a lot of work in the community anyway, so we have that relationship where they'll give us a heads-up if colleagues are going away, or if there's an event going on …' She also wanted to emphasise 'how much of a tight-knit community it really is, which is lovely because everybody knows everybody. It's the same customers that come in week in, week out. But then we also have that excitement of having a number of completely new customers and a new perspective.'

Leaving aside the contrasting methodologies of these two examples, it would be uncontroversial to state that a military base with a large and mobile workforce, which includes dependants and those who have left the army, is likely to have a substantial (if uneven) impact on local amenities such as shops, food and drink, and entertainment. In turn a garrison might be expected to create certain categories of jobs for local residents, as we were reliably informed by a resident of Tidworth: 'If anyone says they can't find a job in this area then they're not looking properly. Because, the fact that you've got, like, Sodexo and Aspire, brings jobs, because they're all the ones doing what the military used to do themselves.'

Feeding the squaddies

As the Chief Executive of Aspire Defence Ltd, Allan Thomson, whom we met in the previous chapter, oversees Project Allenby Connaught through the company's subsidiary business Aspire Defence Services, which provides a wide range of services to the Ministry of Defence defence estate in Salisbury Plain and Aldershot. Aspire has about 980 employees and works alongside another company, Sodexo Defence, which employs approximately 1,700. Together they are contracted to deliver mess catering, accommodation, restaurants, conferencing, bars and pubs for the military community. For this reason it was useful to draw on Allan's long experience of overseeing the commercial side of military management, from a practical as well as an economic standpoint.

One of our first questions was inspired by Sir Henry Malet's dream that the garrison would revive Wiltshire's fruit and vegetable market. The response was that, although the company tries to source fresh produce from local suppliers in the Aldershot and Salisbury Plain areas, it employs a major national food supplier. It's difficult to define the fine grain of these arrangements, he told us, but, before Brexit, around 30 per cent of the firm's fresh fruit and vegetables came from mainland Europe and 70 per cent was sourced from across the UK. 'Sodexo do try and resource locally as much as they can but we're almost too big,' he explained.

Meanwhile, Jacqui, a 56-year-old resident of Tidworth, had confided to us that she had been apprehensive about taking a job with Sodexo in one of the sergeants' messes in Tidworth. Although she had lived and worked for many years in the town she was 'quite nervous about working behind the wire for the first time, feeding the squaddies'. She had heard that the soldiers could be rude to civilian workers and was concerned about getting by on a minimum wage, hourly paid contract. She needn't have worried, though. She was not in the habit of taking nonsense from anyone and had found that there was no shortage of shifts on offer. She received annual leave and sick pay, and her bosses were kind to her.

Jacqui's experience was by no means universal. One employee we spoke to reported that 'the boys are rude, they swear a lot'. Another indication that this was a factor was the sign displayed by the till in the soldiers' mess at Bulford barracks reminding personnel not to be rude to the catering staff. Despite this perception, however, many found that working for Sodexo was no different from working for any other company.

A Nepali employee told us that she had been working for the company since she arrived in England 12 years earlier. It was convenient, because she could walk to work from home, and, unlike security jobs where the majority of retired Gurkhas worked, there were no night shifts. 'Aside from this,' she went on, 'there is nothing special about working for Sodexo. It is a lot of labour for the minimum wage. There are no additional benefits and privileges and I have not attended a single language or any other training courses so far.'

Sodexo appears to employ a significant number of Nepali nationals to work in its catering and cleaning roles. In the past the company struggled to hire enough cleaners and caterers in Wiltshire, and sent shuttles to collect Nepali workers from as far away as Aldershot, which hosts the largest Nepali settlement in the UK. The small but steady increase in the number of Gurkha soldiers, veterans and their families in Tidworth, as well as neighbouring towns of Amesbury and Andover, has meant that this transportation arrangement is no longer needed and so has been terminated, although some Nepali employees were still commuting from as far away as Salisbury and Swindon.

Construction has also been a significant sector for local job creation, involving a number of significant and long-term contracts for designing, building, maintaining and servicing the new housing estates. Allan described the money poured into constructing new housing between 2017 and 2020 as 'the biggest investment into South Wiltshire in any way, shape or form'. Much of this investment was temporary, of course, as jobs tailed off after construction work was completed.

Contracts were not always given to companies based in Wiltshire, either, and construction workers came from as far afield as Southampton and Wales. Aspire did make an effort to sub-contract out to local companies for smaller jobs like building a gym, but the fire doors came from a company in Portugal.[24]

These details provided by the CEO of Aspire Defence were extremely helpful in estimating the value of the khaki pound in the immediate vicinity of the 'super garrison'. They pale into insignificance, however, when considered next to both regional and national levels of defence spending emanating from the government itself.

The defence industry

Tucked away inside the rows of nondescript warehouses in Andover's Walworth Business Park is Scientific Management International Ltd. SMI is a military contractor whose exact operations are of a classified nature, but include the manufacture of military vehicles. Situated on the town's eastern edge, SMI applied for permission to expand its operation in 2021. The plans for the interior of the two extensions were necessarily vague, but the proposal to build an enclosed smoking hut caused consternation amongst the environmental health team at Test Valley Borough Council.[25]

Scientific Management International Ltd is just one example of the many defence and aerospace contractors based in clusters around the borders of Hampshire and Wiltshire. At the other end of the scale is the multinational company QinetiQ headquartered in

Farnborough, Hampshire, which leases the MoD Boscombe Down airfield and all of its infrastructure as part of a twenty-five-year Long Term Partnering Agreement. This site includes the longest military airstrip in the UK, the Empire Test Pilot School and the QinetiQ Apprenticeship Training School. It provides around two thousand jobs whose main focus is on maintaining, repairing, operating and testing military aircraft. For Wiltshire Council this represented huge potential for providing jobs in the aerospace industry and boosting the regional economy.

Porton Science Park, a 10-hectare development on the campus at Porton Down near Salisbury, represents one of the newest investments in the field of defence-related research and development in the county. Like the Castledown Enterprise Centre in Ludgershall, Porton is one of Wiltshire Council's 'innovation centres' provided by The Enterprise Network. At its opening in 2018 the council leader, Baroness Scott of Bybrook OBE, hailed it as 'a platform for science and technology innovation and new business start-ups. Creating modern space here in our county for science and defence technologies places Wiltshire firmly on the map and strengthens our status as a great place to do business. This means more high-skilled local jobs and is more good news for Wiltshire's economy.'[26]

What she did not say was that Wiltshire was already on that particular map, even if the county was not normally associated with industry of any kind. This phenomenon is part of the economic and labour market change that arose from the economic recession in the 1970s. In their book *Sunbelt City? A Study of Economic Change in Britain's M4 Growth Corridor* (1986) the authors Martin Boddy, John Lovering and Keith Bassett explained why this particular sector of manufacturing was protected from then Prime Minister Margaret Thatcher's economic restructuring. Defence expenditure is typically based on long-term contracts with follow-on sales, development and modification, and this kept the aerospace industry afloat, attenuating the job losses in other areas. As a result there was a technological renaissance with significant research and development activities devoted to the development of guided weapons for export.[27]

While a large proportion of manufacturing industries disappeared under Thatcher, investment in the arms industry continued, alongside building relationships with foreign governments who could buy British weapons.[28] However, this was not merely a relic of Thatcher's government but built on innovations put in place by the postwar Labour government which established the Defence Export Services Organisation to co-ordinate the sale of British arms across the world.[29] This segue into arms dealing was part of an internal strategy to allow Britain to continue to act as an important global political actor after losing its status as imperial power.[30]

None the less it was the light-touch regulatory environment created in the 1980s that enabled such significant advances in the development of new military technology and private security firms. Today private companies in the UK are working on cutting-edge cyber warfare technologies and are assisted by the government in accessing foreign markets through advice and introductions to potential customers. UK Defence and Security Exports – which is the latest iteration of the Defence Export Services Organisation – is visibly present at arms shows, helping visitors understand the latest technologies produced by British companies like BAE Systems, and delegations are invited to the government's Defence Science and Technology Laboratory in Porton Down to discuss how it could further support its customers.[31]

As we saw earlier, Wiltshire Council has been enthusiastic in embracing these opportunities for defence investment. In 2009 the first report on the economic significance of the military presence in the South West region suggested that Ministry of Defence expenditure supported almost seventy thousand direct and indirect jobs in the defence industry and contributed around £3 billion GVA to the regional economy.[32] It also revealed that 25 per cent of overall Ministry defence expenditure was spent in the region, and, of that, £5 billion was associated with the presence of bases in the area whilst £4 billion was associated with the defence industry. Added together, defence-related employment accounted for 4 per cent of all jobs in the region. At the time the 'defence industrial cluster' in the South West was second only to the South East, with more than a hundred medium- to large-scale defence-related manufacturing and consultancy companies located in the region.[33]

A decade later the disparity between regions had grown to astonishing proportions. From every pound of Ministry of Defence expenditure on industry in 2018/19, £0.27 effectively went to the South West while less than £0.01 each went to Northern Ireland and the North East.[34] To put it another way, that same year Ministry average expenditure equated to £290 for every person living in the UK. This rounded-up number masked the extent of a vastly unequal distribution. In the North East, for example, the figure was £40 per person. In London it was £170. In the South West it was £930.

These figures show that the reach of the khaki pound goes far beyond the immediate spending power of soldiers and their families living on and around a base. As Curtis and Kennard show in their investigation of Britain's 'warfare state', British governments have long viewed the arms industry as a mechanism to shore up the economy. Successive defence reviews and research sponsored by the Ministry of Defence like the Oxford Economics report routinely present the arms industry (packaged as the defence and security sector) as an effective means to enhance productivity across the UK. Universities, local authorities, police, government departments and other stakeholders from industry are brought together in 'enterprise partnerships', working in 'clusters' to support and expand the country's aspiration to be a world-leading arms manufacturer.[35]

In the South West the University of Exeter plays a particularly important role in co-ordinating the regional 'Defence and Security Cluster'. In 2023 the campaigning group Demilitarise Education revealed that the Physics and Astronomy Doctoral Training programme was being designed in line with Ministry of Defence priorities in the field of electromagnetic materials, and rolled out in partnership with the US Air Force, Thales and QinetiQ. In another example, between 2017/18 and 2020/21 the University of Bristol accepted £12 million for research projects, the titles of which are withheld, from BAE Systems, Rolls-Royce, GKN and Northrop Grumman. Over this period the university received over £500,000 from the same companies for 'consultancy' services rendered.[36]

In December 2023 a report by Open Democracy revealed that at least 36 arms company officials had positions on advisory boards in 12 Russell Group universities, including boards advising on academic programmes.[37] Equally concerning is the role of universities in promoting the establishment of free ports, the controversial low-regulation zones created under the Tory government. For instance, on its official website, the Plymouth and South Devon Freeport was billed as an opportunity to 'supercharge the South West economy by building on our region's unique national capabilities in marine, defence and space to form globally impactful clusters and a UK Innovation Superpower'.[38] As co-ordinator of the South West Region Defence and Security Cluster, the University of Exeter was expected to play a leading role.

It also appears that a proportion of the Ministry of Defence expenditure in the South West is spent on joint surveillance operations with the USA. The GCHQ installation at Bude, Cornwall, which intercepts communications from transatlantic cables carrying internet traffic, is operated in partnership with the US National Security Agency. The NSA paid £15.5 million towards developing the site, according to documents leaked by Edward Snowden.[39]

While the presence of significant military bases across the South West might provide the rationale for increased defence spending in the region as a whole, what does this bring to the rural towns and villages of Salisbury Plain?

Special treatment

We began this chapter on the khaki economy with individual stories showing how hard it was for military dependants to develop their own careers – or even earn a living – due to the particular nature of army life. A business selling pink hair-bows to little girls might seem an odd place to start. But Wiltshire's new business networks that target enterprising spouses and veterans, while also attracting local civilian initiatives, cannot be understood separately from the wider economy of the country's burgeoning defence and security budget. Training soldiers is an expensive investment, and it pays to keep them in the organisation for the longest possible time. Haemorrhaging personnel from fighting-fit units due to pressure from frustrated partners to leave after five years could be seen as a waste of taxpayers' money, not to mention a mark of gross inefficiency.

In May 2021 Lieutenant Colonel Jamie Balls, the retired garrison commander for Tidworth, was able to give us a realistic appraisal of the expansion programme. It transpired that, out of the 1,017 new service family homes made available, over 450 remained unoccupied: many families simply did not want to live there, preferring to buy or rent in surrounding civilian communities. In his opinion there was 'a massive void between where the talk is, and what the reality is, on integration' between military and civilian communities and interests. In his view there needed to be significant investment in shops, entertainment and leisure facilities to induce dependants to move to the new housing. However, this was not on the cards. The council claimed it was the Ministry of Defence's responsibility but the Ministry argued that, since its employees paid council tax, it was up to the council to invest in the area.

While there might be some advantages for non-military people living in close proximity to a base, whether it is access to business premises, start-up advice or work in retail, might there also be some tangible economic disadvantages? In Tidworth opinion was divided on the fairness of the military discounts offered by retailers. These discounts can be applied to all members of the armed forces community eligible for a Defence Privilege Card, which includes the families of serving soldiers, veterans, Ministry of Defence civilians, cadet forces and NATO personnel in the UK. Shops advertise the discount by placing signs in their windows. While some felt that it was deserved, and a way in which the wider society could 'give thanks', others reported that these discounts caused grudges and 'little complaints'. But this isn't all about who receives cheaper sandwiches at Subway or discounted entry tickets for certain facilities.

Lieutenant Colonel Balls had a particular take on this subject which he shared with us. When he retired from his position as garrison commander in early 2021, he took over management of Tedworth Equestrian, a former Ministry of Defence equine centre. He reformulated the business as a charity providing recreational and welfare support to the entire local community. However, the stables were located on Ministry land, which meant that, although the new lease was set at a commercial rate, it came with an obligation to offer heavily discounted services to army families. But the charity was viable only if the public were charged the full amount, with no discount, a situation that appeared to him as 'reverse discrimination'.

As he pointed out, the Armed Forces Covenant established the principle that members of the armed forces, including veterans, should not be disadvantaged in any way. It does not call for special treatment over and above the services and benefits that civilian communities are able to access. However, the Ministry of Defence's programme of 'defence estate optimisation' includes a strategy to lease land to public and private civilian entities with the proviso that they provide discounted services to military families.

Together with the routine discounts offered in shops and other businesses, this arrangement effectively diminishes the value of the khaki pound, especially in the larger 'super garrison' areas. As we saw, the Oxford Economics report on 'the wider value of the British Army' used research carried out at Catterick garrison to assert that military bases 'can represent an extremely important source of spending and income for the surrounding local communities'.[40] Yet if a charity aimed at the local population has to charge members of the public higher fees in order to compensate for the service discount, this casts a slightly different light on the levels of prosperity supposedly created by a large military presence.

Once again, it's an almost trivial example close to home that can help to test, or at least interrogate, these kinds of claims. The truth is that it is very difficult to ascertain the value of the khaki pound in isolation from other costs and benefits associated with this particular company workforce. A large military employer might boost a predominantly rural economy by contributing to retail and entertainment, and even providing a number of administrative jobs for civilians. But there are questions relating to the nature of the work itself – and indeed the workforce – which have profound implications for the social and cultural life of the 'surrounding community'.

6

Living next to a pipeline

Armed Forces Day, held each year on the last Saturday of June, is not a long-standing tradition in the national calendar. It began in 2009, replacing its short-lived predecessor, Veterans Day, which had been inaugurated only three years earlier. The change of focus was an outcome of then Prime Minister Gordon Brown's cross-party inquiry, pitched as an opportunity to thank members of all the armed forces for their service and to show public appreciation for their past and ongoing work defending the country. As Paul Dixon has argued, it was all part of the 'militarisation offensive' that sought to generate support for the 'good war' in Afghanistan and to repair the damage caused to the military's reputation by the 'bad war' in Iraq.[1]

Although it was marked by a grand national spectacle, the principle behind the special day was to encourage grassroots participation. Enthusiasts are offered help with funding events, no matter how small, and boosting visibility through selling merchandise and compiling press releases. Each year a different town or city is selected to host the national event, while local authorities are encouraged to organise their own regional celebrations. Given the large military footprint in Wiltshire, this annual fixture has become a permanent ritual across the county.

In 2018 it was Trowbridge's turn to host the regional Armed Forces Day. Now the county town of Wiltshire, it was built on the wool trade from the fourteenth century and due to the proliferation of cloth-weaving mills was once known as the Manchester of the West before the decline of the industry some five hundred years later. More recently Trowbridge was the base of the Bowyer meat operation, source of the famous sausages, which drew many migrant workers to the town in the 1960s and 1970s. The firm was bought up and the works closed down two decades ago, but Trowbridge is still home to the largest Moroccan-heritage community outside of London.[2] There was little sign of this industrial history as we made our way to the town park.

This year marked the culmination of the First World War centenary, and the theme of the day was designed not so much to thank troops for their service in Afghanistan as to commemorate those who fought and died in the trenches a hundred years previously. The festivities included numerous interactive displays restaging the conditions faced by those young men, a significant number of whom had been trained on Salisbury Plain. We followed signs to the 'front line' and found the entrance point to a trench system, apparently situated somewhere between Ypres and Mons.

Visitors were invited to climb through tunnels formed of painted styrofoam and papier mâché festooned with dangling rats. The designers had spared no detail to achieve an authentic look. In the medical tent a bloodied, life-sized dummy was lying on a stretcher on the ground. His freshly amputated hand was in a porcelain bowl next to him. A tour guide, sitting in the corner of the dark and musty tent, informed us gloomily that 'that is how it was'.

Outside, children milled about with their parents. One man spoke passionately to another guide, visibly sweating in his First World War uniform, who was standing at the entrance to the trench. He looked down at the man's son and held out his imitation rifle, asking him kindly, 'Would you like to hold my gun?'

This question was repeated across the site, especially on the north side of the park where there was an assortment of contemporary military vehicles. Children were hoisted in and out of camouflage helicopters and armoured trucks against the sonorous backdrop of the Battle of Amiens being re-enacted behind a barrier.

A fairground was visible on one side of the park with an area reserved for market stalls selling sundry war-related objects. Punters could browse antique memorabilia consisting of medals, cap badges, stuffed boar heads and antlers, or thumb through used books on military history. Next to these were imitation military assault vests in child and adult sizes, and rows of infant rompers emblazoned with the words 'daddy's little soldier'. Interspersed between burger trucks and churros stalls were recruitment stands enticing people to join the regular or reserve forces, or support a military charity. Educational posters recounted the details of preparation for the First World War in Wiltshire and commemorated those who took part, including men from other corners of the British Empire.

The central focus was a parade ground with a stage, and the line-up consisted of the Salisbury Plain Military Wives Choir; Trowbridge Players, an amateur dramatics society; Stagecoach, the performing arts franchise; and the Salisbury City Band of the Royal British Legion. As we approached, the young Stagecoach dancers were getting into formation before launching into a dance routine choreographed to a track by Beyoncé. Parents looked on anxiously, and we fell into conversation with a mother craning her neck to get a better look at her daughter.

Stagecoach was then replaced by a marching band of older men from the Royal British Legion who played 'It's a Long Way to Tipperary' followed by 'Waltzing Matilda'. An unlikely combination of people, many of whom were very young and strapped into push-chairs, clapped their hands or tapped their feet in time to the music. After a day of witnessing children being encouraged to play with lethal weapons, this confirmed our impression that the institution of Armed Forces Day was not so much a chance to say 'thank you for your service' but an opportunity to stage a corporate recruitment fair on a local, regional and national scale.[3]

Many people living in Wiltshire would be alarmed at idea of a giant pipeline running through their towns and villages, but this analogy is routinely used by military recruiters whose job it is to attract young people of the right calibre. As with all pipelines, however, the inflow is partly calibrated by the rate of outflow, not to mention any leakages along its length. Taps can also be adjusted to increase or reduce the flow at any point, the most egregious example being the on-and-off application of the five-year residency rule for Commonwealth

6.1 Armed Forces Day, Trowbridge, Wiltshire, 2018.

applicants. When more recruits are needed, the qualification is lifted, and, when it looks as though the forces can meet their targets with home-grown recruits, it is reinstated. Meanwhile, with hands nervously clutching the purse-strings, and eyes fixed on the horizon, the government of the day is busy calculating just how large or small an army it actually needs or can get away with.[4]

It was hard to avoid the fact that the disparate age groups enjoying a good time on Armed Forces Day were all connected to this pipeline, whether they knew it or not. Wiltshire has long held the reputation for being a military county because of the British Army's presence on Salisbury Plain. In 2011 this was enhanced when Wootton Bassett, located in the southern part of the county, become the first English town for more than a hundred years to be granted the title 'Royal'.

Due to the closure of RAF Brize Norton in 2007, the route to the hospital in Oxford from RAF Lyneham passed through Wootton Bassett, where local residents, including the town mayor, felt it appropriate to pay their respects to the funeral cortèges of soldiers whose bodies had been repatriated from Afghanistan. As the number of deaths soared, Wootton Bassett rapidly became a focal point for expressing a range of public attitudes, not just to the war itself but also to what it might mean for soldiers to risk their lives for such a contentious cause. In August 2011 the 167th (and final) repatriation took place, taking the total number of men and women who were repatriated through the town to 345.[5]

In 2013 Wiltshire Council, already committed to the Military Civilian Integration Partnership as we saw in Chapter 4, was one of the first local authorities to sign the Armed Forces Covenant, 'a promise from the nation that those who serve or have served and their families, are treated fairly'. And as Councillor Chris Williams had explained, the county had long been favoured as a place of retirement for many ex-forces people, like himself and several other local politicians whom we met. 'There's a good percentage have got a military connection or their father or somebody would have worked for the army in some way or another,' he told us. Born in Birkenhead, he had joined the army's Royal Corps of Electronic and Mechanical Engineers in 1965 against his family's wishes.

This local connection to the military was confirmed at a more symbolic level when Lieutenant General Sir Andrew Gregory KBE CB DL was chosen as the new Vice Lord-Lieutenant of Wiltshire in 2023. A man 'with a distinguished military career', Sir Andrew was the chief executive of SSAFA (the charity originally known as the Soldiers' and Sailors' Families Association) as well as the head of the Royal Regiment of Artillery, historically based at Larkhill.[6] In addition to the local effects of the outflow, however, it seems relevant to ask about the inflow. In other words, is Wiltshire a rich recruiting ground for the army, and if so, how does it do it?

The inflow

We are sitting in one of the converted Victorian buildings in Tidworth garrison, trying not to stare at the stuffed ram with impressively curled horns standing on a wooden base in the corner. Guy Benson, Wiltshire council's military–civilian integration lead, is explaining that the 'youth element' is key to the whole strategy, right across the UK. The programme purportedly seeks to build good community relations in areas with large military populations, he tells us, and hopes to increase public support for the armed forces by showing the economic benefits and jobs generated by having a large standing army. We learn that, when there is a recruitment and retention crisis, the army finds it beneficial to increase its public engagement as a way to replenish its workforce.

Guy is an ex-regular, now serving as a reservist and working on a variety of initiatives across the South West, from health and safety, fuel, data collection and crypto-security to 'engagement opportunities'. His team was involved in the clean-up operation in Salisbury and Amesbury following the Novichok poisonings, but engagement, particularly with young people, takes up most of his time.

Guy tells us that the army is conscious that it is important to start looking for and nurturing potential recruits from a young age as many have decided their next steps by the age of 16. This is why the Ten Tors Challenge, an annual trek held in the moors in Dartmoor and organised by Army HQ in Andover, is designed for young people between 14 and 21. His team also delivers 'leadership development training' in schools, alongside organising less predictable activities like music workshops, poetry classes and even meetings with elite sports personalities, all designed to attract their target audience. He drops in the fact that the team is particularly keen to access schools in Bristol because the city represents the potential for recruiting more young people from diverse backgrounds.

While Guy is speaking, he motions to a taciturn man sitting across the table, telling us that his job is to co-ordinate a team of former soldiers who run week-long residential courses for 16- to 21-year-old students studying for BTEC nationals (public services). Students who attend these courses are given the chance to find out whether the forces might be for them, or whether they might prefer a career in nursing or the police. His colleague is evidently an old hand, and not inclined to speak to us directly or even make eye contact with us, despite the fact that the presentation has been arranged for our benefit. Nevertheless, we make a note that we should interview him in the coming months as he is much more involved in the process. We are in the early stages of our research and are not yet aware that this would be our only official briefing.

We were grateful for this introductory talk, and anticipating finding out how this 'engagement' with young people worked in practice. Did the fact of living so close to an army base mean that the local school students were automatically viewed as potential recruits? Were the children of soldiers more likely to join up than their peers who did not have a parent in the forces? Did the parents of the 16- and 17-year-olds object to their kids being targeted for 'engagement'?

Unfortunately our request for further discussion on the subject was subsequently turned down at the highest level on the basis that the book we were planning to write was unlikely to be a best-seller.[7] Informally we were given to understand that, unless our publication offered young people a positive inducement to enlist, it was simply not worth their while to speak to us. The fact that we were motivated to investigate the wider ecology of a 'super garrison' was irrelevant.

This rebuff, delivered by an apologetic member of the media and communications team based in the Land Forces HQ in Andover, suggested that the army might be fighting a losing battle to attract new recruits, or at least those of sufficient calibre. This is not just a matter of changing the advertising pitch from time to time and adjusting employment policy to meet legal requirements. It is a reminder that military service is not like any other job and, while the public is encouraged to respect the armed forces regardless of what they are instructed to do, it should still mind its own business when it comes to holding them to account on home ground. So much for improved civil–military relations. As a result we were obliged to review the recruitment situation across the country, supplementing this overview with independent analysis provided by journalists and other specialist researchers.

The first point to note is that the army is invariably suffering a recruitment crisis. Numbers of young people applying to join the armed forces are affected by many factors, from the general level of unemployment across the country to perceptions of military life and labour. This has been the case since National Service was abolished in 1960 and the armed forces became an all-volunteer, professional organisation competing with industry and other employment sectors.

Figures released in 2024 showed that the army fell below its target size for the first time since it was set. Overall, the UK armed forces were 5,440 personnel (1 per cent) below target. Between the financial years 1999/2000 and 2023/24 there have been only six years when the number of personnel joining the UK Regular Forces was higher than the number leaving.[8]

Second, like everyone else in the public sector, the armed forces have been subject to multiple cuts and restructuring over the past two decades, the most stringent of which began in 2008 while soldiers were still deployed in Afghanistan. We should also note here that the military workforce is barred from forming a union and going on strike, unlike other public sector employees. Although there were outraged media reports about soldiers receiving redundancy letters in Afghanistan as far back as 2011, news of these cuts is often overshadowed by government pronouncements on Britain's role in a changing world.

During Prime Minister David Cameron's coalition government it was announced that, in terms of overall numbers, the 'Future Army' would be reduced to 117,000 soldiers, of whom 82,000 would be regulars and 30,000 would be reservists. The Strategic Defence and Security Review 2015 announced further restructuring under the banner Army 2020, increasing the planned number of reservists from 30,000 to 35,000, while remaining committed to 82,000 regulars. Another five years later, this target was scrapped. By this time the 'trained strength' of the regular army had dropped to 76,300. On 22 March 2021 the Secretary of State for Defence, Ben Wallace, promised to reduce it further to 72,500 by 2025. Just a few months later, however, he adjusted the target to 73,000, and in time this number would change again, depending on the contingencies of foreign policy and public spending.[9]

The point of relaying this information is not to make an informed judgement on the size of the army at any one time. The issue of recruitment is certainly relevant to the tempo of life on or near an army base, but it also has implications for the rest of society that are seldom acknowledged.

Moral exploitation

According to a 2022 report by *Byline Times*, the government invests heavily in military recruitment, spending more money per person recruited to the armed forces than it does on recruiting teachers and nurses.[10]

Over two years (2019 to 2021) the Ministry of Defence spent nearly £70 million on recruiting new personnel to the Royal Air Force (RAF), the Royal Navy, and the Army. In the same time frame, 31,660 new people signed up to join the armed forces. This was more than double the amount that NHS England spent on recruitment advertising, at £32 million, in which period it recruited 104,638 new nursing staff, health visitors and midwives. The military's spending also dwarfs that of teacher recruitment: in this period the Department for Education launched a £22 million campaign to attract new trainee teachers, while 66,700 teachers joined the profession.

In addition to the amount of money allocated to replenishing the inflow, there is also the question of where these efforts are directed. Occasionally articles are placed in the local media, highlighting the advantages of a successful army carer, and openly encouraging applicants to come forward.[11] It is at secondary school that the army really steps up its recruitment efforts, when students are doing their GCSEs and A Levels and making decisions about their futures. But if young people are to be persuaded that this is the right career path for them, they must first be acquainted with the nature of the work.

A report on the recruitment crisis in 2017, compiled by Mark Francois MP (former Minister of State for the Armed Forces 2013–15), noted that 'unless they have served in a cadet unit, or already come from a military family, young people leaving school have very little, if any, experience or exposure to the Armed Forces. Surveys show, for instance, that the Army is regarded as considerably less important by 18–24 year-olds than by those aged 40 and upwards.'[12]

For those in charge of replenishing the pipeline, this lack of interest and exposure was part of 'a perfect storm', according to the report. Other contributing factors included near-record employment (in 2017 the unemployment rate in the UK was 4.5 per cent, the lowest since 1975) and also demographic change: the UK has 'an ageing population with those of military age declining as a proportion of the total'. Even more worryingly, the perennial search for more BAME members was still proving elusive, almost twenty years after the New Labour government mandated all public institutions to employ a workforce that reflected the ethnic make-up of the country as a whole. Francois admitted that it was worrying that this section of the population was forecast to rise, 'in a segment of the community which has, hitherto, shown a low propensity to apply for military Service'.[13]

In the light of all these factors, one of the main recommendations proposed by Francois was 'to make the role of the Armed Forces a part of the national curriculum, so that every child leaving school will have at least a basic understanding of our Armed Forces and the role they play defending our nation'. However, this is a contentious proposal that makes many people feel uneasy. In 2019 a report by

Child Rights International Network reported that each year over two thousand children aged 16 and 17 were recruited mostly for the army and particularly for the infantry; more new army recruits are 16 than any other age. The UK is the only state in Europe and among only a few worldwide allowing enlistment at age 16.[14]

This makes the UK 'an international outlier', wrote Jonathan Parry, 'an honour it shares with Iran, North Korea, and Zimbabwe'.[15] In his critical response to Francois's report he noted that this policy of recruiting 16- and 17-year-olds has earned criticism from humanitarian organisations – including the UN Committee on the Rights of the Child. And the UK public seems to agree – nearly 80 per cent think the age of enlistment should be at least 18. As a philosopher who lectures in global ethics, his concern was that they are being prematurely exposed to 'moral exploitation', which he defined as 'unfairly offloading or outsourcing moral burdens onto those who are vulnerable'.

Recruits who are under 18 are trained at the Army Foundation college in Harrogate, where welfare arrangements are rated as 'outstanding' by Ofsted. But in 2023 the *Guardian* journalist Dan Sabbagh revealed that 13 sexual offences had been reported to North Yorkshire Police in just over a year.[16] David Gee, an adviser with the Child Rights International Network which had requested the information, told Sabbagh he believed that 'on this record, Harrogate cannot be regarded as safe'. No matter how the welfare arrangements were structured, difficulties were exacerbated by the young age of the recruits. 'This is not a British problem,' he said. 'This is a problem all over the world when young people are recruited to the military. It is not something you can solve by imposing a zero-tolerance policy and hope it will go away.'

The details emerged after an internal army inquiry report found that a 19-year-old Royal Artillery gunner, Jaysley Beck, was believed to have killed herself at Larkhill camp after a period of relentless sexual harassment by one of her superiors. The report found significant evidence of inappropriate sexual behaviour from male soldiers towards female soldiers at the Larkhill garrison. One witness described receiving routine comments from male soldiers that were 'vile' and 'degrading', according to the Centre for Military Justice, which was representing the family.[17]

Other critics have been alarmed at the recruiters' use of social media to target recruitment material towards 16-year-olds, especially around GCSE results day. For example, in a report entitled 'Selling the Military', the co-authors Rhianna Louise and Emma Sangster stated that, in August 2016, the army told young people via Facebook: 'Whatever happens on results day, we'll help you learn, earn and stand on your own two feet.'

The accompanying image showed an open-topped army vehicle against the background of a dramatic sunset. This is one of many ways in which the army uses integrated data-driven digital marketing to reach different audiences, as outlined in their Digital Strategy of 2016. In that year the army spent £640,000 on Facebook recruitment posts alone. The total digital advertising spend was £3,280,000 – covering job boards, website adverts, advertising on search engines, social media platforms and media sites like YouTube.[18]

'Selling the Military' also cites health professionals and campaigners for the rights of child soldiers who have argued that the military deploys an understanding of adolescent psychology in its marketing campaigns in a way that exploits developmental vulnerabilities and social inequalities. They have also presented evidence that these young people are most likely to be adversely affected by military training and service with regard to both their mental and physical health.

For instance the target audience of the 'This Is Belonging' campaign launched in 2017 was described by the marketing brief as 'young people between the ages of sixteen and twenty-four with an average household income of £10,000 per year', amongst the lowest in the UK. The research by Forces Watch showed that particular cities were targeted, including Manchester, Doncaster, Birmingham and Sheffield, all of which have relatively high levels of deprivation. Another interesting finding was that recruits for the three services were identified as slightly different categories: 'The 16–24-year-old target audience of the Royal Navy are also described as "easily influenced" and lacking knowledge of the armed forces. The campaign targets young people from specific areas around the UK as each advert names a place where the recruit is from.'[19]

Statistics that record levels of recruitment by geographical area tell a different story about who really joins the military compared to the message relayed in expensive advertising videos. Between 2013 and 2018 the top five constituencies for recruitment into the regular army were all in areas with a significant military presence either in the South West around Aldershot and Tidworth garrisons, or in the North West around Catterick garrison: Aldershot, Richmond (Yorkshire), Hereford and South Herefordshire, Lancaster and Fleetwood, and Salisbury.[20]

This picture remains very much the same, with some regional variation. In the 12 months to 31 March 2022, for instance, 77 per cent of those recruited to the UK Regular Forces were recruited from England, while 7 per cent were from Scotland, 5 per cent from Wales and 1 per cent from Northern Ireland. (The location of the remaining 10 per cent was not known although this includes recruits who entered from outside the UK.)

Of the total, 25% were recruited from either the South East or South West regions, whereas only 3 per cent were recruited from London. The five former parliamentary constituencies with the largest intake to the UK Regular Forces in the 12 months to 31 March 2024 were Devizes (120); Aldershot (110); Gosport (80); Richmond (Yorkshire) (80); and Sleaford and North Hykeham (70).[21]

Once again Aldershot garrison is a rich area for recruitment, while Devizes, in Wiltshire, is on the north-eastern edge of the Salisbury Plain Training Area. Although we were not permitted to observe any of the official recruitment activities locally, fortunately some of the local schools were more welcoming, allowing us to talk to some of the 'youth element'. How did they feel about living so close to the mouth of the pipeline?

School visits

Avon Valley College is in Durrington, just north of Larkhill garrison. The lunchtime routine was starting and groups of year-eight students started to take their places in the canteen. One girl was looking slightly disoriented and uncomfortable in her group of peers. She told us, in a strong Welsh accent, that she had just moved here because her mum had married a soldier.

Her classmates start to tease her about having to do an assault course when the army comes to visit the school later on in the term. 'Last year one girl nearly passed out!' said one. Another sought to reassure her that their dad is also in the army: 'The thing you'll really notice is the noise of guns and explosions, especially at night'. They all agreed that this sometimes kept them awake but they also complained about the cars driving very loudly around their estate. It was as if the constant rumble of distant gunfire was no more annoying than the sound of traffic.

The assault course in question was part of an annual career day organised by the public outreach team based in Army HQ in Andover. Many of the young people shared a common dream of a future career with the military. One girl, Sara, used to want to enlist when she finished school and joined the cadets as preparation for that day. But then she went on exercise and got really scared being shot at in the dark and decided it wasn't for her. She now wanted to be in the police and train sniffer dogs. Julia planned to join the RAF. 'But they're such snobs!' someone exclaimed, 'they think they're better than everyone else.' The bell rang for the end of lunch and they filed away to their lessons.

Secondary school pupils across Salisbury Plain are used to the regular interruption of military uniforms in their curriculum. Once a year in the autumn term, the army gives a careers presentation at Avon Valley College, explaining all the different jobs you can apply for and how much you can earn. The pupils have to pick a job and write a cover letter explaining their choice, and then submit to a mock interview with serving personnel – the least popular aspect of the exercise. As this was such a routine and relatively innocuous feature of their schooling, however, many did not even remark on it.

Nevertheless, this presentation appeared to make a big difference. One year there was no one available to do the session and only one person enlisted after finishing their GCSEs. Otherwise, about four or five pupils apply directly to the army each year. This might seem like a relatively small number, yet in a year group of approximately 120, that is about 5 per cent of the whole cohort. It was known too that some students went on to take A Levels and then applied to join the army at officer rank. It could hardly be said that school-age children on Salisbury Plain represented Mark Francois's nightmare scenario of young people leaving school with scant experience or exposure to the armed forces.

Perhaps more alarming than a direct approach by army recruiters is the scheme to recruit teenagers with computer skills, often via gaming magazines.[22] However, there is a much more comprehensive attempt to recruit young people for careers in the security services organised under the banner of Cybersecurity Challenge UK. Although nominally run by the police, this is a multi-partner scheme (including BAE Systems, the Open University, Northrop Grumman and the National Crime Agency) that aims to recruit young people with coding and hacking skills. In 2018 the *Guardian* reported that a group of young people, some as young as 14, was brought to 'a military base in Wiltshire' to 'counter fictional but sophisticated cyber-attacks'.[23]

These are some of the considerations involved in the army's engagement with the 'youth element' in the expanding 'super garrison'. Once the recruits have undergone the relevant training, they are officially recorded in the statistics as inflow as they pass through the pipeline into whatever roles they choose or are chosen for them. Yet, as the writer Joe Glenton has pointed out in his book *Veteranhood*, a trained soldier is eligible to be a veteran from the first day of their contract, regardless of how short a period they have served.[24]

In spite of the efforts to retain trained staff, outlined in the previous chapter, there are many reasons why individuals might leave prematurely or drop out, from sustaining injuries and other health issues to pressure from families or simply as a result of personal choice. On being classed as outflow, for whatever reason, each individual then joins a new cohort whose identity has become increasingly politicised in the wake of the Iraq and Afghanistan wars.

Outflow

In its 2009 audit of the military footprint in the region Wiltshire County Council attempted to understand the economic significance of the outflow from the pipeline. It estimated that four thousand people left the services in the South West each year, 1,600 of whom were based in Wiltshire when they left, and the majority of whom were in junior ranks. Survey data also revealed that more than half were intending to settle in the region. This suggested that service leavers accounted for a 7 per cent annual increase in the regional labour force and 15 per cent of the annual net migration of working-age people into Wiltshire from the rest of the UK.[25]

In 2017 a national survey of veterans – which included men and women who were conscripted or who joined up in the 1930s–1940s, or who did National Service – showed that there were an estimated 2.4 million veterans of the UK armed forces in the country as a whole. The statistics also indicated that over a quarter (29 per cent) of these resided in the South East and South West regions of England, where they made up 12 per cent or more of households.[26] Although Wiltshire was not in the top six counties, with many preferring to spend their retirement in Devon and Cornwall, there was no doubt that the historic presence of the army on Salisbury Plain made veterans feel at home in the area.[27]

Like many others we had interviewed, Chris Williams was living proof that a good proportion of those with service backgrounds felt drawn to local politics in the region, and were invested in working towards better relations with the military in the communities where they lived. Just as 'army wives' were able to articulate the different realities of living within a rigid social hierarchy, so the veterans whom we met were ready to offer a diverse range of perspectives, not least as a result of their relationship to their former employer – ambivalent or otherwise.

Old soldiers

Fraser, whom we met in Café Delight, was a good example of the shifting status of the army veteran over the past two decades.

He works for a small local taxi company and mostly makes his living ferrying people from the railway stations in Andover, Grateley and Salisbury to the towns and villages around the eastern part of Salisbury Plain. Unlike Kofi, whom we met in the previous chapter, he is not restricted by childcare obligations, which makes it easier to earn a living. Taxi driving is a good job in this area where people are dependent on cars to get around, and the fares – established by local government – are remunerative. But other factors arising from military service affected his choice of job.

He was born in a small town in the west of Scotland and ended up in Wiltshire after finishing his nine-year army career in the early 1990s. He admits that he was 'off the rails' for a while after he left, but eventually found his feet again, thanks to a supportive family. At that time, there was very little transition support for those leaving the forces, and it would be at least another decade before the Military Covenant campaign began to draw attention to veteran politics.[28]

If he were leaving the forces today, Fraser would be encouraged to attend an Armed Forces Leavers Career Day, which had become an annual event held in Tidworth Leisure Centre. Among the prospective employees' stalls, he would find a number of companies working in logistics, such as Kuehne+Nagel, which is based in Wiltshire and often hires service leavers for driving jobs. There would also be stands with representatives from Wiltshire College and the Salisbury NHS Foundation, or companies like Fran Forces which are explicitly devoted to supporting veterans starting their own franchise business.

Welfare services for leavers would also be evident, with representatives from the Army Families Federation and Homes4Wiltshire providing advice on accommodation and family life too. The council housing team is able to start providing financial support for service leavers as soon as they receive their discharge papers – usually 93 days before they are due to move out. Across the UK councils are able to prioritise veterans for social housing, but in Wiltshire there are so many who choose to settle in the area that only those receiving a lower final pay-off, less than £16,000, are eligible. Local construction firms also offer special deals, fulfilling their contracts to contribute to local community services and facilities.[29]

Fraser was fortunate in having a family to support him when there was relatively little help from charities or local health and welfare services, let alone private companies, but at least his profile was a recognisable one. For some of the older ex-servicemen living locally it was a different story.

Today there is stiff competition among ambitious young Nepali men for a few hundred places in the Brigade of Gurkhas every year, but it has not always been like this. Bhakta, whom we met in Chapter 2, is a veteran of one of the country's little-known wars in south-east Asia. Having defeated the communist insurgency in Malaysia, in 1962 Britain embarked on a conflict with Indonesia over the future of Brunei and North Borneo which lay across the border from Kalimantan. Aware that the British Army was desperate to recruit young Nepalis to fight in jungle terrain, the young Bhakta had to meet native recruiters in secret before joining the 10th Gurkha Rifles.

When Bhakta was aspiring to change his family fortune, against the will of his parents and older relatives, painful memories of tens of thousands of young Nepali men killed or severely wounded while fighting for Britain in the two world wars were still fresh in people's minds. Many young men from his own village had never returned.

Fresh from a hasty training in Sungei Patani (Gurkha HQ in Malaya), Bhakta's platoon joined five battalions of British and Gurkha troops, later augmented by support from Malaysia, Australia and New Zealand. Under the command of Major General Walter Walker, they were committed to defend a frontier that extended for nearly a thousand miles of jungle-covered mountain. While fighting in this harsh and treacherous environment, the young Bhakta witnessed the brutal death of one of his close kin. Thanks to his village deities, he managed to escape with his life and limbs intact.

The conflict – known today as the Indonesian Confrontation – ended in 1965, at which point the decision was taken summarily to reduce the Gurkha forces. Like five thousand others, Bhakta was prematurely dismissed from service and sent back to Nepal. Since he had not completed his 15-year contract, he did not qualify for a pension, nor did he receive any compensation or relief for early release. Long-standing Gurkha terms and conditions of service, made explicit in the 1947 Tripartite Treaty, mandated the compulsory retirement of Gurkha soldiers in Nepal. Some of them did eventually find employment in other countries, such as Malaysia, Belize, Hong Kong and Brunei; however, until the review of Gurkha immigration policy in 2004, retired Gurkhas were rarely permitted to live and work in the UK.

Bhakta did not have the financial resources to seek a second career overseas. Instead he struggled to support his large extended family by labouring in the unwieldy farmland that he had purchased with his meagre savings in the British Army. Over time two of his adult sons went to work in the sweatshops of Malaysia and Qatar as a way of bringing in much-needed cash. Then in 2010 the news spread that many veterans, including some older than himself, were being permitted to live in the UK, from where they could send their welfare benefits back to their families. Two years later, following a costly visa process, he arrived in England, accompanied by his wife, who was ten years his junior.

Today, Tidworth has 15 to 20 retired Gurkhas and their spouses who migrated in their late sixties and early to mid-seventies, but in the past decade, however, there has been a gradual increase in younger Gurkha residents living in Tidworth, Amesbury and Andover. They comprise men in their late forties and early fifties, including some who have served in Iraq and Afghanistan. The chair of the Tidworth Nepali Community, for instance, had been deployed in Afghanistan four times after being posted to an artillery regiment in Larkhill in 2009. Like many veterans, he chose to settle close to his last posting and bought a house in Tidworth.

Although the experiences of Fraser and Bhakta could not have been more diverse – not least in terms of where they served and under what conditions – the contrast between them brings us back to the pipeline analogy. The fact that this is a technical term, long used by the Ministry of Defence as well as by recruiters, confirms that this is no ordinary career. The institution demands a ceaseless flow of raw materials into one end of the pipe, candidates who are relatively fit, trainable and open to the privations and perks of a residential job with guaranteed travel. But how does a military career prepare the individual for life at the other end?

Being classed as 'outflow' suggests anything from a finished product, ready for a radical change of lifestyle, to a form of waste, unable to function as a 'civvie'. Both Fraser and Bhakta had turned to their immediate families for support once they had emerged from the pipeline, one temporarily 'off the rails' and the other a traumatised young man returned to the gruelling life of a hill farmer. In the meantime, however, the whole understanding of 'veterans' as a particular class of citizen had been transformed.

Mental health

In March 2018 Rob, 35, started an internship as a motor mechanic with Forces Re-Engineered, a charity based in a small garage in a quiet corner of Walworth Industrial Estate, to the east of Andover. He was about to gain a qualification as a Vehicle Technician which, though not massively remunerative, represented an opportunity for him to turn his life around.

As he explained, 'I haven't been earning my keep in the past few years, but luckily the garage has made it possible for me to start again. It's quite exciting … I am really hopeful that this will help me cope with my mental problems. When I was diagnosed with PTSD in 2018, I thought my life was over. Now there's some hope I can live a more normal life.'

Rob was young when he joined the army in 2000, at merely 17 years of age. Following a spell of training in Germany, he was deployed to Iraq and Afghanistan. His seven-month tenure in Helmand in 2008 was relatively easy as he did not have to fight; but it was the four months he spent in Iraq the previous year that left the biggest mark. Known to his friends as 'Suicide Rob', he became famous for volunteering to detect and remove possible improvised explosive devices identified along their route.

He left the army in 2012 and joined a high-risk marine security business, before re-enlisting in 2018. Unfortunately he then suffered a serious accident while training on Salisbury Plain and underwent disc surgery which left him housebound for a number of months.

Loneliness, boredom and the effect of heavy medication precipitated a sequence of terrible nightmares, followed by insomnia, during which the events he had experienced in Iraq played over and over again in his mind. He became increasingly paranoid and eventually suicidal.

After receiving a diagnosis of severe PTSD at an NHS trauma centre, he was offered treatment by Help for Heroes, which ran a rehabilitation and recovery centre at Tedworth House nearby. He participated in the scheduled activities that included wheelchair rugby and archery, but without finding them helpful for his particular issues. Towards the end of his stay, his case officer asked him to join a volunteer service in Tidworth and this led him to the small non-profit organisation Forces Re-Engineered.

Stephen West, the proprietor, had used his savings to launch Forces Re-Engineered in January 2017 after he became aware that many of the veterans living in Andover, Tidworth and Salisbury were suffering from undiagnosed PTSD along with social anxiety and depression. This was one of a number of local initiatives, including a gym in Andover called Combat Fuel Fitness, which aimed to bring veterans out of their homes and get them to exercise alongside civilians. 'I could have easily enrolled 60 or 70 men,' he told us.

On first impression it was more like going to a clinic than an auto repair centre. The smells and sounds were carefully controlled and the interns worked indoors, invisible from the forecourt. Stephen and his daughter, who worked as receptionist, mostly dealt with the customers and a retired psychotherapist – who happened to be Stephen's mother – ran weekly counselling sessions in an upstairs room. An acupuncturist was also available occasionally, free of charge. If there were bigger issues, Stephen organised appointments with charities that provided more specialised mental health support, including a local branch of Combat Stress. The project is evidently supported by many local businesses as well as other major charities like the Royal British Legion, which had been reporting on the phenomenon for some time.

It took a little longer for the raised incidence of PTSD to be officially recognised so that more resources could be directed towards treatment. In 2018 research from King's College London confirmed that the conflicts in Iraq and Afghanistan may have led to an increase in the rate of 'probable PTSD' among members of the UK Armed Forces.[30] This was especially the case with those deployed in a combat role. Among former serving personnel interviewed, 17 per cent reported symptoms suggesting probable PTSD compared to 6 per cent of those deployed in a support role such as medical, logistics, signals and aircrew.[31]

Rob's experience was fairly typical of the problems faced by individual veterans in terms of accessing treatment for his symptoms. Meanwhile military charities constantly raised the issue of funding with governments of the day, complaining that they were unable to keep up with the increased demand for mental health support. In response, in 2021 the NHS chief executive Sir Simon Stevens announced a new fast-track service called Op Courage. This committed doctors, nurses and other NHS staff to working with military charities to provide therapy, rehab services and, in extreme cases, inpatient care to hundreds of former soldiers, sailors and RAF personnel each year. Those needing urgent help would receive a same-day referral.

The following year the Ministry of Defence launched another short-term service, Op Fortitude, which was specifically designed to end veterans' homelessness.[32] A total of £8.55 million funding was set aside to provide more than nine hundred veteran-supported housing units with specialist help. Despite the then Minister for Veterans Affairs, Johnny Mercer, pledging that the scheme would end veterans' homelessness by the end of 2023, an article published in the last week of December revealed that homelessness among military veterans in England had actually risen by 14 per cent in the last year.[33]

Research on the long-term consequences of traumatic brain injuries has also continued to produce worrying results. In 2023 the military charities BRAVO VICTOR and BlindVeterans UK produced three reports indicating that many older veterans faced a higher risk of dementia. According to Professor Renata Gomes, chief scientific officer at BRAVO VICTOR, 'Even now, many years on, there are concerns about the lasting effects of traumatic brain injuries.

This may include long-term impairments and disabilities, such as delayed sight loss and dementia, which may not have been linked to a serving soldier or veteran's original injury.'[34]

Despite the fact that the crisis of veteran health is sporadically mentioned in the media, the reality is, writes Joe Glenton, who considers himself a critical veteran, that, 'like any group of people, veterans are a vessel into which people pour assumptions and half-truths'.[35] This underlines the importance of understanding military veterans as a category of expendable labour power that is not only transformed by the institution of war-making, but also implicated in its continuity.

Ken MacLeish is an anthropologist who spent several years carrying out ethnographic work in the US military during the Iraq and Afghanistan wars. During the course of many interviews with men whose lives had been transformed by the experience of military service, he noted that they too used the word 'churn' to refer to the particular character of service life. But instead of referring to the effects of being constantly relocated, as we saw in the previous chapter, they meant something else entirely: 'the rhythm of impersonal institutional demands and the feeling – often as satisfying and validating as it is exhausting and wounding – of being used and used up by those demands'.

Churn, writes MacLeish, 'is a sign that using up and getting rid of soldiers is as crucial a condition of possibility for war as finding and making soldiers in the first place, and the two processes are bound together in ways both highly technical and viscerally intimate.'[36] This offers an alternative to the analogy of the pipeline, which does not quite capture this sense of complicity in the business of lethal violence.

Red, white and blue

In 2019 the Wiltshire city of Salisbury was chosen as the host for the national Armed Forces Day celebrations. This was undoubtedly an effort to rehabilitate the city's reputation following the chemical attack on Sergei Skripal which took the life of the Amesbury resident Dawn Sturgess in 2018. For security reasons this was a ticketed event and the tickets sold out quickly because the Kaiser Chiefs were billed to perform in the evening.

We arrived in time to join large crowds of people lining the road to watch the military parade through the city. People cheered and waved Union Jack flags, especially when a Red Arrows flypast roared overhead, leaving their requisite blue, white and red smoke trails. Armoured trucks and tanks rolled through the winding medieval streets, followed by marching bands and troops in differently coloured ceremonial uniforms. A young boy, sitting on his dad's shoulders, was clearly enthralled. 'Are those the Germans?' he asked, receiving no answer.

In order to get to Hudson's Field where the Armed Forces Day fair was taking place, we piled into free buses behind the city's Market Square. Once we had passed through the metal detectors at the security gates we were presented with a wide green space hemmed by uniform white tents and pavilions with titles like 'Technology' and 'Innovation'.

This time the event was polished and corporate: gone were the kitsch memorabilia and gory dummies of the regional event the previous year. Instead it was possible to buy artwork and souvenirs inside a tent called the 'Business Village'. In the Innovation tent there were displays advertising UK military partnerships in forensic science research, with stands show-casing the UK construction group Kier, communications business Roke, and key defence industry player Babcock. Elegantly dressed folk sipped champagne inside a VIP area whilst we contented ourselves with an array of different 'street food' stalls.

After eating a delicately spiced Caribbean snack, we settled down on the grass to watch the RAF parachute drop into the field's central display area. The glare from the sun – this was the hottest day of the year so far – made it hard to look up, although we could feel the vibrations from the approaching plane before we saw it. Eventually dark specks materialised as humans in parachutes who let off more blue, white and red flares as they descended.

The usual array of armoured cars, helicopters and jeeps stood in a separate part of the field. Soldiers stood at the tented gateway to this area handing out maps that punters could hang round their necks with colourful string. We could see children as young as toddlers crawling in and out of cockpits, enthusiastically studying the maps to identify each vehicle. We walked on, only to end up in another medical tent where a soldier was exhibiting a lifelike model of a human body. Instead of representing a figure maimed by lethal weapons, this time the corpse was offering a different lesson. Its body cavity was open to allow the soldier to help a group of young people identify the different organs.

One of the events that made the national headlines was the presence of the Defence Secretary Penny Mordaunt, who gave a press conference in the 'military village' in Hudson's Field. She told the media that Salisbury 'always had an amazing connection to our armed forces'.

> I remember visiting Salisbury just a couple of weeks after the [nerve agent attack] last year, and it's done an amazing job as a city – it's really pulled together, all of the services and agencies here, providing that reassurance. The public coming in at these events, it gives them their chance to say 'thank you' to our armed forces who stepped in, provided that reassurance, clearly did some really difficult jobs over those weeks and months – it's their chance to say thank you to those people.[37]

Meanwhile an alternative ceremony was being hosted at the Quaker Meeting House in Salisbury town centre. Greg, a retired history teacher, explained that the group had decided not to host an event next to Hudson's Field so as not to upset the military families whom they knew frequented these events in large numbers. Instead, they had invited people to join them at the Meeting House for tea, cake and reflection.

Greg showed us a letter they had sent to the *Salisbury Journal* the previous week. This set out the Quaker position on war, protesting against the military's targeted recruitment of children at events like Armed Forces Day. It began, 'No war, since the dawn of time, has ever been inevitable. Wars happen because of injustice, oppression, inequality and the failure of politics.' The letter went on to suggest that the money spent on the event could have been better used to help homeless veterans in Salisbury and those suffering from PTSD in the psychiatric hospital. They were disappointed that it had not been published.

A video compilation was being screened in one of the cooler back rooms of the Meeting House, featuring familiar faces from the wider UK anti-war movement. Salisbury Quaker Meeting House offered an alternative to the spectacular display of war preparation, this time through the prism of struggles that opposed displays of communal gratitude in favour of genuine peace and healing, starting much closer to home.

The institution of Armed Forces Day in 2009 was, as we have seen, a direct outcome of political intervention during a period of extremely costly and unpopular wars. While public attitudes towards the army might be influenced by these types of measures, the fact remains that the relationship between this sprawling workforce and its neighbours – let alone those who have little or no contact with soldiers – can be extremely hard to gauge at the best of times.

This is partly due to the unbreachable façade of the military workplace, surrounded as it is by barbed wire, checkpoints and armed guards. But it is also the result of shifting attitudes to the work the army is officially required to perform, whether it is considered to be in the national interest or not. In the final section we turn to the aftermath of war itself as we continue to investigate the khaki presence in rural Wiltshire.

Part III

The legacy

7

The shadow of war

Large plastic poppies decorated the frontage of Tidworth Garrison Theatre where men and women in military uniform were mingling with smartly dressed civilians in readiness for the centenary celebrations in November 2018. The traditional symbol of remembrance, which had been adopted by the Royal British Legion in 1921, was a routine sight at this time of year. In nearby Ludgershall and Andover, both self-proclaimed 'army towns', despite having much larger proportions of civilians, extensive displays of poppy paraphernalia would remain for weeks, if not all year round. Yet in the garrisons and camps they would soon be taken down before the mundane activities of war preparation recommenced.

The garrison commander, Lieutenant Colonel Jamie Balls, began the proceedings by reflecting on his role liaising between the army, the local authority and the community. After commenting on the progress of construction work on the new estates, he made the point that Armistice celebrations should give more consideration to the role played by foreign and Commonwealth soldiers, especially in the light of the multinational history of the Plain. He then distributed awards to personnel recognised for their extraordinary performance in different fields, including a Ghanaian soldier who was recognised for musical excellence.

The emphasis on the contribution of foreign and Commonwealth troops continued in the next part of the event. A local Fijian gospel choir, dressed in matching brown and green sulus, performed a devotional song in English as the audience listened in polite silence.

After this a Nepali officer, Captain Surya Gurung, spoke of his community's pride at serving the Queen in such a 'wonderful' part of England. This was followed by more devotional singing from the Tidworth branch of Christian Family Ministries, an evangelical church based in Wiltshire. The performers were West African and Fijian.

The army padre then concluded with a short, non-denominational service, and a section of the crowd made their way to the war memorial in the park nearby. After a minute's silence the chaplain read out the names of the soldiers inscribed on the new memorial. The ceremony ended with the laying of a wreath and a prayer.

Despite the ubiquity of war memorials in towns and villages across the UK, the garrison town of Tidworth had no official monument until late 2017 when Wiltshire Council unveiled this particular memorial in the corner of Wylie Road Community Centre field. Constructed from black Indian granite, the circular structure contains a spire surrounded by eight monoliths etched with scenes that depict Salisbury Plain during the first half of the twentieth century.

Students from local schools were invited to take part in the competition to design the panels which include images of a biplane fighter aircraft swooping over Stonehenge; a group of infantry soldiers posing in front of a tented camp; and scenes from Tidworth's past, including the railway station which had since been replaced by the large branch of Tesco. There are also messages of remembrance and stylised poppies with inscriptions such as 'The Ones We Loved Become a Memory and the Memory Becomes a Treasure'. An evanescent figure in uniform performs a military salute as he fades into the sunset under the words 'Rest in Peace'.

The memorial was a collective project led by Wiltshire Council and funded through the Army Basing Programme. The two-year consultation process was inevitably rambunctious but there was one text selected for the memorial that was particularly controversial. Narrating the poet's longing to escape, over seven verses, its irreverent message made some people feel uneasy. It began:

7.1 Tidworth War Memorial in the Community Centre field, with engravings chosen by local residents.

> There's a certain place called Tidworth
> In the wilds of Salisbury Plain,
> If I could only but escape
> I'd ne'er go back again.

The humorous tone was actually chosen to offset Robert Laurence Binyon's more sombre work, 'For the Fallen', which contained the familiar lines:

> They shall grow not old, as we that are left grow old:
> Age shall not weary them, nor the years condemn.
> At the going down of the sun and in the morning
> We will remember them.

Subsequently referred to as the 'Ode of Remembrance', Binyon's poem was published in September 1914 and is the first known work to infuse the word 'Fallen' with connotations of sacrifice for the greater good of the nation. Seven years later it was adopted by the British Legion (later the Royal British Legion).

The emphasis on diversity at Tidworth's centenary celebrations was something that the garrison commander felt very deeply about on a personal level, having fought alongside Commonwealth troops in his younger years. But it was not just a question of individual loyalty and affection. By this time it had become routine to include Fijian and other non-UK nationals in cultural activities at army events. To the outsider this might appear an encouraging sign that military multiculturalism was alive and well, and that the institution had embraced its legal obligation to represent the wider population as inclusively as possible. But not everyone was convinced.

A group of nearly two dozen retired Nepali veterans and their spouses had gathered at the war memorial and their disgruntled murmuring highlighted the limits of local cultural diversity on display. They were pleased that Captain Gurung had been invited to speak in the garrison theatre, assuming that this was the result of their decision the previous year to organise a parade where they held up their national flag. But this year they were disappointed because the man who owned the flag had refused to lend it them again. He was forthright about his reasons.

He did not feel that Remembrance Day was an occasion that respected Gurkhas, who were not only recruited in Nepal but labelled as 'foreign', since Nepal was not a member of the Commonwealth. 'Why should we be proud?' he asked, 'we are merely Britain's hired soldiers.' He was particularly vexed by the fact that the service was conducted entirely as a Christian ritual, without reference to any other religion. 'We are not Christians; we are Hindus and Buddhists. Gurkha regiments have both of these houses of worship, even in overseas posts like Brunei. If they recognise our contribution to the British Empire, why don't they perform Hindu and Buddhist services, too?'

Hari Gurung, a 75-year-old veteran of the 6th Gurkha Rifles, agreed. Originally recruited in the town of Pokhara, western Nepal, he had come to England as a veteran in 2011 and had been living in South Tidworth ever since. As a young man in the mid-1960s he had fought for the British against Indonesian militants in the jungles of Borneo, and his father had been a decorated hero before him. His choice of attire that day was clearly deliberate. His Gurkha hat was slightly tilted to the left and he had pinned his army medals on his jacket next to a poppy and his regimental tie. He was proud that both Nepali and Fijian communities had taken part in laying the wreaths. But, at the same time, the ceremony left a bad taste.

He too was sad to see that only Christian padres in flowing white robes performed the service, evoking a god he did not worship, in a language he did not fully comprehend. Where was the Hindu chaplain or Buddhist priest who normally officiated at Gurkha ceremonies? The fact that the service was entirely run by Christian officials, with no acknowledgement of other faiths, felt like the systematic denial of the sacrifices his own family had made. According to official figures, over ninety thousand Gurkha soldiers had served in the First World War, with over twenty thousand casualties and six thousand deaths by the end of it.[1]

Yet the centenary had provided many opportunities to expose the history of indifference shown towards 'native' troops who were enlisted to fight alongside the European powers, often volunteering in the hope of freeing their countries from colonial rule.[2] This was particularly evident in the siting, naming and preservation of military graves.

In 2019, for example, the Labour MP David Lammy presented a TV documentary entitled *The Unremembered: Britain's Forgotten War Heroes* which was aired on the centenary of the first Remembrance Sunday in November 1919. Drawing on the pioneering work of the historian Michele Barrett over many years, Lammy visited the military cemetery run by the Commonwealth War Graves Commission in Voi, in southern Kenya. As he stood looking at graves of white soldiers in 'the immaculately kept grounds' he asked the caretaker, Antonny Wachira Kimani, where the bodies of Africans were buried. Official records put the death toll of the Africans who served Britain in the East Africa campaign at around a hundred thousand, although it is thought to have been far higher than that. Kimani pointed to the bush 'beyond the perimeter ... No names, no graves, no dignity'. Barrett's research had established that the politician responsible for 'this morbid form of apartheid' was Winston Churchill, former secretary of state for war and chairman of the Imperial War Graves Commission.[3]

Silent witnesses

The first public monuments commemorating ordinary rank–and-file soldiers were erected in towns and villages across the UK in the wake of the Second Boer War, also known as the South African War. This mushrooming of small memorials created a connection between remote battlefields and the communities from which the soldiers had come, whether as volunteers or conscripts. Memorials became places where people could both mourn their dead and honour their sacrifice; where war could be justified or alternatively decried as futile horror. This novel and often carefully managed approach to war memorialisation offered ways of diverting attention away from the often catastrophic political and military decisions that had cost so many lives, focusing instead on camaraderie and national solidarity.[4]

The centenary of the 1914–18 war was particularly haunting for military communities on Salisbury Plain. Although there were relatively few war memorials, the heritage of the First World War was literally built into the fabric of the larger garrisons like Tidworth, Bulford and Larkhill, as well as the smaller camps that once spread across the training area. As we saw in Chapter 1, this was a tradition that continues into the present.

Bulford's new Plumer estate was named after the much-decorated Field Marshal Herbert Plumer, 1st Viscount Plumer (1857–1932), who distinguished himself in the Battle of Messines in 1917 in charge of troops from New Zealand, many of whom had been based in Sling Camp, as Bulford was once known. The internal streets are named after First World War battles: Passchendaele, Flanders, Beaumont-Hamel. The corresponding new-build in Larkhill, named after Field Marshall Allan Brooke, 1st Viscount Alanbrooke (1883–1963), was built on land where there had once been a First World War training ground.[5] In 2017 archaeologists unearthed a network of tunnels and trenches that had once replicated the conditions soldiers would face in trenches in France and Belgium. Inside was a chalk plaque inscribed with the names of individuals in the Australian 3rd Division infantry, and more than a hundred grenades – still live – that had been used in training. The tunnel walls were covered with graffiti, and the authors' names have subsequently been matched to service records.[6]

Tidworth Military Cemetery provides more conventional evidence of the conditions under which thousands of young men lost their lives, often far from their countries of birth. Now managed by the Commonwealth War Graves Commission, the graveyard was originally laid out in 1903 as an integral part of the garrison. Today you can download the names and military details of more than five hundred individuals buried in a number of different plots, distinguished mainly by Christian denomination and military rank.

The first burials took place in 1914, and by 1919 there were 420 graves. Of these, over half bear headstones commemorating young men from Australia and New Zealand who died in Tidworth Military Hospital after being brought back from battlefields in Europe. A further 106 graves were added during the 1939–45 war. Forty were Polish. There is one grave dedicated to a casualty from the Falklands. In Plot E, labelled as Officers, with a small section for '1914–1914 War Burials' there are at least two women, one of whom was nurse Mary Agnes Langdale, who was buried here with full military honours in February 1917 after becoming ill while working at the hospital.[7] There are also a few graves dedicated to the wives or very young children of army officers.

Smaller cemeteries can be found across the Plain also bearing witness to this history. Durrington cemetery contains the graves of over two hundred men from Larkhill camp who died in Tidworth's military hospital between 1914 and 1918. Many of the graves are of Australian servicemen and there is a separate Australian memorial in the cemetery. The military cemetery in Upavon holds 35 graves of those who were attached to the air services stationed nearby. A striking number of these too were from Australia, New Zealand and Canada. Some of the names jump out: Benno Oscar Linsingen Hahn, 17 years of age, who enlisted in the 1st Regiment South African Infantry but at the time of his death in 1917 had become a second lieutenant, in the Royal Flying Corps. There are two females: Janet Anderson-Hastie, Women's Royal Air Force, died on 24 December 1918;[8] and Josephine Pipon, Women's Auxiliary Air Force, died in 1941 aged 20.

Meanwhile in Ludgershall, the war dead from both the First and Second World Wars were memorialised by the conventional stone plinth located in the town's main thoroughfare. In November 2018, just before the centenary of the Armistice, the traditional obelisk-shaped memorial was crowned with a large red wreath. Oversize plastic poppies were placed in people's front gardens, attached to lamp posts, and adorned the Crown Inn pub, where silhouettes of soldiers were also permanently painted on the frontage and side walls. And in a small memorial garden just off the main road metal outlines of poppies and soldiers with bowed heads dominated the fencing, seating and even the rubbish bin (as shown in Figure 3.2).

Shops and businesses were also involved in the celebration. An estate agent displayed a poster of a saluting soldier, painted in red, white and blue, with the message 'we will remember' appearing above a row of two- and three-bedroom homes for sale. The front window of a tattoo parlour was lavishly plastered with poppy decals. A string of poppy-themed fairy lights hung across the top of the window, and a toothy white skull peered out of a dark hooded garment. A skeletal hand was raised as if in greeting – a relic of Hallowe'en no doubt – encapsulating the more surreal aspects of the dynamic between past and present, military and civilian, local and national.

Glimpsed in the autumn of 2018 when the centenary was coming to a close, the angle of winter light caught the reflection of the old pub across the road, creating the impression that this harbinger of death was watching from an upstairs window. It was yet another indication that places long associated with military culture have their own ways of registering this chronicle of industrial-scale slaughter.

The afterwar

These generic symbols of memorialisation, whether ephemeral scarlet poppies or sombre granite, do little to complicate the neat binary of war and peace that obscures the wider injuries – physical, mental and social – that prevail long after the fighting has ceased. The American anthropologist Zoë Wool proposes an alternative

7.2 Tattoo parlour in Ludgershall, November 2018.

perspective that focuses on the ongoing distortion and dislocation caused to bodies by serious war injury.

Her ethnographic research, conducted at the Walter Reed joint military medical centre in Maryland, USA, emphasises the ways in which war violence is perpetual and disorientating, both within the centre where bodies are pieced back together and on the outside where people attempt to rebuild their lives. This is the 'afterwar', a concept that creates an intimate connection between the battle-ground, however remote, and the 'home front', which extends into all areas of life.[9]

One corner of the 'super garrison' represents this afterwar, serving as a different kind of memorial dedicated to the woman and men who did not die in service but whose lives were permanently impaired by the injuries they received while carrying out orders. Tedworth House is a Grade II listed building set in 30 acres of impressive park-land. Concealed from public view, the grey pillared architecture of the main house was designed in 1828 to reflect the 'restrained Greek revival style' which was becoming popular in the early nineteenth century.[10] Fifty years later its new owner commissioned a stone façade that was more Roman Baroque. It's not surprising that the

War Office was unsure what to do with it when it first acquired the estate in 1897. When pressed into military service, this monument to the conspicuous wealth of the landed gentry veered between providing a glorified play space for the top brass and a dormitory for female staff working under emergency conditions.

In the early years of the 1914–18 war it served as an officers' club before being converted to accommodation for nurses. In the 1940s, when the US Army was stationed in Tidworth, the once stately home became a club for American soldiers. It was then used again by nursing staff who worked at the Military Hospital, but following the closure of the hospital in 1977 it reverted to an officers' social club. In 1984 the building became officially known as The Headquarters I Infantry Brigade Officers' Mess, but after another 25 years the Ministry of Defence decided it was too expensive to maintain.

But in 2011 the mansion was granted an unexpected new lease of life when the charity Help for Heroes negotiated a contract – for a peppercorn rent of £1 a year – to turn the building into a flagship Personnel Recovery Centre, one of five new sites dedicated to the care and rehabilitation of soldiers wounded in Afghanistan. These would be run under the auspices of the Army Recovery Capability, a multi-million-pound joint venture in partnership with the Royal British Legion and the Ministry of Defence.

The refurbishment of Tedworth House, at a cost of £24 million, was hailed as the transformation of a redundant, deteriorating millstone into a gloriously positive focal point for our sick, wounded and recovering soldiers.[11] The design of the new centre, overseen by Francis Terry and Associates (specialists in new-build and restorations of classical Georgian-style architecture and country houses) included an accommodation block of 34 rooms for service personnel and four family suites, a kitchen, presentation room and two lounges.[12] A disused Edwardian indoor skating rink was converted into an adaptive gym with specialist cardio-vascular exercise machines, a movable ski slope and small swimming pool. There would also be a 'Hero Garden', which would offer a space for relaxation and reflection, and a 'revolutionary support hub' for service users, with access to specialist agencies and charities all in one location.

Tedworth House Personal Recovery Centre was formally opened in May 2013 by the Queen's grandsons, William and Harry, who were filmed chatting to injured soldiers and inspecting the state-of-the-art equipment. The 'warrior princes', as they were then called, posed for the national media in front of a sculpture of two uniformed stretcher bearers carrying a wounded comrade with one hand raised in a thumbs-up gesture. The artwork, designed by the Help for Heroes co-founder Bryn Parry and cast in the Morris Singer Art Foundry in neighbouring Hampshire, echoed the charity's trademark symbol. The effect was to create a powerful image of brotherly love for the war wounded, endorsed by endless goodwill from the public whose spontaneous generosity had, in part, helped to fund the whole enterprise.

A decade later the rot had set in. In fact the whole house was falling down, in the words of Captain Steve Hickey, the resident Engagement Officer employed by the Ministry of Defence.[13] A visiting journalist from the *Salisbury Journal* witnessed the deteriorating facilities: dustbins had been placed strategically – along with a

7.3 The Help for Heroes statue in front of Tedworth House.

kayak – to catch water from a leaking roof, the ceiling had collapsed in the dining room and most of the outdoor facilities were unusable. Help for Heroes had left all its equipment, but some of it was dysfunctional due to lack of funds to repair or service it. What on earth had happened?

In April 2021, after laying off dozens of staff during the pandemic, the charity admitted that it could no longer afford to run the recovery centres and would be refocusing its support for veterans on community-based projects and online resources. The Ministry of Defence formally took over management of all five recovery centres, including Tedworth House, on a yearly contract, restricting care to those who were still in service.

According to the *Sun* newspaper, 'Sources said the MoD was now scrambling to work out how to use the sites, which it objected to being built at the time'.[14] 'Scrambling' turned out to be an apt word as negotiations over who was ultimately responsible for the Personnel Recovery Centres would continue for two more years. It emerged that the charity was demanding £30 million payment for the four centres that it had famously equipped in the first place.

Finally, in December 2023, a press conference was held at Tedworth House to announce that the government had guaranteed funding for the next ten years. The mixed audience of military and service family welfare staff were informed that the Wiltshire centre would be used to manage 'Personnel on Recovery Duty' – those who are wounded, injured and sick – on the basis that early intervention was key to getting them back to work as soon as possible. At the time there were a thouand soldiers, 4 per cent of the army, unfit for duty.

Assurances were given that the small, dedicated staff would be 'making every effort to keep the House going with many local units coming in and giving time to maintain the gardens and 28 acres of land'. However, there was mention of turning Tedworth House into a 'Defence asset' in order to release more funds. It was also mooted that the Royal British Legion might become involved in the operation of the Personnel Recovery Centre, which would mean that the facilities would be open to veterans.

Although Tedworth House was in danger of becoming a mill-stone once again, its place in the national pantheon of war heritage was ensured by the extravagant wrought iron gates at the entrance, the initials H4H welded into its ornate design. Its brief period in the public eye – despite its remote rural setting – is testimony to the 'afterwar' identified by Zoë Wool, a reminder that the 'torn world' of war can have material consequences on the home front, far from lethal violence experienced far away.[15] And in fact the phenomenal success of Help for Heroes in galvanising public sympathy for soldiers was one of the driving forces behind some of the policy changes already outlined in this book.

Continuum of conflict

At the start of the centenary year, just as British troops were scheduled to withdraw from Afghanistan, the journalists Ewen MacAskill and Ian Cobain pointed out that,

> Since Britain's declaration of war against Germany in August 1914, not a year has passed without its forces being involved in conflict. It is a statistic that has been largely overlooked, and not one about which the government is likely to boast. The past 100 years have seen two world wars, large-scale conflicts in Korea and Iraq, and small-scale actions in Africa, the Middle East and Asia. There have been punitive operations in defence of empire, cold war operations, post-9/11 support for the US, and the Troubles in Ireland.[16]

Their research was a powerful reminder that the UK has been pursuing military objectives in different parts of the world long after the empire was declared officially over. In fact since 1945 there have been 83 interventions by the UK armed forces, in 47 different countries.[17]

Today the threat of global insecurity has led to an unprecedented investment in military power and with it 'an integrated culture of militarism' which, as Paul Rogers has long argued, both conceals and normalises the commitment to armed violence in the name of national and regional defence.[18] The Ministry of Defence put it more bluntly in its response to the first post-Brexit governmental defence review, issued in 2021:

The notion of war and peace as binary states has given way to a continuum of conflict, requiring us to prepare our forces for more persistent global engagement and constant campaigning, moving seamlessly from operating to war fighting.[19]

Mary Dudziak expresses it more concisely still in her book on the history and consequences of permanent war: 'Wartime has become normal time ... Wartime has become the only time we have.'[20]

Ken MacLeish, another anthropologist based in the USA, observes that this sense of permanent war creates a market for military labour that is both cyclical and anticipatory: 'an institutionalized expectation of constant war, with the bodies needed to wage it kept in motion into, through, out of, and often back into the military apparatus'. Having interviewed many individuals who were obliged to re-enlist after being demobilised following serious injuries, MacLeish argued that developing new ways to help troops recover from war is a practice of war in and of itself.

The development of more efficient ways to harm, kill, and destroy has always demanded new ways to protect and heal the human body, sustain and inure the psyche, and extend and enhance capacities.[21]

This statement underlines the significance of Tedworth House as the manifestation of public sympathy and admiration for the men and women who had suffered appalling damage in the Iraq and Afghanistan wars. The boast of 'state of the art' equipment – from indoor ski slopes to prosthetic limbs – seemed to hold out a promise that life could be fully restored to those who would once have been left behind, in the dole queue if not on the battlefield. Perhaps more significant still, the old mansion's reincarnation as a showcase devoted to the 'recovery' and 'rehabilitation' of traumatised minds and wounded bodies evoked notions of resilience, sacrifice and healing, values that help to sanitise the practice of lethal violence for which generations of new soldiers are constantly being trained.

The departure of the charity from this prestigious building is worth examining too, as it can be explained by several factors, aside from the impact of the pandemic. Tedworth House first caught public attention in October 2007 by which time, partly thanks to the Military Covenant campaign launched earlier that year, soldiers were emerging as particularly symbolic figures, both on and off the battlefield. Six months earlier the *Guardian* had run a story of NHS chaos under the headline 'Scandal of treatment for wounded Iraq veterans'.

The article described how the youngest British soldier injured in Iraq (at just 18 years old) spent a night in Birmingham's Selly Oak Hospital lying in his own faeces after staff allowed his colostomy bag to overflow.[22] Jamie Cooper had been serving in Basra in 2006 when he was seriously injured. The Royal British Legion released a letter from his parents who had complained that their son had been 'sent to Iraq straight from training with no real military knowledge and [is] not receiving the care and attention that is needed for his recovery'.'[23]

As more examples were reported up and down the country, the Wiltshire couple Bryn and Emma Parry, whose son was a serving soldier, decided to organise a fundraising network, which they called Help for Heroes. Their first appeal, launched towards the end of 2007, was in aid of building a specialised swimming pool at the Defence Medical Rehabilitation Centre at Headley Court, Surrey. This was a particularly canny choice. The facility had ignited furious media attention after it was alleged that members of the public were objecting to the inmates' use of the town pool as part of their therapy. This was later proved to be false, but at the time it was instrumental in rousing national support for the armed forces. The Parrys managed to raise £8 million to fund a new pool and gym complex, much of it in the first few weeks.[24]

From its inception, the new charity was enthusiastically supported by General Sir Richard Dannatt, Chief of the General Staff, who was aware that British public opinion was crucial to winning the war in Afghanistan. In a letter to the Minister of Defence, Des Browne, written the previous year, he had emphasised that 'Losing popular support at home is the single biggest danger to our chances of success in our current operations'.[25] With endorsement from such high quarters, Help for Heroes rapidly became a focal point for fundraising activities across the country, expanding at a rate that revealed the public's anxiety about the increasing number of casualties.

It was no coincidence that the co-founders Bryn and Emma Parry had a close connection to Tidworth garrison and were familiar with military culture. The couple had lived in Wiltshire since 1995, when Bryn had left the army. Before launching Help for Heroes he had made a living as a sculptor and caricaturist for a field sports magazine, where he acquired a reputation for his skill in poking fun at the rigid social etiquette involved in shooting and hunting, popular sports in those parts. He quickly applied this graphic expertise to designing the Help for Heroes merchandise and publicity materials, creating a series of cartoon figures and mascots that seemed to capture the national mood.

The most memorable of these was a set of uniformed bear-like creatures – representing the three different services – with limbs in slings or plasters, all managing to give a cheery thumbs-up despite their injuries. The iconography immediately resonated with the public mood, and overnight the giant 'hero bear' mascots rattling fund-raising buckets became a regular fixture at sporting events and in town centres.

The Parrys' local connections were important in dreaming up the conversion of Tedworth House too. They were introduced to Francis Terry, the project's architect, by a mutual friend who was an officer based in Tidworth. They worked together to fulfil the couple's dream of turning the building into a dedicated recovery centre.

The warm embrace of the hero bears was not quite the level of public support that Dannatt had had in mind when he sought out amenable journalists to pitch his case in 2006. Four years later, when the UK fatality count in Helmand had almost reached three hundred, a senior officer warned that there was a 'pervasive and resilient culture of pessimism' about the Afghan war back home which was severely undermining troops on the front line. 'We don't want sympathy,' he declared, 'Sympathy is for losers and we are not losing.' The incoming Chief of Defence Staff put it slightly differently: 'The last thing my soldiers want is for the public to go wobbly on them.'[26]

By 2011 the high-profile renovation was heralded as an example of how charitable organisations could work with the state to address the acute problem of injuries to service personnel in a dangerous overseas deployment. Its success showed how narratives around wounded soldiers and traumatised veterans could shape public attitudes to military work, regardless of the war in question. But the surge in public support, combined with the exorbitant cost of the Tedworth House itself, also led to the charge that Help for Heroes was becoming more of an industry than a charity.[27] In 2014 the *Daily Mail* reported that other military charities were finding themselves 'squeezed out' by Help for Heroes, which was granted preferential access to the Ministry of Defence.[28] The following year a prominent feature in *The Times* revealed that the government was also having doubts about the long-term feasibility of all five centres.[29]

This negative publicity coincided with a change of direction for Help for Heroes. In April 2016 Bryn Parry stepped down as CEO to allow someone else to take the organisation into its 'next phase'. Over the next few years his successor took on the task of providing ongoing care for those living with serious and complex injuries as well as supporting veterans whose mental health was affected after they had left the services.[30]

Now based in Downton Business Centre in Salisbury, Help for Heroes operates as a hub for veteran support, as well as a pressure group urging the government to give all those who have worked with the UK military 'a fair deal'. According to its website it runs sporting and social activities across the UK, and online, to combat loneliness and isolation. The charity also provides grants for home adaptations and medical equipment, and its free online courses and self-help guides offer people life skills so they can live independently.

Following the withdrawal of international troops from Afghanistan in 2021, the charity expanded its remit to include Afghan refugees whose lives have been devastated by military violence in their own country. Project Solidarity was set up to work with civilians and their families who were forced to flee Afghanistan on account of their association with UK forces.[31] This response could partly be explained by what one veteran described as 'feelings of loss, anger, confusion, and most acutely, a sense of betrayal' experienced by many former personnel deployed there from 2006 to 2014.[32]

'Don't pity us, give us work'

In addition to its role as a memorial, Tedworth House offers a useful place from which to think about the relationship between war and disability. Along with countless other services and charities devoted to veterans' wellbeing, Help for Heroes must be understood within the ongoing struggle for rights and social equality for all people with disabilities, which began in the wake of the 1914–18 war. The demand for the right to work has been at the centre of this movement in many different countries, and veterans have often been among the most militant protagonists.

At the start of the First World War centenary the union Unite collaborated with UK Disability History Month to bring this history to light. It was appropriate that one of the country's largest trade unions should remind the public not only of the shameful treatment of war disabled people over the intervening century but also of the interventions that led to reform. In 1919 there was widespread social disruption with strikes all over the country as British ex-servicemen became politicised as never before. Unite's broadsheet reminded readers that:

> Discharged soldiers and sailors demonstrated at the Albert Hall in March 1918, with a mass rally of wounded ex-soldiers later in the same month. The Armistice Day celebrations were disrupted by ex-servicemen on several occasions during the 1920s. The Luton peace riot of 1919 was a response to the town council excluding ex-servicemen's associations from the victory celebrations. The Discharged Soldier's and Sailor's Federation (DSSF) lined the path of the parade and hung a banner 'Don't pity us, give us work'.[33]

The reverberations of the 1914–18 war were felt in many unlikely places. A short distance from Tidworth in the Hampshire village of Enham Alamein, an oak statue of a First World War soldier still stands as a memorial to the role that the village played in the rehabilitation of the war wounded more than a hundred years ago.[34] Originally a pioneering centre for ex-servicemen, Enham Trust is now a general disability charity that provides care and advocacy for individuals with a wide range of physical and learning impairments. It was founded in 1919 by an organisation called Villages Centres Council for Curative Treatment and Training of Disabled Men, initially providing a 150-bed rehabilitation facility.[35]

Enham Village Centre was intended to illustrate that, with the right environment and training, any man disabled by war could return to work. Funding from the Red Cross provided the centre with thermal baths, physiotherapy and a gym for the use of men suffering from chronic fatigue syndrome, shell shock and amputations. Additional private donations poured in, including £100,000 from King George V, and by the end of 1921 more than five hundred veterans had returned to employment, or made significant steps towards recovery.

Enham's physicians prescribed a programme of hard physical labour and fresh air, attempting to demonstrate the benefits of country life for rehabilitating so-called 'unemployables'.[36] Men disabled by their injuries were trained in traditional village crafts such as carpentry, farming and poultry-rearing. The Quaker physician Fortescue Fox, working at Enham, promised that he would restore masculine virtues to these men, and 'bring back self-control and courage, in the unspeakable desolation and despair left by the war'.[37] In 2017, after it had received a grant of £20,000 from the Armed Forces Covenant Fund, a statement from Enham Trust said: 'We're like the original Help for Heroes ... People back then could be given a house and a job to help them re-enter Civvy Street. And, in many ways, given a new purpose in life.'[38]

Digging for Britain

In the grounds of Tedworth House a replica of an Iron Age roundhouse stands as a legacy of Help for Heroes's finer days, when celebrities like Prince Harry were regular visitors. Over 18 months, a group of 50 service personnel and veterans worked with a master craftsman who taught them carpentry and ensured that the building would be authentic. When it was completed in summer 2017, the team dressed up for an Iron-Age-themed party, complete with hog-roast. The celebration ended at Stonehenge where they joined the crowds to mark the summer solstice.[39]

The roundhouse project was successful for several reasons, not least because of the profound difference it made to its collaborators as they negotiated the afterwar. Now a woodworking hut, it performs a similar function to the Men's Shed that we encountered in Ludgershall in Chapter 2, offering a space for learning carpentry skills and avoiding social isolation – the difference being that all the users of the Iron Age roundhouse have found their way there through the auspices of veteran care. But it was also a sign that the Ministry of Defence had finally accepted that the rich heritage of its expansive rural estate, whether under or above ground, was one of its most precious assets.

The buried trenches discovered in Larkhill, complete with live grenades and graffiti scrawls of individual names, were part of this remote environment as much as the modernised Victorian barracks in Tidworth, the names of streets and buildings across all the camps and garrisons, and the cemeteries and monuments found throughout the Plain. The landscape offered a historical tableau open to being investigated, commemorated and celebrated in ways that centre war as an enduring and honourable human occupation.

Perhaps this phenomenon can be best symbolised by the marks that soldiers have inscribed on the ground itself, whether in protest or out of boredom. On Beacon Hill, near Bulford, there is a 130-metre-long shape of a kiwi carved into the chalk by soldiers from New Zealand who were impatiently waiting to be demobilised after the First World War.[40] Of all the dominions, New Zealand troops had suffered the highest percentage (5 per cent) of its military-aged men killed in the war, and the 4,600 stationed in Sling Camp, next to Bulford, were tired of military discipline and desperate to get home. When their requests for a relaxation of rules were refused, the men rioted, stealing food and all the alcohol from the officers' mess. The ringleaders were punished, and the rest given the job of creating this monument in order to keep them busy. The shortage of transport ships and the influenza pandemic meant that the last group of New Zealand soldiers did not arrive home until May 1920.[41]

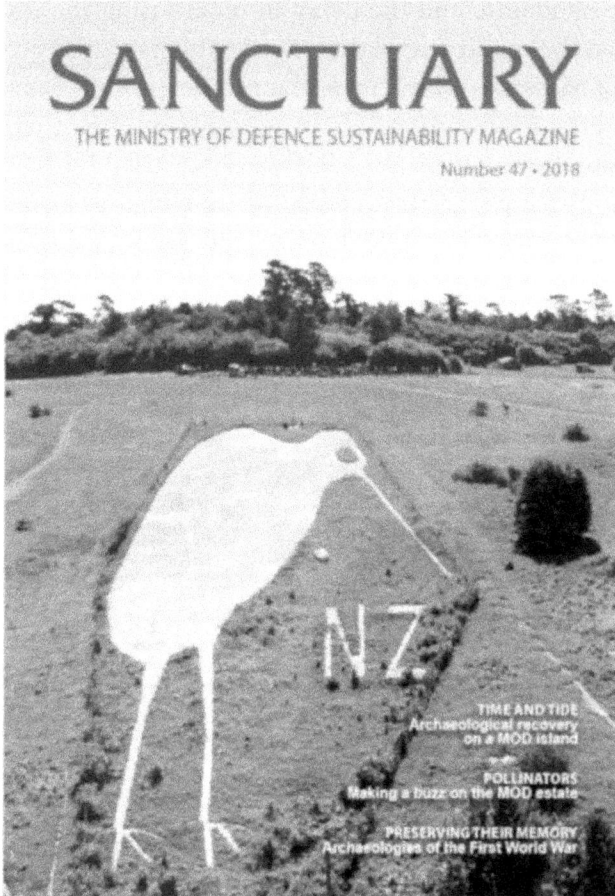

SANCTUARY
THE MINISTRY OF DEFENCE SUSTAINABILITY MAGAZINE
Number 47 · 2018

TIME AND TIDE
Archaeological recovery
on a MOD island

POLLINATORS
Making a buzz on the MOD estate

PRESERVING THEIR MEMORY
Archaeologies of the First World War

7.4 Front cover of *Sanctuary* 2018, showing the Kiwi carved into the chalk landscape by troops from New Zealand in 1919.

Now a scheduled monument, the Bulford Kiwi is regularly maintained by its current custodians, 249 Gurkha Signal Squadron, in conjunction with Landmarc Support Services ('supporting safe, sustainable training solutions for the armed forces') and local conservation groups. In 2022 Exercise Kiwi Refresh was attended by an officer from the New Zealand Defence Force, personnel from the New Zealand High Commission and a small representation from Ngati Ranana, the London-based Maori cultural group.[42] The news story issued by the Ministry of Defence omitted the detail about the rioting, the pandemic and the delay in repatriating the traumatised men. Instead the report stated that 'Kiwi soldiers played a key role in the Battle of Messines which took place in Belgium in 1917. The soldiers carved the Kiwi into the chalk to commemorate their achievements during the battle.'[43]

And this disparate heritage, with all its global associations, can be made instrumental in UK defence and security policy, providing a backdrop for international diplomacy, corporate diversity, veteran rehabilitation, or – finally – exemplary stewardship of an extraordinary national treasure, Salisbury Plain.[44] In the next chapter we explore the ecological and political implications of military occupation for the land itself.

8

This land is our land

It's an early summer morning in 2019 and a team of professional archaeologists and volunteers have come together at the top of Barrow Clump to take part in a new phase of the excavation. The site is on a hill overlooking the Avon Valley, which separates the eastern and western sides of the Salisbury Plain Training Area. For many centuries the grasses and scrub concealed rich evidence of a Neolithic settlement overlaid by Bronze-Age and Saxon burial grounds dating from at least 3500 BCE to the sixth century CE. Although the site was classified as a scheduled monument in 1991, giving it protection from further farming or military activity, it has remained at risk from badgers tunnelling into the mound and throwing up precious evidence in the form of human bones and funereal artefacts. The volunteers are former soldiers, and they are there to participate in the dig.

There is a long history of military involvement in archaeological research which is not so well known. In 2006 English Heritage marked the centenary of the first successful aerial photograph of a prehistoric site, an achievement that would irrevocably transform the whole science of archaeology. As it happened, this experiment was carried out by British Army officers on military-owned land on Salisbury Plain.

According to Martyn Barber's fascinating book *A History of Aerial Photography and Archaeology*, 2nd Lieutenant Philip Henry Sharpe, a junior officer of balloon technology in the Royal Engineers, was moved from Aldershot to Bulford Camp in 1906 under the command of Colonel J.E. Capper, whose expertise in ballooning technology was honed during the Boer War.[1] It is not known whether Sharpe had a particular interest in photography but he was given the job of wielding the camera from a hot-air balloon floating over Stonehenge, which at that time had been photographed only at ground level. The successful results were accordingly exhibited at a meeting of the Society of Antiquaries in December 1906.

Barber's book shows that the history of aerial survey techniques developed rapidly during the course of successive wars, although the co-operation between civilian archaeologists and military pilots was not sustained. [2] But in 2011 the Defence Infrastructure Organisation, Historic England and Wessex Archaeology formed a partnership that combined plans for a full excavation of the site with a scheme to use archaeological research as a way of rehabilitating injured personnel.[3] The renewed interest shown by the Ministry of Defence in the archaeological treasures on Salisbury Plain represents an altogether different approach to investigating the prehistoric past, one that involves looking at the ground as opposed to surveying it from the air.

Known as Operation Nightingale, this new collaboration began with month-long excavations, which took place annually between 2012 and 2014 and involved over a hundred injured soldiers from the Rifles regiment. Alongside the dig itself, an initiative called Project Florence, supported by Heritage Lottery funding, worked with local families and volunteers, many from the garrison communities, inviting them to join the work at Barrow Clump.[4]

Gemma is a forensic archaeologist who specialises in conflict archaeology. She steps carefully around a trench where someone is using a masonry trowel to ease compacted earth away from the newly uncovered skeleton of what is thought to be a thick-set and unusually tall adult Saxon male. She is holding an artefact box containing a few bones that revealed themselves the day before, following an arduous few hours spent sifting through boxes of soil. She wants to show the contents to her colleague Ben, who is not professionally trained but an army veteran who developed an enthusiasm for archaeological research during the excavation of a Second World

War training camp used by US paratroopers. Although Gemma is the professional here, she knows that soldiers can sometimes have expert knowledge, particularly at sites relating to war.

For many of those involved in Operation Nightingale, the experience has been life-changing, exposing individuals to profound moral, psychological and metaphysical concerns about mortality and the fallibility of human memory. The tools employed in archaeological digs – the sieve for sifting soil for fragments of pottery or bones, the drill to break down compacted earth, DNA swabs that can potentially connect the dead to living descendants – are the same as those used in forensic investigations, as well as in more mundane activities like farming and gardening. Sieving, drilling and swabbing involve meticulous attention to detail but also hard physical labour that non-experts can learn to perform. This combination of skills can offer a sense of catharsis to those involved in a dig, amplified by the fact that they are performing an act of care and respect for the dead whom they are working to exhume and memorialise.[5]

Many veterans have been inspired by this combination of heritage and recovery to study archaeology at university. Dickie Bennett, a former Royal Marine, who took part in the 2013 excavation at Barrow Clump, went on to study for a master's degree, and then founded his own charitable organisation to support the work of Operation Nightingale. The aim of Breaking Ground Heritage is to provide former servicemen and servicewomen with 'a safe environment to reintegrate, test their physical limitations, create peer networks, and once again feel like part of a team'.[6]

By 2020, according to an article in *Sanctuary* magazine, the Ministry of Defence's annual publication covering environmental issues, the project had 'made discoveries of national importance, written well-received publications and even has an intellectual property mark owned by the Secretary of State for Defence!'[7] The excavation of the original stable block at Catterick garrison, where an important horse hospital was built in the First World War and subsequently demolished, was an opportunity to underline the Ministry's 'commitment to the historic environment'.

Meanwhile Exercise REDCAP RECOVERY on Burrow Island (known locally as Rat Island), in Portsmouth harbour, related to the burial site of convicts who died on the prison hulks in the early nineteenth century. Overseen by the Royal Military Police, the ongoing project was hailed as not only helping to protect the remains of the convicts which would otherwise have been lost as a result of tidal erosion, 'it also trains and develops a crucial policing capability – Disaster Victim Identification – which continues to be beneficial to the RMP as more human remains are revealed by storms each winter'.

As the *Sanctuary* report made clear, the most important outcome of Operation Nightingale was, from the military's point of view, less the contribution to archaeological knowledge than its enduring benefit to the military. 'The programme has also developed', it says, 'to increase partnerships with external organisations, to work with groups that can examine precisely what works from a recovery perspective and also to design fieldwork that facilitates training opportunities.'

Operation Nightingale offers an impressive example of civil–military co-operation, one that brings significant benefits to the heritage industry as well as to the military. But it did not originate as a spontaneous act of generosity on the part of the Ministry of Defence, either on behalf of wounded veterans or from a deep concern for endangered Saxon artefacts. Considering the competing claims and priorities entailed in managing such a large expanse of rural England, it is important to understand how so many different agencies manage to negotiate the joint stewardship of the rich and complex ecology of Salisbury Plain.

Vandals in uniform

In his castigation of the 'blighted Plain', one of the few contemporary critical accounts of the military's presence in Wiltshire, Jonathan Meades was not just referring to the shoddy architecture of Ministry of Defence buildings. As we noted in earlier chapters, the photographer and film-maker had nothing positive to say about the army's treatment of the land either. It is 'further defaced by vandals in uniform who treat it as a playground and scrapyard', he wrote in 2022, singling out the 'danger areas and their alarmist signs; unexploded ordnance; live firing (260,000 rounds per annum); burned-out tanks, like an installation by a pyromaniacal Anselm Kiefer; rusting planes; racetracks for armoured personnel carriers; overgrown unidentifiable kit; the ghost village of Imber, requisitioned, like Tyneham, in 1943 and now largely destroyed in gung-ho exercises'.[8]

Melanie Friend is another photographer with local connections whose extraordinary portraits of the landscape guide viewers to look beyond the panoramic vistas and dramatic skies to find evidence of military activity in every frame. Tank tracks delineated in snow, chalk, mud and water; incongruous signs warning of explosives in waving grasslands; pale weather-beaten flags hanging limply from random flag poles in the middle of nowhere; abandoned buildings surrounded by saplings and the beginnings of scrub.[9]

As Meades testifies, these imprints and objects can render the Plain both blighted and defaced. But in Friend's photos the more obvious signs of the detritus of war training are sometimes harder to spot, camouflaged by a line of passing sheep or a sprawling herd of cattle, seemingly without any field boundaries or human supervision. In one a murmuration of starlings on the horizon draws the eye away from the rutted tracks that score the earth in the foreground.

In an essay accompanying her images Matthew Flintham writes that 'Friend's forays into the plain are careful but resolute steps in a zone of military simulation and real danger, across an invisible boundary of martial power'.[10] Directing the viewer towards other ways of looking at, as well as searching for, the jarring intrusion of war violence in such an unexpected place, he explains that the photographs 'identify the subtle markers of military power, exclusion and danger, and the uneasy union of the martial and pastoral'.

Meades's reference to the 'ghost village of Imber' brings us back to the unsuccessful struggle to reclaim land back from the War Office in the period after 1945. One of the consequences of the disparate campaigns to restore the right of public access to the Plain and to conserve natural resources was the Nugent Committee report, published in 1973. As we noted in Chapter 1, this created a mandate for the Ministry of Defence to liaise with a wide range of statutory, voluntary and other public bodies responsible for, and committed to, the wellbeing of Salisbury Plain and other training areas in the UK.

Today this history has been incorporated into the narrative of military environmentalism found in *Sanctuary*, launched in 1976. The success of Operation Nightingale, for example, can be traced back to concerns voiced by Wiltshire archaeologists that military training was causing irreparable harm to sites across the Plain. An article in the 2015 edition of the magazine, celebrating its fortieth anniversary, chronicled exactly what steps were needed to bring the Ministry of Defence into line.[11]

Under the heading 'Forty years on Salisbury Plain, how the battle to save archaeology was won', Roy Canham, former County Archaeologist and leading member of the Imber Conservation Group, explained that problems were first flagged up when archaeologists began to compile the Wiltshire Sites and Monuments Record in the mid-1970s. 'Salisbury Plain was a particular problem, because although it was renowned for its heritage the presence of the military made it difficult to access.' Members of conservation groups being formed at that time also reported that training exercises were potentially harming some of the ancient sites.

By 1982 the media had picked up on the danger that this presented to national heritage. The Romano-British settlement at Chisenbury Warren, for example, as the *Sanctuary* article made clear, was unprotected and 'highly vulnerable to units hiding in the warren then dashing forward to ambush opposition forces'. The headline 'Tanks train on Roman village' caught national attention, and thus began a dialogue between the Ministry of Defence, English Heritage and Wiltshire Council.

It transpired that there was no true record of archaeology on the Plain, despite the Ordnance Survey maps showing numerous barrows and tumuli throughout the training area. While some sites were Scheduled Ancient Monuments, the army had never been provided with a list, let alone any guidance on how to protect them. An extensive survey was carried out in 1985, funded by English Heritage and subsequently by the Ministry of Defence. The database and mapping recorded over 2,200 sites, including around six hundred prehistoric burial mounds. Roy Canham remembered the 'bold decision' to classify over five hundred sites as Scheduled Ancient Monuments as a precursor to agreeing how they should be protected.

For decades the Ministry had marked some obviously vulnerable sites with metal star-signs, and this technique was extended by placing a ring of signs around the monument rather than a single star at its centre. But the real challenge was 'to protect clusters of earthworks covering substantial areas', and so the term Archaeological Site Group was coined. Between 1986 and 1993 a number of similar measures were introduced with the intention of guiding military units through these zones rather than imposing exclusion.

One group of archaeological earthworks was elevated to top status, labelled as Important and Fragile Sites. They numbered seven and included some of the best preserved and rarest features found in the country. Only training on foot was permitted within them, and they are marked on the training area map as no-go areas.

Improvements, according to the *Sanctuary* article, also included introducing signage, creating new tracks and closing old ones, fencing enclosures and plantations to block movement and partly clearing existing plantations to redirect movement: 'whatever was needed to fulfil the management plans'. One of the most significant outcomes of these deliberations was the recognition that the preservation of ancient sites must be combined with the protection of the wider ecology of the Plain.

In 1981 English Nature (now Natural England) registered a vast zone with the status of Site of Special Scientific Interest. As we noted earlier, the Salisbury Plain SSSI, Special Area of Conservation and Special Protection Area cover 19,690 hectares, which is about half of the wider military training area. According to the most recent site assessment (2014–15), it is notified for 25 features: chalk grassland, the Nine Mile River, juniper habitat, rare plants, invertebrates including marsh fritillary butterfly and fairy shrimp, and birds including stone curlew and wintering hen harrier.[12]

Martial lore

In Chapter 1 we sketched the origins of the term 'military environmentalism' which was identified in the 1970s after the Ministry of Defence was obliged to 'justify its presence by recognising and meeting its duty as a holder of some of the richest lands in the country in terms of wildlife, heritage and natural beauty'.[13] In the intervening years, just as the military has been required to co-operate more closely with Wiltshire Council under the rubric of the Military Civilian Integration Partnership, or with Wessex Archaeology and a host of other national heritage organisations responsible for safeguarding the Plain's prehistoric riches, the Ministry of Defence is now an established partner in projects to protect and support vulnerable life forms across its entire training estate worldwide.

The pages of *Sanctuary* regularly carry headlines such as 'MoD supports the native British black honey bee' alongside stories of birds, butterflies, spiders, insects, plants – and not forgetting the elusive fairy shrimp – that are now apparently flourishing as a result of these collaborative efforts. One of these initiatives features the stone-curlew which is benefiting from a system of nesting plot management managed by the Royal Society for the Protection of Birds for over twenty years, with the co-operation of local farmers as well as the Ministry of Defence. Nationally populations have fallen since the 1930s, although small numbers have continued to survive in Wiltshire. In 2023 the RSPB published an article on the Wessex stone-curlew project, claiming that the species was 'bouncing back' as a result of joint intervention:

> These elusive birds traditionally bred on tightly grazed grassland and foraged for invertebrates in permanent pasture, but much of this suitable grassland habitat has now given way to agriculture. As a result, more pairs are nesting in cultivated fields, and due to the excellent camouflage of the eggs and chicks they are vulnerable to farming practices. This, along with other issues such as being highly susceptible to human disturbance, has seen stone-curlew populations plummet since the 1930s. Luckily, the population has persisted on Salisbury Plain, partly due to the military training area retaining much of the grassland habitat which stone-curlews love.[14]

8.1 Stone curlew, *Burhinus oedicnemus*, at autumn roost on a carefully managed (in co-operation with the land owners) 'stone curlew plot'. The birds are crepuscular, being more active in the twilight, and generally sleepy in daylight hours.

The RSPB is right to be jubilant about the success of the project, but it is important to interrogate the word 'luckily' more closely. The stone-curlews, black bees, marsh fritillaries, great bustards and microscopic shrimps might well be the beneficiaries of good fortune, thanks to their ability to thrive in areas that have been protected from intensive farming. But they can still be examples of 'khaki conservation' or victims of 'camouwash', as we suggested earlier. In other words the creatures that survive on acres of so-called 'unspoiled' grassland and other protected habitats are indeed fortunate by-products of national defence policy, but any successes can truly be measured only against other forms of harm caused by the military whether on Salisbury Plain or any other training area.

This argument looks more convincing the further we stray from the particular ecology of Salisbury Plain. As Chris Packham enthused in his foreword to the 2017 edition of *Sanctuary*, the Ministry of Defence is to be congratulated for proper management and protection of its estate around the world. He singled out 'the potentially positive aspects of the reactivation of military training in Belize', for example, a country 'with significant but imperilled natural resources'. Belize gained independence from Britain in 1981 but the UK government maintained a military presence there until 1994, when it established the British Army Training Support Unit Belize. It then scaled down its activities, only to ramp them up in 2016 when a fifteen-year agreement allowed this Unit to train up to 3,750 personnel per year in an area the size of Wales. Belize receives no payment for hosting the UK training programme.

An article in the same edition of *Sanctuary* explained that, in order to secure consent from the Belize Department of the Environment, it was necessary to undertake an environmental impact assessment to evaluate the likely negative and positive environmental impacts of military training. After a detailed description of risks and dangers to wildlife, heritage and tourism, the piece listed the various commitments that the army was prepared to make in order to secure the contract.

Jaguars would be protected with anti-poaching patrols, for example, and assurances were given that the risk to vegetation and waterways from live fire and riverine training would be short-term, and that arboriculturally sensitive areas would be out of bounds. The article ends, 'This integrated approach was critical to the success of the project in securing consent to train across a unique and extensive overseas training estate, which is essential for preparing British troops for operating in this uniquely demanding and often hostile environment'.[15]

A subsequent investigation by journalists from DeclassifiedUK pointed to the army's own finding that its contribution to the economy of Belize was negligible. Job creation, especially in the hospitality sector, was minuscule compared to the impact of tourism, accounting for just 0.1 per cent of Belize's GDP against 38 per cent. They also noted that the British presence had led to protests and was reminiscent of the country's experiences with Coca Cola, which bought up cheap land and, following resistance, was forced to sell.[16]

Conflicts of interest

While wildlife organisations cheer the absence of intensive agriculture as a factor in preserving wildlife, the environmental management of the Plain has a slightly more complex history than mere fortunate neglect. It is true that, thanks partly to the grazing of livestock over the centuries, large areas of permanent pasture can be managed with regard to scrub and woodland, which is beneficial for many rare species as well as suitable for army training. This is the case on much of the defence estate, including the Castlemartin range in Wales. Yet this arrangement is not simply a matter of custom and convenience.

The army's takeover of the Plain's agricultural areas was not a straightforward process of purchasing the land and leaving the same farmers in place. The army reorganised farming practices to suit its own needs.[17] One major difference was that, since training had to be carried out throughout the year, arable crops would inevitably be damaged. As for livestock, which were still required on the land to keep it grazed, the risk was mitigated by dividing the land into three categories, last formalised in 1927.[18]

Schedule 1 is land let to farm tenants under agricultural tenancy agreement, over which training rights are reserved, subject to compensation being paid to the tenant in the event of damage. These lands are generally closer to the settlements and include the cultivated fields around Tidworth, Bulford, Amesbury and Larkhill. As Schedule 1 lands are relatively safe from live firing and less likely to be run over by tanks and other military vehicles, they serve as a buffer between the towns and training grounds.

According to *Plain Soldiering*, N.D.G. James's account of how the military encampment was first established on Salisbury Plain, Schedule 2 was land that was arable when purchased but laid down to permanent pasture by the War Office, with the army providing seed and the tenant agreeing to maintain the area. Schedule 3 lands are still leased out to farmers under strict conditions and farmed at the tenants' own risk. These are situated close to the training area, including the impact zones where artillery firing occurs regularly, and the army is not required to provide compensation for any damages. The tenants know that Schedule 3 land can be reclaimed by the army if it is required for training or other purposes.

Although it has been updated, this basic system of land management means that the co-operation of farmers is required to maintain the training environment for a number of reasons. On Schedule 3 land, for example, pastures are allocated on specific weeks and months with the view to clearing the space for military exercises – and keeping the grass low so that these can take place easily and efficiently. This is why grazing is sometimes permitted within the impact zones as well, despite the risk of injury to the livestock.

What these arrangements mean for farmers on the Plain was brought home to us by Bruce Waight, whose family has been working the land there since 1874. Today he farms over 4,000 hectares of land, much of it rented from the Ministry of Defence, with land quality and rent varying hugely. He also receives a subsidy and stewardship payments.[19]

The Waights live in Compton, in the north-eastern part of the Salisbury Plain, and are well known and respected locally. In an article in *Farmers Weekly* Bruce described some of the implications of farming in close proximity to the military, whether for the soil, the terrain or the livestock: 'Cattle are so important to this environment. They open the ground up treading seeds in each year. Without cattle, bushes and bigger plants dominate and shade out the rare flowers.'[20]

When we spoke to him in 2019, he recalled a night the previous year when he had been busy calving the cows. Just before 4 am he received the dreaded call from the army at Westdown Camp. Some soldiers had – yet again – driven right through one of his pastures, breaking the temporary electric fencing and allowing a hundred cows to stray outside the enclosure. Bruce knew that it would be impossible to collect them if he waited till morning; some of them might enter the firing zones in the Training Area and risk being killed. 'Cursing the bloody squaddies', he remembered, he staggered out of bed, climbed into one of his 4×4 jeeps and spent the rest of the night sorting out the problem.

Unlike absentee landlords of large rural estates, the military land-owner is omnipresent. Till recently, a designated army officer was responsible for dealing with the farmers, but that post no longer exists. The farmers attempt to resolve their issues collectively, but they are inevitably overridden by the army. In a 2011 interview with BBC Radio 4 a senior officer commented that 'We do our best to let the farmers get on with their work. But if a conflict of interest arises, we always win.'[21]

Some of the military personnel we spoke with accepted, off the record, that, despite their efforts to prevent encroachment, incidents like this do sometimes occur. The land under cultivation is often interspersed between training areas. Since there are few hedges, and electric fencing is hard to see at night, accidents take place due to carelessness and inattention as well as the inability to appreciate the difference between arable crops and grass.

According to another BBC report, in 2014 a large artillery shell missed its target by five miles and hit a farm near Devizes, creating a 6-feet-wide crater. Luckily no one was injured, although it occurred a mere 300 metres from a railway line. Visibly shaken, a local farmer called Andrew Snook acknowledged that such accidents were possible on the Plain, and requested an apology from the Ministry of Defence – which never came.[22]

While none of Bruce's fields has been struck quite as badly as that, his crops have often been damaged by trespassing tanks and trucks. This not only destroys crops, it also compacts the earth, rendering the chalky soil even harder. Repairing the soil costs money as well as requiring a lot of effort to make it usable again. He was able to produce a photograph of the damage incurred when a Challenger 2 tank ran across one of his fields, flattening the ploughed earth which had been levelled prior to sowing barley. The ground took a long time to recover, but he never received an apology from the army. As this was Schedule 3 land he was not entitled to any compensation.

Even without these incidents, farming on the training area is generally challenging, as Bruce confirmed. He was obliged to invest in expensive farm machinery just to get around his land, especially when it was wet. Tanks and other heavy military vehicles make the tracks impossibly muddy, creating potholes and deep ruts which are difficult to navigate. Worse still, some sections of the farms closest to the impact zones have limited access every year.

As Bruce explained, 'some parts we are not permitted to enter over two hundred days a year – when live firing occurs'. These restrictions are obviously essential for safety reasons, but they makes farming difficult. Sometimes farmers cannot sow seeds on time, or the harvest may be delayed. The laying of pipes of any kind is also not permitted anywhere on the defence estate because of the danger of hitting unexploded devices when putting them in. This makes irrigation difficult, and water has to be driven to the animals.[23]

Strict military rules and regulations add to these obstacles. For example the army may have planted certain objects on the roads and byways for training purposes. If the farmer is not careful and destroys or damages those installations, he has to pay immediately. Bruce was convinced that farmers with a smallholding would find it impossible to survive. His own enterprise was large enough to withstand the potential risks and losses.

If growing crops on military land has its drawbacks, rearing sheep and cattle is even more challenging because of the unpredictable nature of air drops and live artillery firing, and other potentially lethal activities.[24] One perennial problem is being ordered to relocate sheep or cattle at short notice. Bruce recalled:

> In early 2019, one night an army officer called me and asked me to move my 80 or so cows grazing on a particular plot to another location. He said this was urgent as an air drop was planned on site. Fair enough! I again asked him when I needed to clear the space. He said by tomorrow noon. I said OK; what else could I say? But in my head I was cursing him.

In spite of the challenges of farming on military land, there are certain hidden but important mutual benefits as well. The farmers benefit from the relatively low rents, especially for Schedule 3 land. Bruce reckons that lower rents have helped him expand his operation quite rapidly over the years. When the crops are not damaged and the weather is reasonably good, farmers are able to make a profit. They can earn a good income from livestock too. Marlborough Downs and

Salisbury Plain are considered to be among the best pastures in the whole country for high-quality lamb and beef.

Red flags

Being seen to be willing to share space has been essential to the Ministry of Defence's image as a responsible and caring custodian of the environment. We learned from a conversation with the team responsible for advising on environmental support and compliance for the Ministry, that, by the 2000s, the Ministry was spending about £1 million every year on ecology, public access, archaeology, forestry and woodland management.

As we saw in Chapter 1, the process through which the Ministry was forced to co-operate with statutory and voluntary bodies responsible for preserving and protecting the plain, as well as ensuring public access, is now well established. Yet 'the uneasy union of the martial and pastoral' raises many questions about how the space is shared. When it comes to recreational activities, there is a presumption in favour of public access. This was another important consequence of the Nugent Report which laid the groundwork for civilians to be granted more access to Ministry-owned land.

In 2006 the Salisbury Plain Rights of Way Volunteers was established by the Range Safety Officer for Salisbury Plain Training Area, Lieutenant Colonel (Retired) Nigel Linge MBE. The group continues to share responsibility for maintaining public rights of way and permissive access routes by repairing signposts and clearing any obstructions to paths and roads open to the public.[25] The Defence Infrastructure Organisation, which manages the estate on behalf of the Ministry of Defence, publishes a monthly Salisbury Plain Training Area Newsletter with a firing calendar and information about planned changes to public access. It reminds civilians of the rules – public rights of way are closed when red flags are flying and the Imber ranges are always closed unless specifically opened – and encourages people to report illegal activities to the police.[26]

Many users of the Plain complain that the Ministry of Defence is intimidating, however, despite these forms of public access. The lack of safety information and the proliferation of 'MoD – keep off' signs effectively deter many ramblers, naturalists, cyclists, horse riders, joggers, quad bikers and dog walkers who also want access to the many pathways crisscrossing the Plain. But managing the risks posed by civilian incursions in the impact area remains a big issue for the Ministry, and there are certain categories of users who regularly run into law-enforcement agencies on the Plain. On a typical weekend in spring as many as five hundred 4x4s and three hundred motorbikes might arrive, driven by people specifically seeking the chance to ride on unmade roads. This activity is known as greenlaning, and is permitted on the training area subject to certain restrictions.

A leaflet issued by the Ministry of Defence in 2020, for example, asks drivers 'to travel at a quiet and unobtrusive pace. When travelling in groups keep to a small number: four cars or six bikes maximum. Larger groups should split up and use alternative routes rather than using the same trails to avoid causing excessive damage.' It also asks users to follow the Countryside Code and 'Remember that wildlife faces many threats and Public Rights of Way can be valuable habitats. Take special care in spring and early summer.'[27]

In 2018 Wiltshire Police launched Operation Aston in an attempt to curb illegal motoring activity on the Plain. The local media reported that 'Throughout the operation officers stopped over 20 vehicles, including four motorcycles seized for being driven with no insurance, and three fixed penalty notices issued for vehicles being driven off-road without landowner permission, with the drivers issued warnings for anti-social or inconsiderate driving'.[28]

For those wanting a legitimate tour on wheels, a company called Salisbury Plain Safaris offers two- to three-hour drives across the training area. Its publicity highlights the rough terrain as 'so much fun!' although the main draw seems to be 'the stunning countryside which is home to rare birds and plants and rich archaeology and military history, all in the company of an experienced tour guide'.[29]

An example of a more traditional pursuit can be found in the pages of *Shooting UK* ('the home of *Shooting Times* and *Sporting Gun*'). Writing in 2013, the journalist Charles Smith-Jones accompanied the Netheravon shoot, which operates under licence on the eastern side of the training area. Formed in 1972, the Guns, as they are known, are 'an eclectic mix, ranging from retired generals and serving soldiers to local farmers'. The journalist was assured that they co-ordinated closely with the military authorities to avoid training exercises every time they went out, and liaised with everyone else. 'We keep our ears to the ground and stay flexible – it works, at least most of the time.' He still found it surreal to listen to the nearby sound of machine-gun fire 'as troops trained somewhere over the ridgeline'.[30]

Despite these various forms of recreational activities which draw residents and visitors to the Plain, many civilians find it difficult to forget 'the subtle markers of military power, exclusion and danger' that Flintham observes in Friend's images. Yet people who live locally often describe the Plain as somewhere that offers solace and restoration, despite these obvious symbols of military authority which both act as a deterrent and render it unlike anywhere else.

The Gurkha veteran whom we met earlier, Bhakta Limbu, for example, regularly walks in the open country surrounding his home in Tidworth. Having been a subsistence farmer in eastern Nepal, he enjoys the peace and quiet he finds outdoors, and this allows him to feel some sense of belonging in a country that otherwise seems hostile to him. Whereas many other veterans have been attracted by the vast open spaces of Salisbury Plain, he has fallen in love with the wooded ridges flanking the town. But he never loses sight of the fact that the sole purpose of this encampment is to keep the men and women in uniform fit and battle-ready. Ever alert to the sound of explosives in the distance, he wonders if these young soldiers today truly grasp what they have been preparing for, and how their involvement in warfare can potentially damage their lives.

At the other end of the social spectrum Claire, a seasoned army spouse, also finds the proximity of open space a blessing for her mental health and relaxation. Walking the family dog had undoubtedly helped her to integrate into army life. Catterick was still her favourite place, not because it was the largest British garrison in the world but because of its proximity to the North Yorkshire moors. Being able to go on long walks had made up for losing her financial autonomy and professional identity. Now having grown accustomed to her role as an officer's wife, she had discovered that this was about not just integrating into army life but also finding strategies to survive it. Exploring the very different landscape of Salisbury Plain on foot had helped her through a number of personal crises. But there are undeniably risks when it comes to living within the confines of a military training area.

Local communities often react in anger when they feel the environment is being damaged by their military neighbour. In the summer of 2018, for instance, a wildfire erupted in Impact Area 15 during a live firing practice. Known locally as 'The Smoke', it lasted for many days as it could not be extinguished because of the risk of unexploded ordnance. Eventually the leader of Wiltshire Council, Baroness Scott, had to ring the general at Army HQ in Andover to protest, telling them it was setting back military–civilian relations in the area.

Four years later live firing exercises started another conflagration during a period of unprecedented heat and drought. A few days later Dorset and Wiltshire Fire and Rescue Service announced that the fires had been extinguished after Ministry of Defence helicopters had dropped water on the site – the fire service was unable to intervene because of the risk of unexploded ordnance. But the following day the fires had reignited. The Salisbury Journal reported that large amounts of smoke were billowing across Wiltshire, and, despite the high temperatures, the fire service was advising people to close their windows and doors. One shop-owner in Tidworth was quoted saying that the town 'was enveloped in this fog'. He added, 'It does make you worry that it's possibly closer than it really is'.[31]

Residents might have been more alarmed if they had been aware of the impact of wildfires on the British Army training area in Kenya, where in 2021 a cooking accident by UK troops set fire to Lolldaiga Hills, a safari resort near Mount Kenya. The smoke plume was so large that ash particles reached Lake Victoria on the Tanzanian border, some two hundred miles away. At least 7,000 acres, an area larger than the 11 square-mile London borough of Lambeth, was 'torched'. The army claimed immunity from prosecution on the basis that communal lands were not affected. However, 5,563 Kenyans filed compensation claims at the end of 2022, and are awaiting the verdict.[32]

Training ground

Over the last decade, *Sanctuary* (with its new strapline 'The Ministry of Defence sustainability magazine') has published a steady flow of articles detailing the Ministry of Defence's efforts to integrate 'climate resilience' into its practices and policies. Interspersed between reports from conservation groups working in different pockets of the global defence estate, or items about heritage preservation and public access, headlines such as 'Water Consumption reduction: Managing a precious resource' (2017), 'The anxious and most perplexing problem of oil fuel' (2018), 'Carbon efficient accommodation on the Defence Training Estate' (2020), 'Introducing the Directorate for Climate Change and Sustainability' (2021), 'DST Leconfield The British Army's first solar farm' (2021) and 'Climate Hit Parade, the climate resilience team's top hits' (2022) offer glimpses of the Ministry's commitment to taking the climate crisis seriously.

As we argued in Chapter 1, *Sanctuary* is an invaluable tool for the institution, allowing it to be represented as a responsible custodian of land in partnership with many national and local organisations with which it has learned to collaborate, and in accordance with official UK government policy. This public image, which far exceeds the efforts to promote 'khaki conservation' that began in the 1970s, needs to be challenged as a form of 'camouwash' rather than being accepted at face value. War-fighting is not by any description a sustainable activity. The available data suggest that the total military carbon footprint accounts for approximately 5.5 per cent of global emissions. To put it another way: 'If the world's militaries were a country, this figure would mean they have the fourth largest national carbon footprint in the world'.[33]

This grim reality seems to have been acknowledged in the most recent edition of *Sanctuary*, published in 2023, which had a 'new look and feel'. Gone are the corporate logos of arms companies, and the foreword is provided by Lieutenant General Sharon Nesmith,

Deputy Chief of the General Staff, British Army. 'Every single person in Defence has a role to play in tackling climate change,' she wrote, and her own role, 'alongside that of my fellow leaders in the British Army, is to drive the culture needed to respond to the challenges and risks posed by climate change, addressing both the causes and consequences'.[34]

Elsewhere in the journal, another senior army officer acknowledged that the defence sector accounts for 50 per cent of central government's emissions, and the army accounts for nearly 20 per cent of these. His conclusion was rather more impersonal and unconvincing than his colleague's: 'The Army's demonstrable investment in sustainable initiatives will help to achieve its ambition to contribute to a net zero carbon emitting estate by 2050'.

And while the range of collaborations with ecological and heritage groups suggests a readiness to integrate with civil society, this is not the case when it comes to carbon emissions and other climate-related issues. A 2020 report on the environmental impacts of the UK military sector, published by Scientists for Global Responsibility and the media organisation DeclassifiedUK, reveals that the Ministry of Defence, including the armed forces and the Ministry's civilian agencies and contractors, are not automatically covered by civilian environmental regulations. The author Stuart Parkinson states that 'if the MoD decides there is a "defence" need: then they are exempt. Instead the MOD aims to "minimise" its environmental impacts through the application of a set of environmental management systems. External verification of these systems seems to be patchy.'[35]

Parkinson's report centres on the military missions themselves. These are likely to have major environmental impacts, he writes, 'but no data is publicly available on the full extent of these impacts, nor on measures taken to reduce them. Indeed, attempts to assess such impacts seem not to be undertaken routinely by the MoD.' The examples he provides range from managing radioactive and other hazardous waste, on which the Ministry and its contractors have a poor record, to the impact of the arms industry and other Ministry suppliers, and, not least, the 'catastrophic global environmental impacts should the UK government ever launch its nuclear weapons'.

The inclusion of nuclear weapons in this discussion takes us far from the good news stories about thriving wildlife and restored heritage on Salisbury Plain. But the two are connected, of course, and often in ways that are not publicised quite as enthusiastically, at least not in the pages of *Sanctuary*. This might be illustrated by, for example, the UK government's decision in 2023 to send depleted uranium shells for use in the Challenger 2 tanks gifted to Ukraine. A documentary released by the Ministry of Defence in 2023 showed Ukrainian troops on Salisbury Plain, and other UK training areas, being taught how to handle depleted uranium shells, although these were marked 'inert'.[36] Organisations like CND have condemned the use of these weapons as an additional environmental and health disaster for those living through the conflict.

> A by-product of the nuclear enriching process used to make nuclear fuel or nuclear weapons, DU emits three quarters of the radioactivity of natural uranium and shares many of its risks and dangers. It is used in armour piercing rounds as it is heavy and can easily penetrate steel. However on impact, toxic or radioactive dust can be released and subsequently inhaled.[37]

In addition to the impact of military weapons and activity on the environment, there are ways in which the Ministry's stewardship of the Plain can be used as a diplomatic tool to further the military interests of its allies in Europe. A clear example of this took place in Montenegro after it was admitted to NATO membership in 2017.

In 2019, despite public outrage across Montenegro, the parliament announced the creation of a military training area in the Sinjajevina-Durmitor mountain range, the second largest mountainous grazing land in Europe. The Sinjajevina plateau is part of the Tara Canyon Biosphere Reserve and is bordered by two UNESCO World Heritage sites. Two months before an international scientific research team presented its findings to UNESCO, the European Parliament, and the European Commission, explaining the bio-cultural value of Sinjajevina, NATO troops arrived to train. In December 2019 the Save Sinjajevina association was officially launched.[38]

The following year, about 150 farmers and their allies set up a protest camp in the highland pastures to block the soldiers' access to the area. They formed a human chain in the grasslands and used their bodies as shields against the live ammunition of the planned military exercise. They resisted for more than fifty days in freezing conditions until the new Montenegrin Minister of Defence announced that the training would be cancelled.

But in 2022, as the pressure continued, the British ambassador to Montenegro, Karen Maddox, visited the area, and tried to reassure protestors that military training need not jeopardise the precious environment. Her argument was that the biodiversity of both Salisbury Plain and the UNESCO heritage site at Stonehenge had been protected by the presence of the military over the course of many years.

The Save Sinjajevina movement issued a statement rejecting Maddox's argument as inappropriate. Industrialisation and urbanisation had ravaged wildlife in the UK, so it was understandable that the ecosystem of Salisbury Plain had benefited from the absence of intensive farming. In contrast the Montenegrin mountains, especially Sinjajevina, have remained almost untouched by the processes of modernisation; its rich biodiversity is a direct result of the sustainable pastoral lifestyle, which is 'the best and only guarantor of its protection and preservation'.[39] Montenegro was much smaller than the UK and did not have the luxury of turning 120 square kilometres of unique mountain pasture into a training and shooting range, 'thereby neglecting its citizens and depriving them of their age-old hearths'.[40]

The ambassador's failure to tell the difference between an area which had been virtually expunged of pastoral farming communities and a region currently supporting a sustainable ecosystem is perhaps surprising. Yet the British military's record on its overseas bases tells a different story about its stewardship of the land and its people, one in which different standards are applied outside the borders of the UK.

In Kenya, for example, the government has recently launched an inquiry into allegations of abuse by the British Army. The investigation will examine the activities of the British Army Training

Unit Kenya (Batuk), whose soldiers have been accused of murder, sexual abuse and damaging land close to its base in Nanyuki, about 125 miles north of the capital, Nairobi.[41]

While the inquiry will examine historic cases from earlier decades, there have been more recent incidents that demand investigation. For example British soldiers on training exercises have used white phosphorus on 15 occasions since 2017. The British Army states that its own use of white phosphorus there does not breach international law, and insists that it is used only for illumination or smokescreening purposes. However, this controversial munition has been used at Archers Post, a vast area of communal land in Kenya that is frequented by farmers, children and elephants.

Although the army claims to clear firing ranges of 'all persons and wildlife' prior to training exercises, no specific assessment is made of the environmental impact of firing white phosphorus. One witness, who watched a recent exercise at Archers Post, told the journalist Phil Miller: 'You still find some nomads there who are very illiterate, they don't know what's happening or what could be the effect of grazing on such areas … The last time we were there, there were still people grazing their animals on the same areas that they were using to carry out the training.'[42]

We always win

Ordnance Survey maps of Salisbury Plain bear testimony to the way in which it has been reshaped, controlled and occupied over many years. One from 1939–40 shows that by then the area had been given over entirely to war preparation. Red lines indicating firing zones, cross-hatched sections showing where live explosives were being used at Boscombe Down, and other symbols of restricted access, are dramatically distributed throughout the training area. Dense areas of hatching represent the built estate, such as the barracks of Tidworth, Bulford and Larkhill.

The distinctive contours of the Plain are harder to trace, but the more you look, the more you see. The terrain is marked by downs, bottoms, hills, clumps and vales, each bearing a name that would have once meant all the world to its inhabitants. Farms can be seen across the whole county, as they are on all OS maps on this scale. And prehistoric remains are scattered throughout, whether tumuli, mounds, earthworks or the evidence of Roman settlement, all waiting to be catalogued, investigated and protected, as they would be, some decades later.

The annual event known as Imberbus makes it easy to forget the years of struggle that took place as military command of the Plain began to take effect. As we described in the first chapter, the village of Imber was requisitioned by the Ministry of Defence in 1943 with assurances that this was a temporary measure, although it was never returned to its former inhabitants. Today the crumbling, overgrown ruins remain accessible to the public during certain days of the year when the church of St Giles is opened to visitors.

8.2 The Imberbus provides an annual bus service from Warminster to Imber and other points on Salisbury Plain.

First launched in 2009, the Imberbus provides an annual bus service from Warminster to Imber and other points on Salisbury Plain. It has been so successful that the number of buses has increased to more than 25, and the route itself has been extended to other remote destinations, such as New Zealand Camp and Brazen Bottom. As the operation has grown, it has become a regular fundraiser for the Imber Church fund, the Royal British Legion and Macmillan Cancer Support.[43]

Commemorating the original bus routes that began to open up the Plain in the early twentieth century, the cavalcade of scarlet double-deckers snaking over the downs offers a spectacular glimpse of a militarised landscape that has been totally subdued by the incessant drive to practise warcraft. The highlight of the tour, the shattered ruins of Imber village, has been well and truly incorporated into a narrative of authentic, wounded rurality, the fierce resistance of its supporters and former residents all but forgotten. They were merely victims of the army's unnegotiable rule: 'if a conflict of interest arises, we always win'.

Conclusion: Security and danger

We began this book by describing the way that a sprawling military base lies, barely visible, just off the arterial roads that run through southern Wiltshire. A guided tour along back routes, away from the magnetism of Stonehenge, reveals a windswept landscape that has been irrevocably altered by the army's presence. From the recently excavated First World War trenches to the ambiguous 'terrorist or refugee camp' constructed in 2016, the disparate training sites not only reflect the changing practices and technologies of warfare. They also represent crude definitions of the enemy. By the time we had ended our tour, a multinational force had been assembled to train recruits from Ukraine in a new chapter that recalled memories of the early years of the First World War.

While the names of roads and buildings in the camps and garrisons offer lessons in imperial military history, the new housing estates perched on the edge of open country point to the vast infrastructure of service family life required to maintain the modern army. This might be the largest training area in the country, but Salisbury Plain is not the only British Army base to have been categorised as a 'super garrison'.

Catterick in North Yorkshire currently houses six thousand service personnel working for the British Army, with an overall population of about thirteen thousand. At the time of writing, troop numbers at Catterick are expected to rise by more than 50 per cent over the next decade, with corresponding plans to upgrade and expand the army quarters as well as the town itself. In recent years the construction of new service housing has also had a noticeable impact on the town of Aldershot in Hampshire and the city of Colchester in Essex, both historic garrisons in their own right.

The Salisbury Plain Training Area must also be considered within a global network of Britain's bases. In Canada, for example, the training area at British Army Training Area Suffield measures approximately 2,700 square kilometres, three times the size of the Salisbury Plain Training Area. Armoured battlegroups, each containing approximately 1,400 soldiers, conduct live firing manoeuvres there every year, according to the British Army website. In addition the UK armed forces have access to five training areas in Belize, two jungle training sites in Brunei and 13 in Kenya, as we saw in the last chapter.

British forces are also based at strategic locations where they are maintained as 'a visible demonstration of the United Kingdom's sovereignty'. The Sovereign Base Areas on the island of Cyprus cover 98 square miles, encompassing Akrotiri, Episkopi, Dhekelia and Ayos Nikolaos. And British forces are located throughout Gibraltar, in the British Indian Ocean Territory and the South Atlantic Islands, including the Falklands, South Georgia and the South Sandwich Islands. This information is freely available on the Ministry of Defence's Directorate of Overseas Bases, published online.

But this official list does not include the 85 facilities run by Britain's allies in countries such as Saudi Arabia and Oman, where the UK has a significant military presence, or those referred to as 'lily-pads' – sites to which the UK has easy access as and when required, as General Mark Carleton-Smith, Britain's then Chief of the General Staff told the *Telegraph* in 2020.[1]

The Wiltshire 'super garrison', like all these bases and quasi-bases, is marked by a pervasive aura of secrecy and inaccessibility. Yet the very rural setting of Tidworth, the original Victorian garrison, and Ludgershall, the small town just outside the boundary of the training area, brings residents and visitors alike into unavoidably close contact with the values and norms of military culture.

The phrase 'civilians in camouflage', originally used by Catherine Lutz in her historical account of a US military base, is a vivid way to

9.1 A local business that survived the pandemic.

describe residents who may not appear to be 'army', but are still very much connected to it, whether as employees, dependants or former soldiers. So it is not surprising that the routine sight of a khaki uniform in the supermarket aisle, a parent in battledress holding an infant or an armoured vehicle pausing at a zebra crossing rarely turns any heads.

Spending time on the high street or the café downtown also supports Zoë Wool's contention that, on this scale, there is no firm divide 'between a military world and a broader sociocultural one'.[2] But, as Cynthia Enloe has long warned, becoming habituated to the sights and sounds of the military in mundane spaces can influence public attitudes to the work that the whole institution is required to do.[3] In other words it is possible that those who live on or next to an army base, whether officially connected or not, are likely to be persuaded by a commonsense view – imprinted daily in the mainstream media – that most problems between nation states can ultimately be solved by the threat of lethal weapons. As we noted in Chapter 7, the long-time defence analyst Paul Rogers describes this as 'an integrated culture of militarism', one that devalues alternative strategies to deal with international conflict.

And if the army is seen as a force that is necessary to protect 'us' at home, then this hodgepodge of ideas, assumptions and beliefs (often condensed under the banner of 'security') is also likely to shape collective understandings of what makes 'us' unsafe.[4] In fact one of the underlying hypotheses guiding this book was the proposition that proximity to a military community was likely to induce – or certainly affect – a distinctly local sense of insecurity. We could not have known what perils lay ahead when we began our research in the autumn of 2018.

Military aid

The Covid-19 pandemic made it unfeasible to visit the area or continue with face-to-face interviews. But it also provided an unexpected opportunity to consider the question of security from a different angle, not least because it highlighted the role of the armed forces in providing 'military aid to civil authority'. On 18 March 2020, shortly before the first UK lockdown, the government announced the formation of a Covid Support Force which placed twenty thousand troops on 'higher readiness'. Military uniforms were regularly on view in formerly unexpected places, often flanking politicians on the podium. In April 2020 the Chief of the Defence Staff, General Sir Nick Carter, appeared on the daily coronavirus briefing for the first time. The fact that he was wearing camouflage fatigues rather than formal dress uniform enhanced the sense of national emergency for which civil authorities were unprepared.

Carter reassured the public that the military's role in the pandemic response was based on a 'tried and tested system that's been used many times in the past', noting that the military's experience in logistics had proved invaluable to the NHS and Department of Health and Social Care.[5] Over the next few months the army was often held up as an example of good practice in dealing with logistical issues. In a Downing Street press briefing in January 2021, for example, the then Prime Minister Boris Johnson said that the army had been drafted in to assist with the rollout of the vaccine, and that they would use 'battle preparation techniques'[6] to keep up the pace.

Two months later, the army media department published a fulsome account of its contribution to this national emergency. 'This year has been one like no other, in that the Army's response to COVID – known as Operation Rescript – has been such a big part of the day-to-day work of soldiers,' it ran, taking care to point out that it was the global nature of the emergency that allowed them to take time away from their traditional roles: 'As some training and overseas deployments were paused, soldiers turned their attention to the pandemic; the most challenging issue faced by the country for a generation'.[7] Stepping in to help 'wherever they were needed', troops had been engaged in a wide variety of activities, 'from testing whole cities, to delivering babies'. The report listed the logistical support provided for lorry drivers stranded at Dover as well as numerous contributions to emergency health-care teams in hospitals and testing centres.

By 2021, according to a report by the Ministry of Defence, approximately 34,000 servicemen and servicewomen had been deployed to support the UK pandemic response over the course of the previous two years.[8] But close scrutiny of these figures by DeclassifiedUK indicates that, although twenty thousand troops were placed on 'higher readiness' for Covid-19 relief efforts, only 150 were actually deployed to the NHS to drive oxygen tankers, and only 109 contributed to building the Nightingale hospital in East London.[9]

This four-thousand-bed facility at London's ExCel centre was one of seven emergency hospitals built by the army in England, starting in April 2020. Known collectively as Nightingale hospitals, they were set up with great fanfare to deal with a predicted surge of Covid-19 cases. The initiative was wound down a year later as they were 'largely not needed'. Many suspected that it was as much a PR exercise to show that the government was in control as a practical response to the crisis.[10] And as time went by it emerged that military recruitment ads were beginning to foreground the 'fight' against

Covid, suggesting that new recruits would be able to contribute meaningfully to pandemic efforts.[11]

Public opinion about the armed forces' contribution seemed less than convinced. In the run-up to Armed Forces Day 2021, SSAFA, one of the oldest charities to support the families of service personnel, published the results of a national survey showing that fewer than half of UK residents were aware of the role played by the armed forces in the fight against Covid-19, and less than a quarter admired the armed forces for their efforts. Citing support offered at Covid-19 testing facilities, in the creation of a PPE distribution network and in the vaccine rollout, SSAFA called on the public to thank the armed forces for the role they had played.[12]

The survey received scant attention in the mainstream press. The *Andover Advertiser* was one of very few regional media outlets to publish a story about it, which was unsurprising given that Andover was a military town, proud of its longstanding connection to the army.

Key workers

In Wiltshire, as elsewhere in the country, pandemic efforts were led by the NHS and local government. In Tidworth the main NHS GP practice asked for help from the local authority with the vaccination rollout. County councillors based around Tidworth and Ludgershall contacted the garrison, who initially proposed making available a disused military building in Bulford for drive-through vaccinations. In the end they settled on the Tidworth Leisure Centre, which we visited in Chapter 2. Patients entered through the front doors and left through the sports hall at the back, travelling on an electric buggy.

Non-military residents told us that they had seen soldiers working behind the wire and knew that some regiments were part of the Link scheme which helped transport people to hospital when they didn't have their own cars. Troops from Tidworth had also built an emergency mortuary in Salisbury and they had heard that some soldiers based locally had helped to build the Nightingale hospital in London. One resident told us, 'The military are jacked up for this sort of thing. You know, dealing with emergencies. They click their fingers and things happen. They don't have the usual bureaucracy. They aren't constrained.'[13]

This apparent lack of constraints was likely to cause problems for everyone else, as we saw in Chapter 4. Between 2018 and 2019 headteachers across Salisbury Plain had serious concerns about the impact of rebasing on pupil numbers, given the limited number of school places and the fact that schools needed at least 12 months' notice in order to plan resources for creating additional capacity. It became a significant problem that military officials were so difficult to pin down and engage in meaningful planning conversations. Despite claims of hyper-competence in logistics, the reality still seemed to be that the army made its own arrangements and everyone else had to fall in line.

This would have repercussions for service families during the pandemic. At a national level, a lack of clear guidance for military employees meant that the Army Families Federation, which, as we saw in Chapter 4, is an independent organisation representing the views and needs of army families to senior commanders and government, was left to field questions. This was no small task since many postings had been delayed, leading to problems relating to houses, school places and spouses' jobs. The organisation created new pages on its website addressing Covid-related questions in the absence of information provided by the authorities, particularly with regard to forthcoming or potential postings.

According to local councillors and military staff, however, the impact of the pandemic had not been too serious, thanks to the area's low population density. Mutual aid groups were set up by local citizens during the first lockdown in March, but these tended to lapse as time went on. Service children were considered to be members of 'key worker' families so were entitled to attend school, and, for many, life appeared to continue as normal, although at a somewhat slower pace. Local schools had to absorb the pressure to accommodate the children of military staff while keeping safety precautions in place.

As for the military themselves, a large proportion of the personnel based on Salisbury Plain were asked to work from home in order to avoid infection clusters in the garrisons. Quite what this work involved is unclear, but according to a former garrison commander this period of working from home left almost a quarter of the force suffering from depression and unfit for duty.[14]

Secret science

It is important not to overlook the day-to-day risks and fears that come with living in the shadow of a military base. An incoming head-teacher, arriving from a military school in Germany, was alarmed to discover that there were no security measures in place. In her previous post service children were categorised as being at risk from terrorist threats. She quickly arranged for gates to be installed to stop people cutting through the school grounds on their way to the shops.

There is also more to say about the extent to which all inhabitants of the base are, or should be, considered to be at risk, especially those who live outside the high security fences. Many service families living locally complained of feeling vulnerable in the absence of support. In one example a wife of an army officer stationed in Tidworth told us that, following a traumatic experience which fortunately turned out to be a false alarm, her family had decided to move into normal housing because they felt too insecure living on an army patch. But this level of insecurity often extended to non-military residents as well.

Prior to its closure in March 2020 when the first Covid lockdown began, the shared facilities in Tidworth Leisure Centre would be bustling with users in and out of uniform from Monday morning to Friday lunchtime. At that point the place would empty out as many single soldiers would either go to their families or venture elsewhere to enjoy the weekend. As we saw in Chapter 2, staff would often joke that, if World War Three broke out on a Friday afternoon, the army would be found missing in action.

While this casual fatalism about living next to a hive of war preparation was fairly typical in Tidworth, at times it seemed that residents were constantly negotiating a sense of danger fed by rumours and hearsay. Walkers, for example, were often warned to stay away from well-known paths, despite there being no evidence of anything suspicious.[15] But while there were undoubtedly very real dangers arising from the army presence – including the fires that we saw in the last chapter – geopolitical tensions emanating far beyond the Plain could also reverberate nearer home.

In March 2018 the attempted poisoning of Sergei Skripal and his daughter Yulia in the nearby city of Salisbury put Wiltshire on the world map in a new way. The use of the nerve agent Novichok as a lethal weapon made international headlines, but many local people were all too aware that the toxic substance was also being produced by scientists at Porton Down, the Defence Science and Technology Laboratory located five miles outside Salisbury. A year later a Tidworth resident tried to explain how she felt when she first heard the news:

> it did make me giggle the way they just looked at little Salisbury. It's like, you have no idea what's here. Porton is down the road, Porton is where that stuff is made, and I know people that work there, so people just may think Salisbury Plain is just this little pinprick on the map, it's not, there is loads here, absolutely loads.

Her comment suggested that living near military facilities can induce feelings of paranoia as well as security. In her view 'they' would want to protect the area because of the numbers of personnel stationed there. This made her feel safe because, 'you know, they're young, fit and healthy men and women'. But still, the risks to ordinary people felt very tangible in this part of the world. 'You're either going to get saved or you're going to get blown up,' she went on. 'You know there's not going to be any half measures, it's either you're a target or you're very, very safe.'

For those with longer memories, the site at Porton Down had acquired an ominous reputation due to the history of chemical and biological weapons research involving humans as well as animals. In May 1953 six volunteers, all with a military background, took part in a trial at Porton Down involving the nerve agent Sarin. One man, Ronald Maddison, suffered a terrible death in 'the most severe case of nerve gas poisoning ever recorded in the western world'.[16] In 2008, after several inconclusive investigations and inquests, the Ministry of Defence announced that it would award £3 million in compensation to a total of 360 veterans who had suffered from chemical weapons tests at some point during the previous fifty years.[17]

The fact that it took so long to establish the truth about this military 'secret science' in the Cold War era was one reason why the name 'Porton Down' continues to evoke suspicion. In 2016, a hundred years after the lab was founded to carry out research into the types of chemical warfare being used in the trenches, it was obliged to publish an article entitled 'The Truth about Porton Down: Answering the Myths and Misconceptions'.[18] And several months after the Salisbury attack the BBC journalist Frank Gardner was permitted to write a report about the UK's 'top secret facility', possibly in recognition of public concern about the lab's fortuitous proximity to the scene of the crime, and the speed with which the poison was identified.[19]

Although Britain ended its offensive chemical and biological weapons programmes in the 1950s, he wrote, 'and the UK had ratified the Chemical Weapons Convention, which obliges all 192 members to destroy their chemical weapons stockpiles, Porton Down does produce small amounts for research 'to help develop effective medical counter-measures and to test systems'.

After a guided tour of the facilities, which covered various topics from deadly pathogens to animal testing, staff safety and potential security risks, Gardner ended his attempt to sound reassuring with this not exactly convincing observation, 'Given world events, we probably haven't heard the last of Porton Down. Whether it's Novichok nerve gas, bubonic plague or microbial-resistant bugs, this secretive Wiltshire base is likely to remain Britain's frontline defence against them for the foreseeable future.'

Needless to say, Porton Down would acquire a whole new significance with the arrival of the coronavirus the following year. Today the newly established Vaccine Development and Evaluation Centre, 'hastily constructed as part of the emergency response to Covid' and now run by UK Health Security Agency, is dedicated to finding protection from new forms of deadly pathogens before they can spread.[20] But there is no doubt that the history of experimentation at Porton Down, combined with high security levels and the occasional leak, has led to intense scepticism about vaccines which continue to be seen by significant numbers of people as part of a government plot to poison, control or otherwise harm a trusting population.[21]

Open prison camp

The creation of 'super garrisons', in the heat of two unpopular wars, was a logistical attempt to consolidate resources, but this has also resulted in selling off land that was surplus to requirements, with profound consequences for local communities, as we saw in Chapter 6. One result was that some disused military bases, predominantly located in rural areas, have been commandeered by the Home Office for housing and containing asylum seekers, often fleeing from the aftermath of wars in which the UK government has been involved. Although the political repercussions of this strategy need to be explored more fully elsewhere, it is worth emphasising that the development opens up a new dimension of the 'khaki countryside'.

Since 2020 there have been several attempts to place hundreds of mostly male asylum seekers in former barracks or temporary buildings on land owned by the Ministry of Defence near rural communities. One proposal centred on the village of Barton Stacey, situated just off the A303 north of Andover, would have housed five hundred men in temporary cabins on a site without electricity or running water. The nearest shop was a service station which was accessible only by foot along the busy dual carriageway. This plan was dropped, but in September 2020 Napier barracks in Folkestone was used to house four hundred migrants in temporary cabins.[22] After a fire broke out the following year, and the overcrowded conditions caused a mass outbreak of Covid, six inmates brought a case against the government; the High Court ruled that it was unlawful to house migrants in a 'squalid' building.[23]

Despite this setback the Home Office has continued to explore the use of disused bases for accommodating unprocessed asylum seekers, often against the wishes of MPs in whose constituencies the sites are located. RAF Wethersfield, a former military airbase near Braintree in Essex, was in the constituency of the then Home Secretary, James Cleverly. Even he remarked, in a social media post, that the site was not 'appropriate'.[24] The facility is ringed by security fences and monitored round the clock by on-site security guards and CCTV. There are no pavements on the roads around the site and no public transport.

In 2023 a report by the Helen Bamber Foundation and the Humans for Rights Network called for Wethersfield – which held 508 men from Afghanistan, Iran and Eritrea, many of whom were survivors of torture and trafficking and had severe mental health problems – to be closed down immediately. The site was described as a large 'open-prison camp' that had caused irreparable and profound harm to residents in the five months since it had opened.[25]

The decision to use dilapidated barracks and airfields as refugee camps was not exactly unprecedented but in the current context it represented a political solution designed to secure popular support.[26] But the same government was less forthcoming about adapting MoD resources for its unlawful plan to deport refugees to Rwanda. In 2022 the plane that was to have taken the first batch of migrants to Kigali

9.2 Protestors at the perimeter of MoD Boscombe Down where a Boeing 767 aircraft was waiting to take asylum seekers to Rwanda, 14 June 2022.

was sitting on the runway at Boscombe Down, just a few miles from Tidworth.[27]

As the government continued to fight legal challenges to the scheme, before it was scrapped by the incoming Labour government in July 2024, it emerged that no civil airline was willing to risk its reputation by association.[28] As a result Boscombe Down, the RAF airfield currently managed by the defence technology company QinetiQ in partnership with the Ministry of Defence, remained the mostly likely departure point. This example illustrates the more furtive ways in which military resources can be commandeered for political expediency.

Endless war

It would be a mistake to assume that the pandemic led to any sort of concrete reorientation in the UK military's security strategy, despite the publicity surrounding military contributions to the pandemic. Published in March 2021, the UK government's next defence review was largely focused on traditional military activities, with a particular emphasis on cybersecurity and the need to boost the UK's nuclear arsenal. Military spending was to be increased by £4 billion a year for the next four years, while foreign aid would be cut. In a review over one hundred pages long, only one and a half pages were devoted to future 'health resilience'.[29]

These regular governmental reviews can make disturbing reading, not least because each new administration is determined to establish that, whatever new threat emerges, the UK will be a world leader in the response to it. But while it is important to be ready to challenge the ever-increasing investment in lethal weaponry including nuclear armaments, it is equally necessary to look closer to home in order to understand what lies behind that commitment to war as a mode of international politics. As this book has tried to show, it is in one of the most rural parts of the country that we might learn at close hand what it means to try to integrate a professional military workforce into the surrounding community, on its own terms.

Put simply, we argue that the county of Wiltshire, which signed up to the Military Civilian Integration Partnership in 2006, provides an ideal locus for investigating the contractual relationship between soldiers and society in the present. One of our first findings was that the Ministry of Defence, which oversees that relationship, remains as intransigent and dismissive of independent scrutiny as ever. Yet close attention to everyday life in the relatively mixed environment of the Salisbury Plain 'super garrison' offered many chances to observe the impact of reforms promised as a result of political interventions like the Armed Forces Covenant, conceived against the backdrop of the public's huge unease about the wars being fought in its name.[30]

At the same time the extraordinary ecological and historical nature of Salisbury Plain provided numerous opportunities to examine the military's commitment to issues of sustainability, public rights of way, safeguarding heritage and protecting rare habitats. Our study is intended as an encouragement to others who might otherwise be deterred by the difficulty of accessing land owned by the Ministry of Defence or indeed making contact with the diverse communities who live on or next to military bases anywhere in the UK.

To conclude, this book has sought to establish two fundamental points: first, that every phase of war blurs the neat dichotomy between civilian and military, even as it produces new categories of wounded, displaced and traumatised people as a result; and, second, that the status and conditions of military labour should be a matter of concern to all citizens whose taxes, votes, values, opinions and feelings of security and danger contribute to ideas about what can or cannot be addressed by the use of lethal violence, sanctioned and organised by the state.

The whole project has been planned, researched and written in the spirit of William Wordsworth, whose poetic genius was inspired by the wild and lawless expanse of Salisbury Plain. Penned in the wake of the French Revolution, perhaps anticipating the carnage of the Napoleonic wars, his words are still echoed by the legendary wind that moans over the grasslands: 'Oh! what can war but endless war still breed?'[31]

Figures

Acknowledgements

This book has been a long time coming and there are many people to thank, not least our own families and friends who encouraged us to keep going. Cynthia Enloe first planted the seed in 2008, providing encouragement and inspiration over many years. We are also indebted to Catherine Lutz and Rachel Woodward for their work and for helping us secure funding for the project at critical times. Paul Dixon has been an important interlocutor from the very start. We would like to acknowledge support from the Leverhulme Trust which allowed us to begin the fieldwork in 2018 and continue into the pandemic.

Thanks to Matthew Flintham, Melanie Friend and Patrick Wright for ongoing conversations on the military-pastoral and to Paul Gilroy for kestrel-eyed research skills. Colin Leys provided prompt and exacting editing advice at the time when it mattered, proving an indispensable reader. Lucia Trimbur and Luke de Noronha guided us through the ethics of collective writing. We are grateful to the MUP production team, especially John Banks and Don Shewan.

Ross McGarry provided expert academic advice as a reviewer. Tariq Jazeel, Adam Elliot-Cooper, Maren Elfert, Tom Sykes, Francis Dodsworth and Egle Rindzeviciute provided valuable opportunities to present the research at UCL, Warwick University, QMUL, KCL, Portsmouth University and Kingston University and Harriet Gray, Marsha Henry and Alex Hyde shared early insights at the Gender Studies Dept, LSE. Anthony Barnett and the late, much-missed Rosemary Bechler at openDemocracy provided space to explore contemporary militarisation. Thanks to Joe Glenton, Rhianna Louise and Emma Sangster at Forces Watch and Jinsella at Demilitarise Education for the podcasts. In fact there are many dedicated people whose research and expertise have provided an indispensable collective resource: not least DeclassifiedUK, Action on Armed Violence, Scientists for Global Responsibility and the Conflict and Environment Observatory. Mitra would like to thank Dhakal Lohani and Phauda Limbu for their help with research in Tidworth, and David Gellner and Dhan Bahadur Sarki for support of all kinds during the entire period of his research.

This project would not have been possible without the initial support of Sir Freddie Viggers and Brigadier (Rtd) Mark Abraham, who bear the responsibility for opening the door, although not for this particular outcome. We are also grateful to Wiltshire County councillors serving the communities in Tidworth, Ludgershall and Larkhill. We owe particular thanks to Cllr Chris Williams, Mike Giles, Tony Pickernell and Lt Col Jamie Balls MBE and his predecessor, the late Lt Col Richard Carman, for their time and patience.

We have made efforts to protect the identity of interviewees on principle, although we acknowledge that some individuals may remain identifiable. With the exception of some local public figures, all names have been changed. However, we are grateful to all of those who took the time to speak to us, including: Guy Benson, Richard Brooks, Lt Col R. S. Clayton, Bill Dowling, Sally Hunter, Major Nigel Lewis, Rick Kavanagh, Kevin Ladner, Richard Osgood, Allan Thomson, Kate Viggers, Bruce Waight and Stephen West. We would also like to acknowledge the helpful steers we received from Carole Rudd, Katherine Houlston and Emma Long (Army Families Federation) and Matt Stevens (Hawk Conservancy).

Thanks to John Chandler, Martin Curtis and the Imberbus Team for allowing us to use for extra material and images, and to Francis Ware for last-minute image editing.

Notes

Introduction

1 Tom Fort, *The A303: Highway to the Sun* (London: Simon & Schuster, 2019).
2 Charlotte Higgins, 'The Battle for the Future of Stonehenge.' *Guardian*, 8 February 2019.
3 Continual Operational Readiness: 3rd (United Kingdom) Division. The Iron Division (2023). Available from: https://lordslibrary.parliament.uk/ warfighting-capability-of-the-british-army-3rd-uk-division/ (accessed 16 August 2024).
4 Guy Shrubsole, 'Defence of the Realm: The Ministry of Defence Land Holdings' (16 April 2016). https://whoownsengland.org/2016/08/14/mod-land/ (accessed 16 August 2024). The defence estate includes 16 major training areas, as well as more than a hundred smaller sites with ranges and camps for training purposes. In 2023 the Defence Infrastructure Organisation awarded Landmarc a new contract, worth £560 million, to manage the entire UK military training estate. The contractor, which had been working for the Organisationsince 2003, is a joint venture of Mitie, the UK's leading facilities management and professional services company, and Amentum, a leading provider of global mission services to the US Government.
5 Rachel Woodward, 'From Military Geography to Militarism's Geographies: Disciplinary Eengagements with the Geographies of Militarism and Military Activities.' *Progress in Human Geography*, 29:6 (2005), pp. 718–740.
6 Rachel Woodward, *Military Geographies* (Oxford: Blackwell, 2004), pp. 3–4.
7 Peter Burt and Dave Webb, *For Heaven's Sake: Examining the UK's Militarisation of Space* (Drone Wars and CND, 2022). Available from: https://cnduk.org/resources/for-heavens-sake-examining-the-uks-militarisa tion-of-space/ (accessed 16 August 2024).
8 Some biographical details have been disaggregated from the information supplied by research participants. The book also makes general reference to unanticipated encounters recorded during the research, where it was

impractical for the researcher to announce their presence and ask people to sign consent forms. Jon Swain and Brendan King, 'Using Informal Conversations in Qualitative Research.' *International Journal of Qualitative Methods*, 21 (2022), pp. 1–10.

9 Where our presence did not disturb the natural flow of life, and where we judged the potential harm to be limited, this allowed us to convey the spirit and mood of what was said and observed, and depict a naturalistic setting with greater verisimilitude. For more information about these ethical and methodological debates see A.S.J. Cree (ed.), *Creative Methods in Military Studies* (London: Rowman & Littlefield Publishers, 2023).

10 Jessica Murray, 'British Army Would Exhaust Capabilities after Two Months of War, MPs Told.' *Guardian*, 4 February 2024.

11 Jason Hughes, 'Wiltshire Hosts the MoD's First Long Range Laser Energy Weapon Trial.' *Wiltshire Times*, 20 November 2022.

12 Tarak Barkawi, among others, has argued that this is a Eurocentric notion that simply elides the history of imperial wars, invasions and occupations. T. Barkawi, 'Decolonising War.' *European Journal of International Security*, 1:2 (2022), pp. 199–214. https://doi.org/10.1017/eis.2016.7.

13 Ministry of Defence, *Defence in a Competitive Age*, HMSO CP411, March 2021, p. 9. Available from https://assets.publishing.service.gov.uk/media/6063061e8fa8f55b6ad297d0/CP411_-Defence_Command_Plan.pdf.

14 Tony Diver, 'US to Station Nuclear Weapons in UK to Counter Threat from Russia.' *Telegraph*, 26 January 2024.

Dan Sabbagh, 'Global Defence Spending Rises 9% to Record $2.2tn.' *Guardian*, 13 February 2024.

Chapter 1

1 Jonathan Meades, 'Blighted Plain.' *London Review of Books*, 44:1 (6 January 2022).

2 Joanne Moore, 'Salisbury Plain Firing Ranges Are "Death Traps" Says Union.' *Gazette and Herald*, 19 April 2016.

3 The National Archives, Military Lands Act 1892, Legislation.gov.uk. Available from: https://www.legislation.gov.uk/ukpga/1892/43/pdfs/ukpga_1892 0043_en.pdf (accessed 16 February 2024).

4 N.D.G. James, *Plain Soldiering* (Salisbury: The Hobnob Press, 1987), p. 9.

5 For similarly uncritical account by a military historian see Arthur Tucker. 'Army and Society in England 1870–1900: A Reassessment of the Cardwell Reforms.' *Journal of British Studies*, 2:2 (May 1963), pp. 110–141.

6 Land Use Consultants, *Wiltshire Landscape Character Assessment: FINAL REPORT*. Prepared on behalf of Wiltshire County Council by Land Use Consultants, December 2004, p. 54; James, *Plain Soldiering*, pp. 9–17.

7 James, *Plain Soldiering*, p. 17.

8 Lieutenant Colonel Richard Clayton, (Retired), 'Wiltshire: Larkhill and Westdown.' *Sanctuary*, 46 (2017), p. 87. This article is based on a comprehensive GIS survey of Salisbury Plain from 1733 onwards completed by Tony Rowlands.

9 James, *Plain Soldiering*, pp. 5–6. The Wiltshire horned sheep had no hair on their underbellies because the chalk was warm and dry.

10 A.G. Bradley, *Round about Wiltshire* (1907), p. 241, cited in James, *Plain Soldiering*, p. 100.

11 Ella Noyes, *Salisbury Plain, Its Stones, Cathedral, Villages and Folk* (London: J.M. Dent, 1913), pp. vii–viii.

12 Carolyn Hart, 'The Beekeeper Keeping Britain's Honey Industry Abuzz.' *Telegraph*, 5 April 2020.

13 The Royal Geographical Society (with the Institute of British Geographers), 'Military Environmentalism: Discover Prehistoric Sites and Rare Species Preserved on Salisbury Plain', *Discovering Britain* (n.p.: Royal Geographical Society (with the Institute of British Geographers), 2012), p. 4.

14 Wiltshire Conservation Team, *Salisbury Plain SSSI Integrated Site Assessment 2014–15* (York: Natural England, 2016), p. 1.

15 BBC News, 'Army to Build 'Afghan Compound' on Salisbury Plain', 21 January 2012.

16 BBC News, 'Fake Refugee Camp Built on Salisbury Plain to Train Troops', 28 October 2016.

17 Joshua Truksa, 'Annual Bus Service Offers Glimpse at Evacuated Village.' *Salisbury Journal*, 22 August 2023.

18 Monica M. Hutchings, *The Special Smile* (London: Hodder & Stoughton, 1951), pp. 107–115.

19 Ibid.

20 Marianna Dudley, 'A Fairy (Shrimp) Tale of Military Environmentalism: The "Greening" of Salisbury Plain.' In Chris Pearson, Peter Coates and Tim Cole (eds), *Militarized Landscapes: From Gettysburg to Salisbury Plain* (London: Continuum, 2010), pp. 135–150.

21 Peter Coates, Tim Cole, Marianna Dudley and Chris Pearson, 'Defending Nation, Defending Nature? Militarized Landscapes and Military Environmentalism in Britain, France and the United States.' *Environmental History*, 16:3 (July 2011), pp. 458, 467.

22 Ibid., p. 459.

23 Rachel Woodward first used the term in 2001, citing Andrew Ross in *The Ecologist*, 26 (1996), pp. 22–24. Woodward, 'Khaki Conservation: An Examination of Military Environmentalist Discourses in the British Army.' *Journal of Rural Studies*, 17:2 (April 2001), pp. 201–217. For an overview of these debates see Chris Pearson, 'Researching Militarized Landscapes: A Literature Review on War and the Militarization of the Environment.' *Landscape Research*, 37:1 (February 2012), pp. 115–133.

24 This was largely as a response to the Dorset-based Tyneham Action Group and Friends of Tyneham which argued that the landscape should be 'managed for the public good by experienced organisations' such as the National Trust or Countryside Commission. Coates et al., 'Defending Nation?', pp. 467–469.

25 Nikolaus Pevsner, *The Buildings of England: Wiltshire* (1963), quoted in Meades, 'Blighted Plain'.

26 Rex Sawyer, *Little Imber on the Down: Salisbury Plain's Ghost Village* (Salisbury: Hobnob Press, 2001). The following account is taken from Sawyer's book.
27 Ibid., pp. 129–130.
28 Coates et al., 'Defending Nation?', p. 460.
29 Patrick Wright, *The Village that Died for England* (London: Repeater Books, 2022), p. 414.
30 George Richard Hodges Nugent, the son of a colonel and great devotee of the countryside, began his career in the army. His previous roles included service in the National Farmers Union and the Ministry of Agriculture, as well as the chairmanship of the Thames Conservancy Board. See Coates, 'Defending Nation?', n. 12, p. 483.
31 Ibid., p. 469; Royal Geographical Society, 'Military Environmentalism', p. 22.
32 Dudley, 'A Fairy (Shrimp) Tale', p. 141.
33 Wright, *The Village*, pp. 506–507.
34 *Sanctuary* magazine is the Ministry of Defence's annual sustainability publication, which has been showcasing conservation activities across the defence estate for over 45 years. https://www.gov.uk/government/publica tions/sanctuary (accessed 5 May 2023).
35 *Sanctuary*, 46 (2017).
36 Ibid.
37 After being posted to Warminster in the early 1980s, Major Nigel Lewis (Retired), a prominent volunteer ornithologist, joined the HQ Director of Infantry IMBER Conservation Group, and continued his lifelong project of erecting and monitoring nesting boxes for owls and other raptors across areas of Salisbury Plain.
38 According to the QinetiQ website, 'Team Pegasus will work in partnership with the MoD for a 10-year period on the transformation project – SOCIETAS – providing a specialist mission data and electronic warfare skills solution alongside training and IT support. The project will accelerate the production of mission data, enabling the UK's military platforms and personnel to be better protected in a rapidly changing threat landscape and enhancing the performance of its advanced military systems. The partnership will also contribute to the UK's export agenda by providing our allies with access to world-class mission data in support of UK Defence sales, enhancing UK Prosperity.' www.qinetiq.com/en-gb/news/team-pegasus-awarded-80m-mis sion-data-partnership-contract-by-mod (accessed 5 May 2023).
39 *Sanctuary*, 50 (2021).
40 Adrian Parr, *Hijacking Sustainability* (Cambridge, MA: MIT Press, 2009), p. 80. See also 'If the world's militaries were a country, this figure would mean they have the fourth largest national carbon footprint in the world'. Stuart Parkinson and Linsey Cottrell, 'Estimating the Military's Global Greenhouse Gas Emissions'. Scientists for Global Responsibility and the Conflict and Environment Observatory, November 2022. https://ceobs.org/wp-content/uploads/2022/11/SGR-CEOBS_Estimating_Global_MIlitary_G HG_Emissions.pdf (accessed 28 February 2024).

41 Parr, *Hijacking Sustainability*.

42 James, *Plain Soldiering*, p. 165.

43 Ibid., p. 127.

44 Ibid., p. 133.

45 Ibid., p. 92.

46 In 1914 there was a prison camp for interned aliens in Bulford as well. Ibid., p. 114.

47 Ibid., pp. 239–240. Lowa is an Indian village half-way between Lucknow and Allahabad.

48 James, *Plain Soldiering*, p. 37.

49 Vron Ware, *Military Migrants: Fighting for YOUR Country* (Basingstoke: Palgrave, 2012), pp. 282–283.

Chapter 2

1 Cynthia Enloe, *Bananas, Beaches, and Bases: Making Feminist Sense of International Politics* (Oakland, CA: University of California Press, 1990), p. 132.

2 Zoë H. Wool, 'Critical Military Studies, Queer Theory, and the Possibilities of Critique: The Case of Suicide and Family Caregiving in the US military.' *Critical Military Studies*, 1:1 (2014), p. 2. http://dx.doi.org/10.1080/2333748 6.2014.964600.

3 Rachel Woodward, 'From Military Geography to Militarism's Geographies: Disciplinary Engagements with the Geographies of Militarism and Military Activities.' *Progress in Human Geography*, 29:6 (2005), pp. 718–740.

4 The Fan Dance challenge, in particular, is very popular with people thinking of joining, or already employed by, the armed forces. It consists of a gruelling 24 km march through the exposed terrain of the Brecon Beacons.

5 X-Forces Enterprise, 'From Barracks to Bistro: Meet the Army Veteran's Spouse at the Helm of a Thriving Family Business.'

6 Catherine Lutz, *Homefront: A Military City and the American Twentieth Century* (Boston, MA: Beacon Press, 2001). See pp. 122–124 for a fuller discussion of this concept in the context of the USA.

7 See this site for update of long-running campaign for parity in pensions: https://gurkhasatyagraha.org (accessed 27 April 2023).

8 Age UK, *The Challenges of Rural Living for Older People*, 22 July 2013. https://editorial.ageuk.org.uk/latest-press/archive/the-challenges-of-rural-living-for-older-people/ (accessed 27 August 2024).

9 Tom Sables, 'How Religious Are Our Armed Forces?' Forces.net, 16 December 2018.

10 Lieutenant Colonel L. T. Quinn, '"No Religion": The Army's Inclusivity Blind-Spot', May 2016. www.secularism.org.uk/uploads/laurence-quinn-red-book.pdf?v=1635956048 (accessed 27 February 2024). See also UK Armed Forces Biannual Diversity Statistics 2021. www.gov.uk/govern ment/statistics/uk-armed-forces-biannual-diversity-statistics-october-2021 (accessed 16 July 2023).

11 Chris Hughes, 'Christianity Has No Place in the British Army Claims Senior Military Officer', *Mirror*, 3 December 2014.
12 N.D.G. James, *Plain Soldiering* (Salisbury: The Hobnob Press, 1987), pp. 52–53.
13 Ibid.
14 Council for Christian Unity, 'National Census 2001 and 2011: Changes in the Ethnic Diversity of the Christian Population in England' (Archbishops' Council of the Church of England, 2014). Available from: www.churchofe ngland.org/sites/default/files/2017-10/north_east.pdf (accessed 25 August 2024).
15 Mahendra Lawoti and Susan I. Hangen, *Nationalism and Ethnic Conflict in Nepal: Identities and Mobilisation since 1990* (London: Routledge, 2013).
16 Mitra Pariyar, 'Caste, Military, Migration: Nepali Gurkha Communities in Britain.' *Ethnicities* (2019). https://doi.org/10.1177/1468796819890138.

Chapter 3

1 Rebecca Hudson, 'Army Management Firm Hits Back at Claims Barracks "Not Fit For Animals" after Leaked Fire Safety Report.' *Salisbury Journal*, 4 January 2019.
2 Tom Newton Dunn, 'Fury as MoD Cover-Up Is Exposed, Revealing Thousands of Soldiers Are Living in Grenfell-Style Fire Traps, Watchdog Says.' *Scottish Sun*, 31 December 2018.
3 Jonathan Meades, 'Blighted Plain.' *London Review of Books*, 44:1 (6 January 2022).
4 Nicholas A. Phelps, *An Anatomy of Sprawl: Planning and Politics in Britain* (London: Routledge, 2012), p. 2.
5 'Reasons why Andover Hampshire Is Such a Great Place to Live.' *Andover Advertiser*, 1 December 2021.
6 N.D.G. James, *Plain Soldiering* (Salisbury: The Hobnob Press, 1987), pp. 47–48.
7 Cynthia Enloe, *Maneuvers: The International Politics of Militarizing Women's Lives* (London: University of California Press, 2000), p. 159.
8 See, for example, the history of SSAFA, the Armed Forces charity that provides professional and voluntary help for families in every garrison, including at the Beeches Family Centre in Bulford. It was founded by Sir James Gildea, a British Army Militia officer who raised money for the families of British soldiers killed in the Zulu War of 1879 and the Second Afghan War of 1880.
9 The taxi office by Andover station had a hand-drawn map pinned to the wall. No GPS was able to keep up with the rapid construction of new streets and houses.
10 Wiltshire Council, *Army Basing Briefing for the Amesbury, Pewsey, Tidworth and Warminster Area Boards* –(September 2015). https://cms.wiltshire.gov.uk/documents/s94075/Army%20Re-basing.pdf.
11 Danielle Sheridan, 'Army Wives Accuse MoD of "Utter Betrayal" over New Military Accommodation Plan.' *Telegraph*, 23 February 2024.

12 Harry Cole, 'Shot Down: Plans to Allocate Military Housing Based on Family Size Rather than Rank Paused in "Welcome Victory for Common Sense".' *Sun*, 27 February 2024.

13 Steve Dancey, 'Town Status Gets the Nod.' *Andover Advertiser*, 19 May 2008.

14 T.S. Crawford, *Wiltshire and the Great War: Training the Empire's Soldiers* (Marlborough: The Crowood Press, 2012), pp. 112–113.

15 The first military railway, for example, was constructed by civilian engineers in the Crimea in 1854–55 'at a time when Government and military organisation for running the war had completely broken down'. Brian Cooke, *The Grand Crimean Central Railway: The Railway that Won a War* (Knutsford: Cavalier House, 1990).

16 Winifred Dixon, *A History of Ludgershall* (Ludgershall: Highfield House Trust, 1994), pp. 97–100.

17 James, *Plain Soldiering*, p. 208.

18 The Army Families Federation advised people that they needed to inform themselves about the rules and costs associated with owning a car and consider whether it was realistic for them.

19 Martina Moscariello, 'More than 400 New Homes Set to Be Built on Former Ministry of Defence Site in Ludgershall.' *Salisbury Journal*, 4 May 2020.

20 See Paul Dixon, *Warrior Nation: War, Militarisation and British Democracy*. Forces Watch, 2018, https://archive.ph/e01wh (accessed 24 February 2024); and Vron Ware, 'Lives on the Line.' *Soundings*, 45 (summer 2010).

21 Ministry of Defence, 'The Government's Response to the Report of Inquiry into National Recognition of Our Armed Forces.' Presented to Parliament on behalf of the Secretary of State for Defence by the Minister of State for the Armed Forces (2008), p. 2. Available from: https://assets.publishing.service.gov.uk/media/5a795f59ed915d07d35b4f3b/govt_response_recogniti on_armed_forces.pdf (accessed 24 February 2024).

Chapter 4

1 See, for example, Hew Strachan, 'The British Army, 1815–1856; Recent Writing Reviewed.' *Journal of the Society for Army Historical Research*, 63:254 (summer 1985), pp. 68–79; Albert V. Tucker, 'Army and Society in England 1870–1900: A Reassessment of the Cardwell Reforms.' *Journal of British Studies*, 2:2 (May 1963), pp. 110–141.

2 Wiltshire Council, *Military Presence and Economic Significance in the South West Region* (Devizes, March 2009).

3 Ministry of Defence, 'The Defence Estate Development Plan', 3 July 2009 (DEDP 09: DE Est Dev 3–2–1–5). This document outlines the rationale for and requirements of a 'super garrison'. 'As a guide, a SG should consist of a hub of sufficient magnitude (ideally over 5000 service personnel) to attract significant MOD and local authority investment and a number of satellite sites within easy travelling distance', p. 5.

4 Wiltshire Council, *Military Population in Wiltshire and the SW Region* (Devizes, October 2012), p. 8, figure 5.

5 Wiltshire Council, *Provision of Services to Wiltshire's Military Communities* (Devizes, June 2011), p. v.
   'A number of agencies working with service families have noted an increase in relationship breakdown related to the current high levels of military deployment, which in some cases leads to spouses requiring support to secure housing and manage financially. Relate mid Wiltshire have reported in the course of this study that they would be keen to offer pre- and post-deployment support to families to help them adjust to the pressures of separation and being reunited to try to address this issue.'

6 Wiltshire Council, *Deprivation in Wiltshire: Indices of Deprivation 2010* (Devizes, June 2011).

7 Gary Cleland, 'MoD Homes "Scandal" as 400,000 Call Helpline.' *Telegraph*, 15 October 2007.

8 Roland Batten, 'Army Housing Worst in UK.' *Salisbury Journal*, 23 September 2007.

9 Ibid. See also BBC News, 'Forces Minister Opens Army Homes', 26 June 2008.

10 BBC News, 'Army Troop Relocations Announced by Ministry of Defence', 10 November 2011.

11 Ibid.

12 Ministry of Defence, 'New Employment Model', gov.uk, 12 December 2012. Available from: www.gov.uk/guidance/new-employment-model (accessed 27 February 2024).

13 Danielle Sheridan 'Unmarried Couples Entitled to Service Accommodation in Armed Forces Housing Shake-Up.' *Telegraph*, 19 September 2023.

14 Danielle Sheridan, 'Army Wives Accuse MoD of "Utter Betrayal" over New Military Accommodation Plan.' *Telegraph*, 23 February 2024. www.telegraph.co.uk/news/2024/02/23/army-wives-utter-betrayal-military-housing-ministry-defence/ (accessed 24 February 2024).

15 Daniel Boffey, 'MoD Apologises over "Unacceptable" Standard of Army Homes.' *Guardian*, 3 October 2022. See also Julian Perreira, 'New Year, New Housing Misery for Military Families Living in Mouldy Homes.' Forces.Net, 4 January 2023.

16 Army Family Federation. 'Housing Success for Army Families', *Army&You*, 11 January 2019. See also *Military Families and Transition* (London: The Centre for Social Justice, 2016). www.centreforsocialjustice.org.uk/wp-content/uploads/2016/05/MILITARY-FAMILIES.pdf (accessed 26 August 2024).

17 According to Defence Infrastructure Organisation Army Basing Project Manager Andy Corcoran. See 'Saxon Cemetery Discovered at Bulford, Wiltshire.' Archaeology News Network (2016), https://archaeology.org/news/2016/04/15/160415-anglo-saxon-cemetery/ (accessed 27 February 2024).

18 Aspire Defence, 'Work Begins on the New Medical and Dental Centre for Larkhill', 18 July 2018.

19 Ministry of Defence, 'Guidance: Service Pupil Freedom: What You Need to Know', 19 May 2023. Available from: https://www.gov.uk/government/

publications/the-service-pupil-premium/service-pupil-premium-what-you-n
eed-to-know. Service children also have access to subsidised private school
education in boarding schools, a benefit that is often taken up at secondary
school level when stability and continuity are so important to good educational attainment. Fees are partially paid for by the Ministry of Defence,
funded through public money.

20 Wiltshire Council, 'Military Population', p. 19.

21 M. Rodrigues, A.K. Osborne, D. Johnson and M.D. Kiernan, 'The
Exploration of the Dispersal of British Military Families in England
Following the Strategic Defence and Security Review 2010.' PLoS ONE,
15 (9) (2020). e0238508.https://doi.org/10.1371/journal.pone.0238508. G.
Huxford, '"School Is Everywhere"? British Military Children, "Turbulence"
and the Meanings of Post-War Mobility.' History of Education (Tavistock),
51:5 (2022), pp. 710–731; K.M.T. De Pedro, et al. Avi Astor, R. Benbishty
and J. N. Estrada, 'The Children of Military Service Members: Challenges,
Supports, and Future Educational Research.' Review of Educational
Research, 81:4 (2011), pp. 566–618.

22 See for example, the support that the charity Little Troopers provides
regarding the impact upon service children of frequent house moves and
periods of separation from serving parents due to training or deployment.

Chapter 5

1 Hilary Callan and Shirley Ardener (eds), The Incorporated Wife (London:
Croom Helm, 1984).

2 The late nineteenth-century decision to allow soldiers to marry and bring
wives with them on postings was an important part of the way in which
Britain sought to manage the transmission of venereal diseases between soldiers and sex workers, particularly in the colonial context. Antony Beevor,
Inside the British Army (London: Corgi Books, 1990), p. 59.

3 Cynthia Enloe, Maneuvers: The International Politics of Militarizing
Women's Lives (London: University of California Press, 2000), p. 159.

4 Vron Ware, 'Thin Ice: Postcoloniality and Sexuality in the Politics of
Citizenship and Military Service.' In Sandra Ponzanesi (ed.), Gender,
Globalisation and Violence: Postcolonial Conflict Zones (London:
Routledge, 2014), pp. 46–63.

5 Further funding has been supplied by the EU (the European Agricultural Fund
for Rural Development) and DEFRA. https://archive.ph/E6mar (accessed
27 February 2024).

6 The Flatcap Story: www.flatcapcoffee.com/ (accessed 23 February 2024).

7 Lucy Fisher, 'Worrying Armed Forces Exodus Triggers Inquiry.' The Times,
5 February 2019.

8 According to the website Payscale, the average salary in Andover in 2020
was £27,000 a year, in Salisbury £26,000 and in Tidworth £25,000 These
figures are derived from payscale.com and check.a.salary.co.uk.

9 BBC News, 'Defence Review to See Dozens Of Sites Close', 7 November
2016. 'In addition to the sale of 35 MoD sites that had previously been

announced. A further eight sites in Scotland, including the Redford Cavalry and Infantry Barracks in Edinburgh, and Fort George, near Ardersier.'

10 Ibid.

11 Clare Buchanan, 'Rosyth: MOD Caledonia Closure Delayed until 2026 but Swimming Pool to Stay Shut.' *Dunfermline Press*, 29 September 2022.

12 Ministry of Defence, The Rt Hon Tobias Ellwood MP, and The Rt Hon Sir Gavin Williamson CBE MP. 'Defence Secretary Announces Five-Year Plan for Key Military Sites', gov.uk, 28 February 2019.www.gov.uk/govern ment/news/defence-secretary-announces-five-year-plan-for-key-military-sit es (accessed 27 August 2024).

13 Ibid.

14 Ministry of Defence and Defence Infrastructure Organisation, *Strategy for Defence Infrastructure*, 2022. Available from: https://assets.publishing. service.gov.uk/media/61f0008ee90e0703787c56f3/20220125-Strategy_for_ Defence_Infrastructure.pdf (accessed 27 August 2024).

15 N.D.G. James, *Plain Soldiering* (Salisbury: The Hobnob Press, 1987), p. 17.

16 Catherine Lutz, *Homefront: A Military City and the American Twentieth Century* (Boston, MA: Beacon Press, 2001), p. 180.

17 Ibid., pp. 171–213.

18 Ibid., pp. 180–185; Kim Sengupta, 'Collateral Damage: British Troops Are Set to Finally Leave Germany But What Will Be the Effect of Their Departure?' *Independent*, 26 March 2013. It is hard to assess the actual impact of the British Army's withdrawal from Germany at the time of writing.

19 Ibid.

20 See for example Oxford Economics, *The Wider Value of the British Army*, Oxford Economics Ltd, May 2021, pp. 42–3.

21 Ibid., p. 41.

22 GVA is an economic productivity model that measures the contribution of a corporate subsidiary, company, or municipality to an economy, producer, sector or region. A net study would calculate the value in a 'counterfactual hypothetical' situation – as in, what if, in this instance, the base did not exist?

23 Lilith Foster-Collins, 'Grocer 33 Store of the Week Tesco Tidworth.' *The Grocer*, 3 February 2023.

24 In 2018 Rollalong was awarded a contract worth over £100 million by Aspire Defence to design, manufacture and install 52 new high-class single living accommodation buildings for service personnel returning from Germany in 2020: the Army Basing Programme 2020.

Rollalong won Best Offsite Project of the Year for this Project at the Constructing Excellence South West Built Environment Awards. The award recognises the outstanding work carried out on Salisbury Plain to support Aspire's delivery for the Army Basing Programme.

25 James Ashworth, 'Classified Business SMI Applies for Andover Extension.' *Andover Advertiser*, 4 May 2021.

26 The Enterprise Network in Swindon and Wiltshire. Porton Science Park. www.theenterprisenetwork.co.uk/centre/porton/ (accessed 25 February 2024).

27 Martin Boddy, John Lovering and Keith Bassett, *Sunbelt City? A Study of Economic Change in Britain's M4 Growth Corridor* (Oxford: Oxford University Press, 1986), pp. 81–84, 122.
28 Matt Kennard and Mark Curtis, 'Britain's Warfare State.' *Open Democracy*, 24 September 2018.
29 Matt Kennard, 'How Britain Has Become a World Leading Manufacturer of the Products of War.' *Action Against Armed Violence*, 20 October 2017.
30 Kennard and Curtis, 'Britain's Warfare State.'
31 Mark Curtis, 'Britain Always Seeks a Profit in Wars.' *DeclassifiedUK*, 5 October 2023.
32 Wiltshire Council, *Military Presence and Economic Significance in the South West Region*, March 2009.
33 Ibid., p. 16.
34 Ministry of Defence, UK Defence in Numbers 2019: 22. Available from: https://assets.publishing.service.gov.uk/media/5f652045d3bf7f723ad68c65/20200227_CH_UK_Defence_in_Numbers_2019.pdf.
35 SouthWest Regional Defence and Security Cluster. https://southwestrdsc.co.uk/ (accessed 27 February 2024). According to the website, 'The cluster seeks to aggregate and raise the profile of regional D&S capability to stimulate greater sector knowledge, business, economic growth and productivity across the South West region. It will attract businesses of all scales with an interest in D&S to deliver new sector and cross-sector capability. It aims to apply a "Team UK" approach to enable more joined up working between industry, academia and government, providing an efficient and accessible route to industry curation and the region's D&S value chain.'
36 Jinsella, 'Explained: The £1BN-plus Deals between UK Universities and the Arms Trade.' *DeclassifiedUK*, 7 February 2023.
37 Jenna Corduroy and Billy Stockwell, 'UK Universities Take Millions from Defence Companies Arming Israel.' *OpenDemocracy*, 19 December 2023.
38 Richard Murphy, 'Freeports: A Pathway to the End of Government as We Know It.' *West Country Voices*, 24 September 2023. See See Plymouth and South Devon Freeport (https://pasdfreeport.com) for more information.
39 Matt Kennard, 'The 183 American Troops Deployed at Secret Locations across Britain.' *DeclassifiedUK*, 9 February 2023.
   See also Nick Hopkins and Julian Borger, 'NSA Pay £100m in Secret Funding for GCHQ.' *Guardian*, 1 August 2013.
40 Oxford Economics, *The Wider Value*, p. 41.

Chapter 6

1 Paul Dixon, *Warrior Nation: War, Militarisation and British Democracy*. Forces Watch, 2018, pp. 2, 18.
2 People began migrating from Oudja in north-eastern Morocco in the 1960s and 1970s to work in factories like the Bowyers meat factory. The town has a mosque, built in 1997. See Sarah Hackett, *Britain's Rural Muslims: Rethinking Integration* (Manchester: Manchester University Press, 2021).

3 N. Danilova, *The Politics of War Commemoration in the UK and Russia* (Basingstoke: Palgrave, 2015), cited in Dixon, *Warrior Nation*. For a more recent ethnographic analysis of Armed Forces Day see R. McGarry, 'Visualizing Liminal Military Landscape: A Small-Scale Study of Armed Forces Day in the United Kingdom.' *Critical Military Studies*, 8:3, (2021), pp. 273–298, and M.F. Rech and R. Yarwood, 'Exploring Post-Military Geographies: Plymouth and the Spatialities of Armed Forces Day.' In Rachel Woodward (ed.), *A Research Agenda for Military Geographies* (Cheltenham: Edward Elgar Publishing, 2019).

4 Dan Sabbagh, 'Head of British Army Could Quit in Row over Further Cuts.' *Guardian*, 29 June 2023.

5 S. Walklate, G. Mythen and R. McGarry, 'Witnessing Wootton Bassett: An Exploration in Cultural Victimology.' *Crime, Media, Culture*, 7:2 (2011), pp. 149–165.

6 Joshua Truksa, 'Lord-Lieutenant Wiltshire Appoints Vice Lord-Lieutenant Andrew Gregory.' *Salisbury Journal*, 18 January 2023. 'He is governor of a school and a patron of many organisations, including "Fighting with Pride," a charity seeking to address the historic wrongs done to LGBT veterans.'

7 Our response from the army media department was polite and frank. 'After thorough consideration, and based upon current Army core communication priorities, the *return* on academic books and projects (noting that resource is tight and not as extensive as it was in 2008), and especially as academic books do not have the same degree of reach as some of the books we have supported over years (some with sales of 52,000 or more), my chain of command has taken the decision that we will not be able to support your current project.'

8 Esme Kirk-Wade. UK Defence Personnel Statistics. House of Commons Library Research Briefing, No. 7930, 13 August 2024, pp. 26–27. Available from: https://researchbriefings.files.parliament.uk/documents/CBP-7930/CBP-7930.pdf (accessed 21 August 2024).

9 These figures are made available through regular publication of Ministry of Defence statistics online, sometimes with useful summaries and diagrams. For example: 'Between 2000 and 2022, inflow of personnel to the UK Regular Forces has only been higher than outflow in six years. In the 12 months to 31 March 2022 there was a negative net flow of personnel – intake was 13,350 while outflow was 14,630. This followed two consecutive years of positive net flow.' Esme Kirk-Wade, UK Defence Personnel Statistics, House of Commons Library Research Briefing, 2022, p. 4.

10 Max Colbert, 'Military Spending on Recruitment Adverts Far Outstrips Teaching and health.' *Byline Times*, 25 August 2022.

11 Mark Paine, 'Banking Crisis Led to Army Career for Sergeant Dennis Kofitia.' *Andover Advertiser*, 13 September 2023.

12 'Filling the Ranks.' A Report for the Prime Minister on the state of recruiting into the United Kingdom armed forces by the Rt Hon Mark Francois MP, July 2017, p. 33.

13 Ibid., p. 2.

14 Child Rights International Network, *Conscription by Poverty: Deprivation and Army Recruitment in the UK* (London, 2019).

15 Jonathan Parry, 'From the Classroom to the Frontline – Schools Must Be Careful What They Teach Kids about the Army.' *The Conversation*, 26 September 2017.

16 Dan Sabbagh, 'Nine Rapes at Harrogate Military College Reported to Civilian Police in 13 Months.' *Guardian*, 5 October 2023.

17 Geneva Abdul, 'British Soldier Took Her Own Life after Sexual Harassment from Boss, Says Army.' *Guardian*, 4 October 2023.

18 Rhianna Louise and Emma Sangster, *Selling the Military: A Critical Analysis of Contemporary Recruitment Marketing in the UK*. ForcesWatch and Medact, 2019, p. 15.

19 Ibid., pp. 13–14.

20 Noel Dempsey, UK Defence Personnel Statistics. House of Commons Library Briefing Paper No. CBP7930, 27 July 2020. Available from: https://researchbriefings.files.parliament.uk/documents/CDP-2018-0016/CBP-79 30.pdf.

21 Kirk-Wade, UK Personnel Defence Statistics, House of Commons Library Research Briefing, 13 August 2024, pp. 26–27.

22 Steven Morris, 'Army Accused of Targeting Children via Gaming Magazine.' *Guardian*, 29 January 2019; Tom Sables, 'What Does the Military See in Gamers?' *Forces News*, 5 January 2021.

23 Mark Townsend, 'Inside the British Military Base where Young Hackers Learn to Stop Cybercrime.' *Guardian*, 19 August 2018.

24 Joe Glenton, *Veteranhood: Rage and Hope in British Ex-Military Life* (London: Repeater Books, 2021), pp. 18–21. See also. Ministry of Defence, *The Armed Forces Covenant* (London, n.d.). p. 4. Available from: https://assets.publishing.service.gov.uk/media/5a78c7b740f0b62b22cbcbd4/the_arm ed_forces_covenant.pdf (accessed 25 February 2024).

25 Wiltshire Council, *Military presence and Economic Significance in the South West Region* (Devizes, March 2009), pp. 72–96. This study was conducted in the months following the financial crash of 2008 and recognised that the large numbers of vacancies in the region, which might well tally with the career aspirations of those leaving the forces, would likely shrink and transform as economic decline continued. Using survey data, the study noted that many expressed a desire to move into technical and engineering, or police and fire services; but predicted that the region's reservoir of labour service would be increasingly funnelled into security and care work which would welcome younger veterans' military experience.

26 Ministry of Defence, *Annual Population Survey: UK Armed Forces Veterans Residing in Great Britain, 2017*, 31 January 2019. Available from: www.gov.uk/government/statistics/annual-population-survey-uk-armed-forces-veter ans-residing-in-great-britain-2017 (accessed 21 August 2024).

27 Annette J. Beveridge, 'Alabare: Navy Veteran Talks Truth about Homelessness.' *Salisbury Journal*, 24 June 2023.

28 David I. Walker, 'Anticipating Army Exit: Constructions of Final Year UK Career Soldiers.' *Armed Forces & Society*, 39:2 (2012), pp. 284–304.

29 In 2022, for example, Lovell offered a £5,000 incentive to buyers with a military connection at Drummond Park, its new development of a mixture of 412 affordable and open-market homes on the former defence medical site in Ludgershall. It also sponsored the Tidworth Armed Forces Day event that year. Julie Bowen, regional sales director, explained that 'Celebrating Armed Forces Day is very important to us, as we recently launched our Veteran Community Build scheme at Drummond Park. This scheme is providing veterans with work, mentoring and the opportunity to secure a new affordable home, which they have helped to build … We are committed to supporting local veterans across Wiltshire wherever we can.' Catriona Aitken, 'Event Held for Armed Forces Day Sponsored by Developer Offering £5,000 Incentive for Members and Veterans at Newbuild Properties.' *Andover Advertiser*, 27 June 2022.

30 Sharon A.M. Stevelink, Margaret Jones, Lisa Hull, David Pernet, Shirlee MacCrimmon, Laura Goodwin, Deidre MacManus, Dominic Murphy, Norman Jones and Neil Greenberg, 'Mental Health Outcomes at the End of the British Involvement in the Iraq and Afghanistan Conflicts: A Cohort Study.' *The British Journal of Psychiatry*, 213 (8 October 2018), pp. 690–697. https://doi.org/10.1192/bjp.2018.175.

31 NHS England (2021), 'NHS Launches "Op Courage" Veterans' Mental Health Service.' www.england.nhs.uk/2021/03/nhs-launches-op-courage-veterans-mental-health-service/ (accessed 26 February 2024).

32 Johnny Mercer MP, 'New Funding and Support Scheme to Finally End Armed Forces Veterans' Homelessness.' Office for Veterans Affairs, 21 December 2022 www.gov.uk/government/news/new-government-funded-hotline-to-end-veteran-homelessness-now-live-across-the-uk--2 (accessed 25 February 2024).

33 Aletha Adu, 'Homelessness among Armed Forces Veterans in England Rises by 14%.' *Guardian*, 26 December 2023.

34 Josh Layton, 'Hidden Toll of Afghan War on British soldiers Being Uncovered 20 Years On.' *Metro*, 22 July 2023. https://archive.ph/iny4s (accessed 25 February 2024); Zara Raza, Syeda F. Hussain, Suzanne Ftouni, Gershon Spitz, Nick Caplin, Russell G. Foster and Renata S. M. Gomes, 'Dementia in Military and Veteran Populations: A Review of Risk Factors – Traumatic Brain Injury, Post-Traumatic Stress Disorder, Deployment, and Sleep.' *Military Medical Research*, 8 (2021), p. 55.

35 Glenton, *Veteranhood*, p. 3. See also Joe Glenton, 'I Survive by Scrimping – The Plight pf Former Soldiers in Britain.' *DeclassifiedUK*, 21 December 2023.

36 Ken MacLeish, 'Churn: Mobilization–Demobilization and the Fungibility of American Military Life.' *Security Dialogue*, 51:2–3 (2020), p. 196. https://doi.org/10.1177/0967010619889469.

37 'Armed Forces Day 2019: Salisbury Celebrates National Event.' *Forces.net*, 27 June 2019.

Chapter 7

1 Hema Kiruppalini, 'Imperial Inheritance: The Transnational Lives of Gurkha Families iIn Asian Contexts, 1948–1971.' *Modern Asian Studies*, 57:2 (2023), pp. 669–690. https://doi.org/10.1017/S0026749X22000191. See also The Gurkha Museum, 'Gurkhas and the First World War' (n.d.). https://thegurkhamuseum.co.uk/blog/gurkhas-and-the-first-world-war/ (accessed 24 February 2024).

2 David Olusoga, *The World's War: Forgotten Soldiers of Empire* BBC Two, July 2014. See also David Olusoga, *The World's War* (London: Head of Zeus, 2014).

3 David Lammy, 'How Britain Dishonoured its African First World War Dead.' *Guardian*, 3 November 2019. See also Michele Barrett, 'Dehumanization and the War in East Africa.' *Journal of War & Culture Studies*, 10:3 (August 2017), pp. 238–252.

4 Megan Howarth, *The Changing Face of War Memorialisation*, Remember Me Project (2017). https://archive.ph/lr1al (accessed 24 February 2024); Peter Donaldson, *Remembering the South African War: Britain and the Memory of the Anglo-Boer War from 1899 to the Present* (Liverpool: Liverpool University Press, 2013).

5 BBC News, 'WWI Practice Tunnels Found under Salisbury Plain', 24 April 2017.

6 Maev Kennedy, 'First World War Training Tunnels and Trenches Discovered in Wiltshire.' *Guardian*, 24 April 2017.

7 Thebignote, 'With the British Army in Flanders & France'. https://thebignote.com/?s=Mary+Agnes+Langdale (accessed 25 August 2024).

8 The Women's Royal Air Force was the first incarnation of the women's branch of the Royal Air Force; it existed from 1918 to 1920.

9 Zoë H. Wool, *After War: The Weight of Life at Walter Reed* (Chapel Hill, NC: Duke University Press, 2015).

10 Francis Terry and Associates, *Recovery Centre, Tedworth House, Wiltshire*. https://ftanda.co.uk/projects/recovery-centre/.

11 Editorial, 'Restoration and Recuperation.' *Wiltshire Magazine*, 2011; The Royal British Legion also assumed part responsibility for some of the costs of running the centre.

12 Terry, *Recovery Centre*.

13 David Falke, 'Future of Tedworth House Secured.' *Salisbury Journal*, 14 December 2023.

14 Jerome Starkey, 'Blow to Heroes. Help For Heroes Gives up Flagship Recovery Centres and Lays off 90 as Income Plunges during Covid.' *Sun*, 7 April 2021.

15 Wool, *After War*, p. 5.

16 Ewen MacAskill and Ian Cobain, 'British Forces' Century of Unbroken Warfare Set to End with Afghanistan Exit.' *Guardian*, 11 February 2014.

17 Mark Curtis, 'The UK's 83 Military Interventions Around the World since 1945.' *DeclassifiedUK*, 10 January 2023.

18 Paul Rogers, *Irregular War: The New Threat from the Margins* (London: I.B. Taurus, 2017), p. 196.
19 Ministry of Defence, *Defence in a Competitive Age* (London: HMSO, March 2021). CP411, p. 9. Available from https://assets.publishing.service. gov.uk/media/6063061e8fa8f55b6ad297d0/CP411_-Defence_Command_Pla n.pdf (accessed 24 August 2024).
20 Mary L. Dudziak, *War-Time: An Idea, Its History, Its Consequences* (Oxford: Oxford University Press, 2012), p. 8.
21 Ken MacLeish, 'The Ethnography of Good Machines.' *Critical Military Studies*, 1:1 (2015), p. 9. http://dx.doi.org/10.1080/23337486.2014.973680.
22 Ned Temko and Mark Townsend, 'Scandal of Treatment for Wounded Iraq Veterans.' *Guardian*, 11 March 2007.
23 Ibid. A spokesman for University Hospital Birmingham Trust, which is inclusive of Selly Oak Hospital, said that 'While we cannot comment on individual cases the types of injuries that soldiers sustain and that we treat are very complex – therefore their pain control is very complex.'
24 BBC News, 'Helping Heroes at Headley Court', 27 July 2010.
25 Dixon, *Warrior Nation*, p. 17; Richard Dannatt, *Leading from the Front: An Autobiography* (London: Bantam, 2011).
26 Kim Sengupta '"Diana Effect" Blamed for War Weariness.' *Independent*, 5 April 2010.
27 John Bingham, 'Charity Watchdog Examining Serious Concerns over Help for Heroes.' *Telegraph*, 7 February 2016.
28 Ana Pozo and Catherine Walker, 'UK Armed Forces Charities: An Overview and Analysis.' *Directory of Social Change*, 2014. https://archive.ph/yvUUZ.
29 Rebecca Cooney, 'Help for Heroes Criticised by The Times for Allegedly Spending Millions on Unused Beds.' *Third Sector*, 29 September 2015. The article referred to an internal Ministry of Defence review that spoke 'of an ambitious project where costs grew and decisions to spend charity and tax money were made without sufficient analysis of where it was needed'. The defence correspondent Deborah Haynes claimed that costs for the project had risen to £350 million from the original £70 million, taking over ten years instead of the planned four. In addition, only half of the available bed-rooms at the two largest recovery centres were used by serving personnel between August 2013 and January 2015.
30 By 2022, for example, statistics showed that more than half of injuries occurred in training, with the greatest proportion of those sustained by recruits struggling to up their fitness levels in their first phase. While a military-related profession entails more risks to health and safety than many other occupations, this can hardly be expected to arouse sympa-thy as much as the life-changing injuries suffered in war. Ministry of Defence, 'MOD health and Safety Statistics: Annual Summary & Trends over Time 2017/18 – 2021/22' (published 7 July 2022, revised 8 September 2022). Available from: https://assets.publishing.service.gov. uk/government/uploads/system/uploads/attachment_data/file/1104101/M OD_Health__Safety_Statistic_Annual_Report_2021-22.pdf (accessed 24 August 2024).

31 Help for Heroes, 'Afghanistan: We Fight for Those who Fought for, and with, Us', 12 July 2022. www.helpforheroes.org.uk/about-us/news/afghanistan-we-fight-for-those-who-fought-for-and-with-us/ (accessed 26 February 2024).

32 Joe Glenton, 'Shame, Confusion, Betrayal: UK Veterans on the War in Afghanistan.' *DeclassifiedUK*, 29 September 2021. https://archive.ph/t5334 (accessed 27 February 2024). Chris Bamford served in the Royal Signals and worked with Afghan translators to intercept radio communications, turning the information into workable intelligence. He told the journalist Joe Glenton that he was unclear what happened to those he worked with. 'I'm not sure any got out, but at least two were told somewhere that their work would get them into the UK. Hence the betrayal being all the fucking worse, because if they have been left behind after being promised asylum …'

33 Unite the Union and UK Disability History Month, 'War and Impairment: The Social Consequences of Disablement for Disabled Ex-Servicemen', November/December 2014. Available from: www.worldofinclusion.com/v3/wp-content/uploads/2014/09/UK-Disability-history-month-2014.pdf (accessed 26 February 2024).

34 'The Remarkable Story of Enham Alamein.' *Great British Life*, 24 October 2017. www.greatbritishlife.co.uk/magazines/hampshire/22580141.remarkable-story-enham-alamein/ (accessed 26 February 2024).

35 See https://www.enhamtrust.org.uk/ for details.

36 Deborah Cohen, *The War Come Home: Disabled Veterans in Britain and Germany, 1914–1939* (London: University of California Press, 2001), p. 123.

37 Ibid., p. 124.

38 'The Remarkable Story of Enham Alamein.'

39 Joe Riddle, 'Veterans Complete Iron Age Project.' *Salisbury Journal*, 22 June 2017. https://archive.ph/KU72N (accessed 25 June 2023).

40 N.D.G. James, *Plain Soldiering* (Salisbury: The Hobnob Press, 1987), p. 113. In James's account the project was dreamed up after 'an outbreak of trouble' at the camp.

41 New Zealand History, First World War Overview, 1919: 15–16 March. 'Troops Riot at Sling Camp' https://nzhistory.govt.nz/war/first-world-war-timeline (accessed 24 August 2024). See also T.S. Crawford, *Wiltshire and the Great War: Training the Empire's Soldiers* (Marlborough: The Crowood Press, 2012), pp. 233–236.

42 Ministry of Defence, 'Bulford Kiwi Is Restored to Its Original Splendour', 16 June 2022. www.gov.uk/government/news/bulford-kiwi-is-restored-to-its-original-splendour (accessed 27 February 2024).

43 The chalk is renewed annually in a joint ceremony with the New Zealand High Commission. In 2023 the Defence Iinfrastructure Organisation issued a statement announcing that 'As the All Blacks prepare to take on Italy at the Rugby World Cup on Friday, DIO has highlighted the connection between the soldiers who created the Kiwi and the "Trench All Blacks" – a team of soldiers from New Zealand who won "The Somme Cup", a special rugby division for those fighting in the war'. The press release repeated that falsehood that 'the New Zealand soldiers still in the UK decided to leave their mark on the countryside before they returned home'. Ministry of Defence

and Defence Infrastructure Organisation, 'Giant Kiwi Monument Shines after Chopper Chalk Drop', 29 September 2023. gov.uk, 29 September 2023. www.gov.uk/government/news/giant-kiwi-monument-shines-after-choppe r-chalk-drop (accessed 24 June 2023).

44 Vron Ware, 'From War Grave to Peace Garden: Muslim Soldiers, Militarised Multiculture and Cultural Heritage.' *Journal of War and Culture Studies*, 10:4 (2017), pp. 287–304. http://dx.doi.org/10.1080/17526272.2017.1396069.

Chapter 8

1 Martyn Barber, *A History of Aerial Photography and Archaeology: Mata Hari's Glass Eye and Other Stories* (Swindon: English Heritage, 2011).

2 Jesse Casana, David D. Goodman and Carolin Ferwerda, 'A Wall or a Road? A Remote Sensing-Based Investigation of Fortifications on Rome's Eastern Frontier.' *Antiquity*, 97:396 (December 2023), pp. 1516–1533. https://doi. org/10.15184/aqy.2023.153.

3 Wessex Archaeology, *Operation Nightingale*. www.wessexarch.co.uk/our-work/operation-nightingale (accessed 25 February 2024).

4 Heritage Fund, 'Project Florence Gains Heritage Lottery Fund Support', 7 October 2014. www.heritagefund.org.uk/news/project-florence-gains-her itage-lottery-fund-support (accessed 26 February 2024).

5 Layla Renshaw, *Exhuming Loss: Memory, Materiality and Mass Graves of the Spanish Civil War* (Walnut Creek, CA: Left Coast Press, 2011), p. 11; Layla Renshaw, Marina Álamo Bryan, Zuzanna Dziuban and Claire Moon, *Tools in the Search for Human Remains: Thinking through Objects in Forensic Practices*. Independent Social Research Foundation, 13 May 2020.

6 'Breaking Ground at Barrow Clump.' *Current Archaeology*, 5 February 2018. See also Paul Everill, Richard Bennett and Karen Burnell, 'Dig In: An Evaluation of the Role of Archaeological Fieldwork for the Improved Wellbeing of Military Veterans.' *Antiquity*, 94:373 (2020), pp. 212–227. https://doi.org/10.15184/aqy.2019.85.

7 Richard Osgood, Alex Southeran and Maj Ryan Parmentar, 'A Decade of Discovery – 10 Years of Operation Nightingale.' *Sanctuary*, 49 (2020), pp. 18–21.

8 Jonathan Meades, 'Blighted Plain.' *London Review of Books*, 44:1 (6 January 2022).

9 Melanie Friend, *The Plain* (Stockport: Dewi Lewis Publishing, 2020).

10 Ibid., pp. 84–86.

11 Roy Canham, '40 Years on Salisbury Plain, How the Battle to Save Archaeology Was Won.' *Sanctuary*, 44 (2015), pp. 26–27.

12 Wiltshire Conservation Team Natural England, *Salisbury Plain SSSI Integrated Site Assessment* (2014–15), p. 1.

13 Marianna Dudley, 'A Fairy (Shrimp) Tale of Military Environmentalism: The "Greening" of Salisbury Plain.' In Chris Pearson, Peter Coates and Tim Cole (eds), *Militarized Landscapes: From Gettysburg to Salisbury Plain* (London: Continuum, 2010), p. 141.

14 The article is no longer available, but for a full account of the conservation programme on Salisbury Plain see the RSPB's Wessex Stone-curlew project, Hampshire Ornithological Society, 2021 www.youtube.com/watch?v=5fQzsgUjQXw.

15 Clare Richmond, 'UK Military Training in Belize, Considering the Environment.' *Sanctuary*, 49 (2017), pp. 8–10.

16 Phil Miller and Matt Kennard, 'Britain Uses Vast Swathes of One of the World's Most Biodiverse Countries for Military Training – and Pays Nothing.' *DeclassifiedUK*, 4 February 2020.

17 N.D.G. James, *Plain Soldiering* (Salisbury: The Hobnob Press, 1987), pp. 22–23. In 1899 the War Office Salisbury Plain Committee decided that 'all land outside the approved limits of the Avon Valley cultivation zone should be laid down permanently to grass, as soon as possible'.

18 Brianna Millett, 'The History of Salisbury Plain "Ghost Village" Left Abandoned since the 1940s.' *Bristol Live*, 31 May 2020.

19 Michael Priestly, 'How a Tenant Farm Manages 3,200ha of Wiltshire Grassland.' *Farmers Weekly*, 30 July 2019.

20 Ibid.

21 Tom Heap, 'On Your Farm: Military Farm', BBC, 11 July 2011, produced by Emma Weatherill.

22 BBC News, 'Salisbury Plain Stray Shell "Misses Target by Five Miles"', 10 March 2024.

23 Water is a relatively unexplored aspect of the Ministry of Defence's historic management of the Plain. Adam Doig, 'Water Consumption Reduction: Managing a Precious Resource.' *Sanctuary*, 49 (2020), p. 50.

24 An FOI request in 2022 showed that there have been no incidents involving damage to animals on Salisbury Plain since 10 July 2020 when eight cows were killed and four injured in a live firing exercise on Castlemartin Army Firing Range in Pembrokeshire, Wales. In 2017, however, an artillery shell landed a few feet from Bruce's herd. Fortunately, it did not harm any cows although two were trapped in a crater.

25 In October 2023, for example, the Defence Infrastructure Organisation, Wiltshire Council and the Salisbury Plain Rights of Way Volunteers signed an agreement to support the ongoing work of volunteers dedicated to improving and maintaining public access across Salisbury Plain Training Area. Benjamin Paessler, 'Agreement to Support Volunteers on Salisbury Plain Training Area.' *Salisbury Journal*, 4 October 2023.

26 DIO, *Salisbury Plain Training Area Newsletter*, December 2018.

27 Ministry of Defence, *Greenlaning Good Practice Guide. Salisbury Plain Training Area* (2020). Ref: MMC13–08–129. Available from: https://assets.publishing.service.gov.uk/media/5fd8c243d3bf7f40cb84c624/20201022-SPTA_Greenlaning_Practice_Guide_2020_Version__Web_-FINAL.pdf (accessed 23 August 2024).

28 'Operation Launched to Shut Down Illegal Activity on Salisbury Plain.' *Andover Advertiser*, 23 September 2018.

29 Salisbury Plain Safaris, https://salisburyplainsafaris.co.uk.

30 Charles Smith-Jones, 'Netheravon Shoot in Wiltshire.' *Shooting Times*, 25 December 2013.

31 BBC News, 'Fire Reignites on Salisbury Plain, Causing "Smog"', 16 July 2022.

32 Phil Miller, 'Ashes of Empire: Britain's Burning Injustice in Kenya.' *DeclassifiedUK*, 19 January 2023.

33 'If the world's militaries were a country, this figure would mean they have the fourth largest national carbon footprint in the world.' Stuart Parkinson and Linsey Cottrell, 'Estimating the Military's Global Greenhouse Gas Emissions', p. 2. Scientists for Global Responsibility and the Conflict and Environment Observatory, November 2022. p https://ceobs.org/wp-content/uploads/2022/11/SGR-CEOBS_Estimating_Global_MIlitary_GHG_Emissions.pdf (accessed 28 February 2024).

34 Lieutenant General Sharon Nesmith, 'Foreword', *Sanctuary*, 51 (2022), p. 2. See also Major General Richard Clements, 'Around the Services: British Army'. Scientists for Global Responsibility and the Conflict and Environment Observatory (November 2022), p. 7.

35 Stuart Parkinson, 'The Environmental Impacts of the UK Military Sector.' Scientists for Global Responsibility and *DeclassifiedUK*, 2020.

36 Phil Miller, 'Ukrainian Soldiers Seen with Depleted Uranium Ammo in UK.' *DeclassifiedUK*, 27 March 2023. There is no evidence that live depleted uranium has ever been used in Wiltshire.

37 'UK to Send Depleted Uranium Munitions to Ukraine.' CND Salisbury, 21 March 2023.

38 'Sinjajevinans Kept Military off the Mountain Again.' Sinjajevina blog, 13 June 2023 https://sinjajevina.org/blog-feed/ (accessed 26 February 2024).

39 See the campaign website for more information: https://sinjajevina.org/blog-feed (accessed 26 February 2024).

40 David Swanson, 'UK Pushes Mountain Destruction on Montenegro as Green Policy.' World Beyond War, 18 August 2022.

41 Caroline Kimeu, 'Kenya Launches Inquiry into Claims of Abuse by British Soldiers at Training Unit.' *Guardian*, 14 August 2023.

42 Phil Miller, 'British Army's White Phosphorus Habit Revealed.' *DeclassifiedUK*, 3 August 2022. See also Phil Miller, 'Kenya Warned British Army about Dangerous Ammunition Decades Ago.' *DeclassifiedUK*, 21 September 2023.

43 Peter Ross, 'A Journey Back in Time to the Ghost Village on Salisbury Plain.' *Guardian*, 25 August 2023. See also History of the Bus Services through Imber: https://imberbus.org/bus-history/.

Conclusion

1 Phil Miller, 'Revealed: The UK Military's Overseas Base Network Involves 145 Sites in 42 Countries.' *DeclassifiedUK*, 24 November 2020.

2 Zoë H. Wool, 'Critical Military Studies, Queer Theory, and the Possibilities of Critique: The Case of Suicide and Family Caregiving in the US Military.' *Critical Military Studies*, 1:1 (2014), p. 2.

3 Cynthia Enloe, *Maneuvers: The International Politics of Militarizing Women's Lives* (London: University of California Press, 2000), p. 219.

4 Cynthia Enloe, *Bananas, Beaches, and Bases: Making Feminist Sense of International Politics* (Oakland: University of California Press, 1990), p. 132.

5 Army Technology, 'UK Chief of Defence Staff Participated in Daily Coronavirus Briefing', 2020 https://www.army-technology.com/news/uk-chief-of-defence-staff-participates-in-daily-coronavirus-briefing/ (accessed 15 January 2024).

6 Prime Minister's Office, 'Prime Minister's Statement on Coronavirus (COVID-19)', 7 January 2021. www.gov.uk/government/speeches/prime-ministers-statement-on-coronavirus-covid-19-7-january-2021 (accessed 10 August 2021).

7 Army.mod.uk, 'A Year of Supporting COVID Response', 23 March 2021www.army.mod.uk/news-and-events/news/2021/03/a-year-of-supporting-covid/ (accessed 26 February 2024).

8 Ministry of Defence, 'COVID Support Force: MOD's Contribution to the Coronavirus Response.' Gov.uk, 2022. www.gov.uk/guidance/covid-support-force-the-mods-continued-contribution-to-the-coronavirus-response (accessed 26 February 2024).

9 Matt Kennard and Joe Glenton, 'The British Armed Forces Are Using Covid-19 to Solve a Recruitment Crisis and to Heal Their Damaged Reputation.' *Declassified UK*, 13 May 2020.

10 Ibid.

11 Ibid.

12 Ryan Evans, 'Less than 1 in 4 Admire Work of Armed Forces' Covid Response.' *Andover Advertiser*, 24 June 2021.

13 Although some mistakes were made. See BBC News, 'Used Coronavirus Tests Handed Out by Mistake in Birmingham', 14 October 2020.

14 Staff working for the Army Welfare Service were also aware that suicide rates amongst personnel had increased slightly during the pandemic. In fact a number of shocking deaths of personnel were reported across Britain's 'super garrison' areas in 2020 and 2021, including the unexplained deaths of Lance Corporal Bernard Mongan in Catterick in January 2020 and an unnamed woman soldier in Larkhill in July 2021. The circumstances around Mongan's death were particularly egregious as his body was not discovered for a number of weeks and it later emerged that he had been complaining of bullying and had been severely distressed – complaints that were not investigated. Jonathan Beale, 'Bernard Mongan: Failings by Army over Soldier's Death, Report Says.' BBC News, 11 July 2021; Holly Christodoulou, 'Police Probe Death of Female Soldier, 30s, Found Unresponsive at Royal Artillery Barracks in Larkhill.' *Sun*, 23 July 2021.

15 In one example a local bus driver, who walked regularly on Sidbury Hill, the site of an Iron Age hillfort and thus a scheduled monument, told us about an occasion when he was approached by some young men on quad bikes who had warned him to go back as there was some kind of army exercise going on ahead. Since he knew that military training was not permitted there, he had ignored them but it still made him apprehensive.

16 Ulf Schmidt, *Secret Science: A Century of Poison Warfare and Human Experiments* (Oxford: Oxford University Press, 2015), pp. 1–2.

17 BBC News, 'Timeline: Porton Down Laboratory' 31 January 2008.

18 Defence Science and Technology Laboratory, 'The Truth about Porton Down: Answering the Myths and Misconceptions.' gov.uk, 27 June 2016. www.gov.uk/government/news/the-truth-about-porton-down.

19 Frank Gardner, 'Porton Down: What's Inside the UK's Top-Secret Laboratory?' BBC News, 13 June 2019.

20 James Gallagher, 'Porton Down: Can This Laboratory Help Stop the Next Pandemic?' BBC News, 17 August 2023.

21 See also the Defence Chemical Biological Radiological and Nuclear Centre at Winterbourne Gunner, on the south-eastern edge of the Plain. www.gov.uk/government/publications/defence-chemical-biological-radiological-and-nuclear-centre-dcbrnc/defence-chemical-biological-radiological-and-nuclear-centre.

22 Jamie Grierson, 'Former Kent Barracks to House Asylum Seekers who Arrived by Boat.' *Guardian*, 15 September 2020.

23 BBC News, 'Napier Barracks: Housing Migrants at Barracks Unlawful, Court Rules', 3 June 2021.

24 Macaully Moffat, 'Home Secretary James Cleverly on Wethersfield Asylum Centre.' *Daily Gazette*, 21 November 2023.

25 Kamena Dorling and Maddie Harris, 'Ghettoised and Traumatised: The Experiences of Men Held in Quasi-Detention in Wethersfield.' Helen Bamber Foundation and Humans for Rights Network, 5 December 2023. www.helenbamber.org/sites/default/files/2023-12/HBF%20HRNF%20Ghettoised%20and%20traumatised_report%20on%20Wethersfield_December23.pdf (accessed 26 February 2024).

26 Jordanna Bailkin, *Unsettled: Refugee Camps and the Making of Multicultural Britain* (Oxford: Oxford University Press, 2020), p. 10.

27 MoD Boscombe Down, RAF, 2024. www.raf.mod.uk/our-organisation/stations/mod-boscombe-down/ (accessed 26 February 2024).

28 Annette J. Beveridge, 'Rwanda Deal May Need Migrant Flights from Boscombe Down.' *Salisbury Journal*, 18 December 2023.

29 Paul Rogers, 'The Latest Military Review Decoded.' *Peace News*, 2654 (1 June 2021).

30 A survey had in 2012 found that 83 per cent of the population had a high opinion of UK troops (rising to 92 per cent of the over-65s), while only half of those questioned supported the war in Helmand. A. Park, E. Clery, J. Curtice, M. Phillips and D. Utting (eds), *British Social Attitudes: the 29th Report* (London: NatCen Social Research, 2012).

31 Here Wordsworth was echoing John Milton's appeal to Lord Fairfax at the siege of Colchester in 1648: 'For what can war but endless war still breed, / Till Truth and Right from violence be freed.' (Sonnet 15: Fairfax, whose name in arms through Europe rings).

Index

www.ingramcontent.com/pod-product-compliance
Ingram Content Group UK Ltd.
Pitfield, Milton Keynes, MK11 3LW, UK
UKHW050957030225
454425UK00021B/74

9 781526 174833